PSYCHEDELIA BRITANNICA

PSYCHEDELIA BRITANNICA

HALLUCINOGENIC DRUGS IN BRITAIN

Edited by Antonio Melechi

With a foreword by Albert Hofmann

 **TURNAROUND**

First edition published in 1997 by
Turnaround
Unit 3, Olympia Trading Estate
Coburg Road
London N22 6TZ

ISBN 1 873262 05 1

British Library Cataloguing in Publication Data
A catalogue record for this book is available
from the British Library

Printed in the UK by Redwood Books
Designed and produced for Turnaround by Book Works
Cover Design by Gwyn Rowlands

Contents

This book is for Julie

Acknowledgements

I would like to thank:
Jeff Hearn and Francesco Melechi for their help and support;
John Witton for the provision of material from the Library of
the Institute for the Study of Drug Dependency, London; Dick
Alpert, John Beresford, James Greene, John Hopkins, Kristof,
Barry Mason, Joey Mellen, Ralph Metzner and Morton
Schatzman for additional information.

For permission to publish material:
Serpent's Tail for material from Simon Reynolds's and Joy
Press's (1995) *Sex Revolts: Gender, Rebellion and Rock 'n' Roll*;
The Estate of Alexander Trocchi for notes and papers from the
unpublished *Drugs of the Mind*.

Foreword

Increasing drug consumption, especially in the western world, is one of the largest problems of the present day. During public discussions drugs are, however, mainly spoken of in general terms, according insufficient distinction between the individual psychoactive substances, leading to mythologies and misunderstandings about the effects of drugs. As different pharmacological attributes, toxicities and psychological effects lead to very different health and social problems, it is important to understand the particular drug group which is being discussed.

The drugs which are the subject of *Psychedelia Britannica* are a group of psychoactive substances which have become known under several descriptions, such as phantastica, hallucinogens, psychotomimetics, psychedelics and more recently entheogens. The fact that so many names have been given to the same substances shows that the psychological effects of psychedelic drugs, as this drug group will here be referred to, are varied, complex and hard to define linguistically.

Psychedelic drugs differ from the classical, euphoriant, dampening or stimulating drugs like morphine, heroin, cocaine and amphetamines, in two particular respects. Firstly, psychedelic drugs are non-addictive. Secondly, even in higher doses they contain practically no chemical toxicity. These two attributes are connected to the fact that psychedelic drugs act upon the deepest, most extensive and most enigmatic core of the human intellect, which is itself also hard to define.

This could lead to psychedelic drugs being considered as harmless, problem-free substances. This is in no way the case. While addictive drugs may only cause physical and psychological harm after heavy use, the first experiment with a psychedelic drug can lead to psychotic fits or cause lasting psychological damage, if the aforementioned deep, consciousness-altering effects are not taken into account. When LSD went on to become the drug of choice in the 1960s, the very real dangers of its use were largely ignored. Consequently, the resultant 'accidents' lead to the enforcement of a total ban on the production, possession and use of psychedelic drugs. It was not, however, only a response to the accidents which resulted in draconian measures bringing to an end the medical use of psychedelic drugs in psychiatry and research, there were also extensive political motives involved. In the United States, the authorities wanted particularly to hit out at the political opposition of that time – the young, the hippy movement and associated groups which were against the establishment and the Vietnam War. In all probability, the legal crackdown would not have occurred if the drug scene had sought to use psychedelic drugs in a responsible and beneficial fashion.

Psychedelic drugs contain active substances which have played a meaningful role in ancient cultures for thousands of years, and in many primitive tribes they are still to be found used in a social and medical context. The substances which are involved here are: mescaline, the active substance from a Mexican cactus, which the Indians call *peyotl*; psilocybin, an active ingredient of a magical, Mexican mushroom *teonanacatl*; and LSD which includes only a minimal chemical modification of the active substance in the old, Indian, magical drug *ololiuqui*. LSD is an abbreviation for lysergic acid diethylamide, the chemical structure closely related to lysergic acid hydroxyethylamide, the main active ingredient of *ololiuqui*. And so as far as the chemical structure and the psychological effect is concerned, LSD belongs to the group of sacred Mexican drugs.

The sacramental use of these drugs by the Indians could have been a model for a valuable and safe usage of LSD and other such drugs. The use of this drug by the Indians was always in the context of a religious ceremony. To them it is a holy drug, the use of which is controlled by the shamans, who work as both doctors and priests.

In our society, the psychiatrist fulfils the role of the shaman. However, membership of the psychiatric profession does not guarantee the ability to deal with psychedelic drugs effectively. This requires special training and individual experience. The need for psychotherapists to have personal experience in the use of psychedelic drugs in their consultancies has already been proved by the pharmaceutical company Sandoz, which distributed LSD for trials before the substance was banned. Through these tests, doctors were given the opportunity to self-experiment and were able to experience the exceptional effects of the drug and learn how to use it appropriately.

It is to be hoped that the total ban on psychedelic drugs will soon be lifted, and that this highly interesting *pharmakon* will again be available to the doctors, in the same way as opium. Then the experiments with psychedelic drugs which came to an end in the 1960s, or were confined underground, could be resumed and furthered. This would not only be important for the further development of a valuable aid to the psychiatric practice, but also to general research into the area of the consciousness.

The large social, ecological and health problems of today are connected to the dual materialistic philosophy of life which shapes the industrial age. The psychedelic experience often produces a change in consciousness which leads towards an integrated experience between humanity and nature, helping to create the intellectual and cultural prerequisites for the necessary change in our threatened world.

Albert Hofmann
Burg i.L.
Switzerland

Introduction

Psychedelia Britannica provides an introduction to the cultural history of psychedelic drugs in Britain, examining the use and influence of the drug experience in the context of literature, psychiatry, popular music and the counter-culture of the 1960s and 1990s.

While the bias of the anthology leans towards the post-war history of psychedelic drugs, Michael Carmichael's essay begins by investigating the drug history of the Reverend Charles Lutwidge Dodgson, aka Lewis Carroll, author of *Alice's Adventures in Wonderland*, and honorary godfather of the psychedelic movement. Carmichael presents convincing evidence that Dodgson's hallucinatory flights of fancy in *Alice* and subsequent tales were drawn from his use of a number of common remedies in the Victorian pharmacopoeia, including henbane, opium, cannabis and digitalis, which he turned to for relief from chronic headaches and insomnia. But not only was Carroll a practising homoeopath with a considerable collection of materia medica, he was also a Russophile. It is this interest which provides a clue to the mystery of Alice's mushroom adventures, as Carmichael suggests how Dodgson could have come to discover the magical effects of fly-agaric mushrooms through Mordecai Cooke's account of Siberian shamanism in *The Seven Sisters of Sleep* (1860).

There is of course a well established precedent for the literary pursuit of visions and reveries as a source of creative inspiration. To this end, the Romantics had employed a number of different tech-

1

niques. The novelist Mrs Bancroft and the painter Paul Fusili indulged in late-night suppers of meat and cheese to provoke wild and vivid imagery for their gothic fantasies. For Wordsworth, trancelike rapture was to be found in the contemplation of the landscape. For others, such as Coleridge and De Quincey it was opium that stoked the imagination. In *Confessions of an English Opium Eater* De Quincey reflected upon the agency which opium wielded upon his dreams. While De Quincey took opium to forget, to lose himself in its soporific stupor, its effects were sometimes quite the opposite: leading him back to a morbid recollection of childhood, which was for De Quincey the *mise en scène* of all dreams. It is this preoccupation with the parallel worlds of childhood and dreams which links the writings of both De Quincey and Dodgson to psychoanalysis, which by the end of the nineteenth century had begun to colonise these subterranean regions of the unconscious in the name of science.

It was not, however, until the 1950s when psychiatry, following its literary precursors, began to seriously explore the potential of psychoactive drugs as a short-cut on the royal road to the unconscious, as researchers discovered in LSD a remarkable facility for generating repressed psychic material in the treatment of neuroses and obsessions. This psychiatric experimentation provides the background to my own essay, exploring the connections between drugs, madness and mysticism since the early 1950s. This brief intellectual history of psychedelic drug use culminates in a focus upon R.D. Laing, who was adopted as a guide into inner space by the firstwave of the psychedelic counter-culture. Laing was himself a keen experimenter, having by 1965 taken LSD on at least twenty occasions, and also used mescaline and psilocybin. The influence of his experimentation upon his work is most apparent in *The Politics of Experience*, which effectively claimed schizophrenia, regression and drug use as different routes to the transcendental.

In Britain, LSD therapy was pioneered by Dr Ronald Sandison, whose essay provides a retrospective on the techniques he developed at Powick Hospital. In the light of renewed media interest in the clinical history of LSD – following the recent spate of reports of ex-psychiatric patients suffering the long-term consequences of LSD's administration – Sandison's essay provides a much needed corrective to the lack of informed debate on the ethics and efficacy of LSD treatment, with a considered defence of its therapeutic use.

In a second essay I turn to a contemporary of Laing's, Michael

Hollingshead, who in 1965 founded the World Psychedelic Centre in London, from where he set about proselytising the consciousness-expanding possibilities of LSD to a stream of well-heeled visitors. If Hollingshead is unique in being Britain's only public champion of the LSD experience, another of his claims to fame was that he was responsible for introducing LSD to Timothy Leary, high priest and propagandist of the American psychedelic movement, at the beginning of the 1960s. After spending more than a decade spreading the psychedelic gospel in Britain and America, Hollingshead penned an autobiographical account of his adventures with LSD, *The Man Who Turned on the World*. The title was, however, ill-deserved, for Hollingshead was in reality more likely to con than convert in the course of missionary work.

Another writer who sought to examine and chronicle the effects of drugs on his own creative process was Alexander Trocchi, a central figure of the 1960s literary underground and a one-time collaborator with both Hollingshead and Laing. The excerpts which have been published here form part of an unfinished book, *Drugs of the Mind*. While Trocchi is most commonly connected with heroin, his writings also present a consideration of hallucinogenic drugs, such as hashish, with which Trocchi was able to open up a new level of experience, 'to come to sense perception in a fresh and structurally innocent way'.

The medium that was most effected by this dislocation of the senses was, however, popular music, which from the mid-Sixties sought to guide its audience towards ecstatic retreat and cosmic oneness. Sheila Whiteley's essay focuses principally upon the material aspect of musical production and the range of effects and techniques which psychedelia has deployed. Simon Reynolds similarly moves from the 1960s to the 1990s, tracing the mythologies of the infantile and pastoral in psychedelic music from Pink Floyd through to the Orb, unpicking psychedelia's various 'strategies of regression'.

Signs of a psychedelic revival in pop and dance culture have been evident since the late 1980s, when Ecstasy fuelled the resurrection and reinvention of much of psychedelia's musical legacy. For Stuart Metcalfe, whose essay assesses the influence of Ecstasy for domestic youth culture, the liberatory ethos of the early days of Acid House and the rave scene has been lost to a consumerist club scene: where musical experimentation and eclecticism have been replaced by the endless repetition of 'functionalist dance', and Ecstasy is guilty of leading House music and the dance scene into a state of creative atrophy.

Lastly, Fraser Clark's dispatch from the frontline of the shamanic insurrection brings the anthology to a close, culminating with an altogether different view of the rave scene. Clark begins by drawing on the evolutionary theory of Terence McKenna, leading us back into psychedelic pre-history, to the primal scene of the fall of group consciousness and the creation of the ego. For Clark, the promise of liberation is now being enacted in rave culture, which is rekindling the tribal bond and propelling us back to the future, towards a new vision of shamanic society.

Antonio Melechi
Bradford
United Kingdom

WONDERLAND REVISITED

Michael Carmichael

The Fall into Wonderland

Arising out of the mist and beckoning unto you, the horizons of Wonderland gradually rise into focus. A luminous white rabbit leads you downward, through a long and darkened hall of doors. You place a precious golden key into the tiny lock of a little door that leads you into a magical garden. You rotate the key, and as the door swings open, Wonderland bathes you in its riveting and hypnotic glow. You are seized with a feeling at once more curious more fascinating, more urgent than any you have ever known. Your mind reels, as you move forward into a looking-glass world. You pause in the beautiful garden with its preternaturally bright flowers, cool, pellucid fountains and fabulous bestiary of supernatural animals. A stupefying collection of characters babble sharply and inharmoniously. Confused and terrified, your eyes dissolve, and you release a torrent of tears. Maddeningly, the size of your body keeps shifting. Immediately before he gives you an extremely powerful drug, a brilliant and imperious caterpillar coldly challenges your identity. Your ego melts. You reel through a high velocity series of manic encounters. Finally, you are accused of crime, placed on trial and sentenced to a violent death. In that cruel moment, you escape Wonderland, a place which can only be visited now and again, in haste. You find yourself lying on the banks of the Isis at Godstow. It is the fourth of July, 1862. You realise that your adventures in Wonderland were unco-ordinated movements of a mind that surged out of control. Released beyond any pattern of interior memory, your mind simply escaped into a dream world, vacant of reason, and absolutely exotic to time as you had known it. Your discovery of Wonderland required more than merely a heroic effort of supplementary imagination – this immense journey propelled you through psychological torture and acute stages of agony as a result of the explosive and unpredictable power of mind-altering drugs. How, in the age of Queen Victoria, was this possible?

'When things went smoothly like a baby drugged.'
Aurora Leigh, Elizabeth Barrett Browning

Drugged English babies were commonplace in the nineteenth century. Mothers and fathers dosed their darlings with soporific drugs, often opium, or that even more popular concoction, laudanum, a cocktail of alcohol laced with opium in order to calm and quiet their sons and daughters. The custom of doping children has centuries of fine tradition behind it. Still a practice in some parts of the Orient, drugging children has, in most cases, been replaced by the dummy in other parts of the world.

If drugged children were not unusual a century ago, neither were drugged adults. A new genre of literature emerged from the nineteenth-century's turbulently panoramic drug scene – the drug saga. The works of Samuel Taylor Coleridge, Thomas De Quincey, Théophile Gautier, Charles Baudelaire, Fitz Hugh Ludlow and Lewis Carroll feature brilliant accounts of drug-induced states of intoxication.

Lewis Carroll was the pseudonym of the Reverend Charles Lutwidge Dodgson, an eccentric and often renegade mathematics don at Christ Church, Oxford. He wrote the most classical story in the entire history of children's literature, *Alice's Adventures in Wonderland*. One of the most eccentric dons during one of the most eccentric centuries at Oxford, Dodgson wrote treatises on mathematics and symbolic logic, four novels for children, several books of poetry and a series of controversial pamphlets concerning both university and humanitarian issues from architecture to vivisection.

The most curious feature of Reverend Dodgson's polyhedral personality was his preference for the friendship of children as his social companions. He preferred the company of young girls to every other stratum of Victorian society. Dodgson regaled his 'girl-friends', as he called them, with kisses, boating excursions on the Isis, visits to London, tea parties, croquet, card games, brilliant repartee and a bardic gift for telling marvellous stories.

Dodgson's social peculiarities have aroused many relevant questions concerning his libido. It is well known that he photographed and made drawings of his pubescent girlfriends *au naturel*. He wrote them lengthy and fervent love letters. He asked their mothers if they were 'kissable' before proposing to escort them. As he advanced in years, so did some of his companions, and he took them to London or Brighton for days at a time, far beyond the powers of their parents to protect them. Some girls testified that his treatment did them no harm, while the parents of others would become outraged, and prohibit Dodgson from the private company of their daughters. Today, he is memorialised by groups of child pornographers and paedophiles in Britain and America, as the patron saint of both child pornography and child sexual abuse. Had he conducted the same activities today, he would have been incarcerated along with child molesters and child pornographers, but that dubious achievement does not diminish his literary accomplishments by one solitary scintilla.

Dodgson claims another dubious pair of distinctions, for he was an abuser of drugs and a panderer of drugs to his child companions. From a postmodern viewpoint, the most striking feature of Dodgson's greatest work, *Alice's Adventures in Wonderland*, is the astonishing accuracy with which he portrays the psychoactivity of powerful drugs. Alice's visions, her floating fall down the rabbit hole, her radical alterations in size, her loss of identity, her hallucinations of animals, her fears, her emotional surges from pathos to blissfulness, are all characteristics of the hallucinogenic drugs: LSD; magic mushrooms and Ecstasy.

In 1955, Todd published a paper, which maintained that Dodgson's visionary imagination could have been activated by several causes from migraine headaches to brain damage, high fevers to hallucinogenic drugs. His paper came before the 1960s, when the list could be quite safely narrowed to the psychoactive drugs that Dodgson frequently placed in the mouth of his heroine.

Two years after Todd's paper, the world's leading mycologists, Valentina and Gordon Wasson, published their monumental work, *Mushrooms, Russia and History*. They suggested that Dodgson had been inspired by the writings of the English naturalist, Mordecai Cooke, who had described the intoxicating effects of hallucinogenic mushrooms in two books, *The Seven Sisters of Sleep* (1860) and *A Plain and Easy Account of British Fungi* (1862). Noting that Dodgson composed 'Alice's Adventures Underground', a sort of Ur-Alice in 1862, the Wassons wrote, 'We leap to the conclusion that Alice's mushroom is the one Cooke serves us. The timing is perfect.' Since 1957, few other writers have drawn attention to this tantalising situation. One of the most obvious exceptions, is Grace Slick, the American songwriter who composed White Rabbit, during the 1960s, imploring her listeners to follow the White Rabbit and the Alice model to 'feed your head'. Perhaps, the best place to commence our revisitation of Wonderland is in the plot of the story itself.

Throughout Dodgson's saga, Alice ingests a series of mysterious and potent elixirs, foods and fruit. After her plunge down the rabbit hole, she arrives in the dark, underground hall of doors and discovers a little bottle labelled 'Drink Me'. Alice drinks the contents and experiences a 'curious feeling ', as she shrinks to a height of ten inches. Realising that she has left the golden key well out of her reach on the table above her, she takes action by eating a small cake invitingly labelled 'Eat Me', which she finds in a small glass box. Now feeling, 'curiouser and curiouser', Alice's height surges upwards. These spatial distortions are accompanied by fits of crying, interjected between episodic hallucinations of charming animals.

While visiting the home of the white rabbit, Alice imbibes the liquid contents of another mysterious bottle, stating 'I know something interesting is sure to happen whenever I eat or drink anything'. This magic elixir brings on another explosive surge of rapid and uncontrollable growth. Now too large to exit via the doors or windows, she finds herself hopelessly imprisoned within the house of the white rabbit. Her claustrophobic predicament is brought to an end when the white rabbit and his retinue pelt her face with pebbles that are magically transformed into little cakes. Convinced that by eating these metamorphic cakes, she will diminish in size, Alice eats one, and, straightaway, her body shrinks allowing her to escape her uncomfortable confinement.

However, she is now so small that an overly playful puppy nearly tramples her beneath his paws, so she designs a plan to enlarge herself again by eating or drinking something new. As she begins her search for a dose of a new elixir, she meets the character who will become her master of metamorphosis – the blue caterpillar. Perched on a mushroom and smoking a hookah, the blue caterpillar addresses Alice in a 'languid, sleepy voice', doubtless the result of the narcotic contents in his hookah. Informing her that the mushroom is magical, he says, 'One side will make you grow taller, and the other side will make you grow shorter'. The blue caterpillar exits, and Alice embarks on the most violent and terrifying shifts in her size thus far. She grows smaller, then taller, towering over nature at a perilous and vertiginous altitude, far above the tops of trees, lost in the clouds. By eating alternately from her two pieces of the magic mushroom, Alice finally learns to control her magical changes in size. She will use the magical properties of the mushroom to change her size several more times in Wonderland. She eats a part of the mushroom to enter the house of the Duchess, and again as she approaches the house of the march hare. Her last dose is taken after she takes the golden key and opens the door to the beautiful garden. In all, Alice has taken oral doses of the magic mushroom six times in Wonderland.

Other characters in Wonderland take their share of drugs. Bill, the lizard is given an oral dose of a drug after his devastating accident. The mad hatter and the march hare are drastically dependent on caffeine, their drug of choice, while the Dormouse prefers the dozy effects of opiated treacle.

Although Carroll avoided drug motifs in his sequel to Wonderland, *Through the Looking Glass*, the aphasia of the poem 'Jabberwocky' displays a frequent side-effect of psychoactive drugs. In his last two novels, *Sylvie and Bruno* and *Sylvie and Bruno Concluded*, there are only scattered references to pills and medicines. The elfin fairy, Bruno, indulges in one minor escapade of medicine 'tasting', and there are numerous references to the universal drug, alcohol. One of the principal characters, the professor, who is the Royal Physician of Outland, produces drugs that are so popular that he restricts their availability by providing them on only one very special day per week, known simply as, 'Medicine Day'.

In *Sylvie and Bruno*, Dodgson states that one must experience an 'eerie feeling' in order to see fairies. Throughout both of the saga-length *Sylvie and Bruno* books, Lewis Carroll, as the narrator, moves in and out of this eerie state of consciousness to come into contact with his two child-fairies, never explaining the psychological technique he uses to concentrate his attention. Throughout all of his many writings, Dodgson describes a phantasmagoric reality populated by gentle but mischievous fairies and ghosts drawn into magical exploits by adventurers who establish contact with this maddening but blissful world. The biographical evidence suggests that while writing the exploits of *Sylvie and Bruno*, Dodgson was dosing himself with powerful tinctures of psychoactive drugs extracted from digitalis (foxglove) and opium (poppies), as well as others.

Gordon Wasson, the first scientist to publish the hallucinogenic effects of magic mushrooms, recorded numerous reports of mushroom-induced visions among the Indians of Mexico. In their testimony to Wasson, Mexican shamans described their magic mushrooms as 'children' and the visions they induce as populated by myriads of small children. A Zapotec shaman described a vision thus, 'Two little girls appear dressed all in white to reply to the questions that are put to them'. The visionary oracles are '[children] of both sexes but are small, of the height of the mushrooms themselves'. In *Sylvie and Bruno*, the fairy Sylvie sits on a mushroom to make an enchanting form of percussive music on the petals of a daisy.

Dodgson's final book was entitled, *Three Sunsets*, a work of serious poetry. It is adorned with illustrations of fairies by E. Gertrude Thompson. These fairies are all nude girls aged between four and thirteen and drawn from live models engaged by Dodgson. Wasson states that the little people of the shamanic visions triggered by the most well known of psychoactive mushrooms, the *amanita muscaria*, are often girls, and in Siberia, where the fly-agarics (*amanitas*) are prolific, 'The fly-agaric girls... answer questions and play all sorts of tricks'. One of Thompson's illustrations depicts a nude girl sitting on the top of a mushroom. The final illustration in the last of Dodgson's many books, published in the year that he died, depicts three nude girls sheltered from a rainstorm under a mushroom.

In 1885, when Dodgson was beginning to write his first *Sylvie and Bruno* book, he escorted his niece, Nellie, on a walk. In later years, F. Menella Dodgson wrote, 'He took me Newlands Corner way, and when we came to the "fairy rings" among the many trees there, he asked me, "Do you believe in fairies?" I answered that I didn't know, to which he replied: "Ah, that is because you have never seen one." Fairy rings are large underground circles of fungus that cause lush growths of mushrooms to spring up in these fertile and mysterious places.

Wasson regarded the cult of mushroom shamanism as the final vestige of a profound, global Ur-religion of hallucinatory visions induced by a variety of plant drugs. Is it possible that the mild-mannered eccentric, Reverend Dodgson, rediscovered this powerful, ante-diluvian religion of hallucinogenic visions and fairy godchildren?

Dodgson was a man of catholic interests. He was a pioneer and master of photography, when it was an infant artform. He visited a lunatic asylum, and pondered the causes of insanity: 'when we are dreaming... do we not say and do things which in waking life would be insane? May we not then sometimes define insanity as an inability to distinguish which is the waking and which the sleeping life'. Shortly after writing this passage, Dodgson was walking through the Anatomical School Quadrangle at Oxford, where he witnessed a student undergoing the spontaneous effects of an epileptic seizure. This incident kindled an intense medical curiosity in Dodgson's mind, and he accumulated an immense personal library of medical textbooks. This interest led him to the operating theatre of St Bartholomew's in London to witness the effects of general anaesthesia, the medical miracle of its day. He wrote, 'The chloroform took several minutes to act fully, producing first convulsions, and then stupor like that of a man dead drunk'.

Dodgson read voraciously. During his early years at Christ Church, he read the works of Thomas de Quincey, the brilliantly articulate opium addict. He owned a fourteen volume set of De Quincey's works, which were auctioned after his death. In early January 1858, he read Barrett Browning's, *Aurora Leigh*. He read the works of Edgar Allen Poe, who had suffered addiction to opium, and who referred to the depression of drug dependency in his writings. In September, 1857, Dodgson went to Glasgow, where he attended a production of Goethe's *Faust*, a play which contains numerous references to powerful drugs and the hallucinatory world of apparitions, witches and demonic magic.

From April 1858 to May 1862, there is a puzzling and troubling hiatus in his diaries. His family have been accused of purging his diaries of unsavoury passages while they prohibited scholarly access to them until 1953. In 1898, there had been thirteen volumes of holograph diaries, but by 1930 only nine survived. His family have never permitted an unexpurgated edition. The Dodgson biographer, Roger Lancelyn Green wrote, 'The fact that the diaries have been inaccessible to the general critic, biographer, and research student has led to the suggestion that they contain information about Lewis Carroll which his pious relatives wish to keep from the world. That rumour can now be set at rest'. Green went on to recount the destruction of the great mass of Dodgson's papers. Most including any manuscripts of the *Alice* books, had been consigned to the flames by his surviving family members, immediately after his death. Apparently, Dodgson had left instructions to destroy massive parts of his archive, and only a mere handful of his photographs of nude girls have survived. Green speculated, quite correctly in my opinion, that the family might have wished to destroy evidence concerning the personal life of their eccentric relative.

Strong evidence supports Green's suspicions. Dodgson did have a fleeting affair during the blank period covered over by the missing diaries. His survivors clearly wished to eradicate all trace of the Reverend's sexual and other assorted transgressions.

His last book, *Three Sunsets*, reveals the affair during the period covered by the hiatus in the diaries. Additionally, he experimented with powerful psychoactive drugs. His poem, 'Stolen Waters' reveals some of the suppressed activities that engaged Dodgson during the years from 1858 to 1862. Dated 9 May 1862, 'Stolen Waters', twenty-six stanzas in length and composed in iambic tetrameter, is the most important poem in Dodgson's final work. It records his rite of sexual passage in a perennial story of enchantment, intoxication, ecstasy, remorse, madness, catharsis and resignation to the inevitable melancholia of life as an adult. Dodgson tells his story of meeting a ravishingly beautiful sorceress, who hypnotised him and gave him a highly intoxicating dose of a powerful drug that produced a deliciously searing form of pain prior to orgasm. This effect achieved cataclysmic proportions in the mind of the young and innocent clergyman, producing immediate regret, anxiety and an acute psychotic reaction. His once charming seductress transformed herself, into a hideous and revolting old crone. The shattering denouement to the heights of drug-intensified, sexual ecstasy disgusted him and compelled him to bolt headlong, fleeing helter skelter into the 'ghastly night'. Recognising the profundity of his transmutation, Dodgson contemplated suicide. Upon hearing a song that glorified the innocence of childhood, he experienced a catharsis and resigned himself to, 'Be as a child', in a form of atonement for his psychic and spiritual violations. 'Stolen Waters' is the crest of Dodgson's early life, and it vividly reveals the transformation of his libido from adult sexuality to his love for children. That this perverted form of love for his child-girlfriends was fundamentally sexual in character, there can be no serious doubt.

According to his diaries, Dodgson only visited the great Oxford library, The Bodleian, on one occasion, 18 June 1862. Sixteen days later, he told the drug-saturated tale of Wonderland to the three daughters of Dean and Mrs Liddell: Alice, Ina and Edith. Dodgson's visit to the Bodleian coincides perfectly with Wasson's suggestion that he had been influenced by the books of Mordecai Cooke, which were both on deposit at the library at the time of Dodgson's singular visit.

While performing the research for this essay, I examined the Bodleian copies of Cooke's two books. The physical condition of the earlier one, *The Seven Sisters of Sleep*, provides important evidence for Wasson's theory. At first glance, the Bodleian copy of *The Seven Sisters of Sleep* appeared to be unread, for the pages were joined together at the top. For a regular reader at the Bodleian it is uncommon to find unopened volumes from the nineteenth century, although I have found several. The books were originally deposited in uncut form, and many are still unread to the present day. However, on closer examination, I discovered that certain pages had been opened by an earlier reader. The first pages of the book that contained the table of contents had been torn apart quite carelessly, the tops of their pages are jagged and broken, apparently pulled apart rapidly and forcibly by hand as some reader had all too eagerly wished to examine the table of contents. The other signatures in the book are intact and uncut, except for the one containing the ultimate chapter, 'The Exile of Siberia'. Here the tops of the pages are smoothly cut, as if they have been carefully and deliberately severed, coolly and specifically selected for their subject matter. Was Charles Dodgson the first reader to open these few pages in the Bodleian copy of *The Seven Sisters of Sleep*? The question is pertinent, for the chapter deals with the use of magic mushrooms as drugs of vision and ecstasy by the tribal shamans in Siberia, and Dodgson was fascinated by Russia. The Crimean War made a deep and vivid impression on him in the mid-1850s. His diaries resound with notes about the war in Sebastopol, Balaklava and the Malakoff Tower. He viewed an exhibition of Crimean photographs in Ripon and made a note of the signing of the peace. In later years, he invented a game for children he called 'The Ural Mountains'. The only journey Dodgson ever undertook outside of Britain was to Russia. Dodgson was a fully qualified Russophile, and Cooke's chapter on Siberian mushroom shamanism would have drawn his immediate attention. Dodgson would have been immediately attracted to Cooke's *The Seven Sisters of Sleep* for two more obvious reasons: he had seven sisters and he was a lifelong insomniac.

The final pages of the Bodleian copy of Cooke's narcotic text have been opened as well. Cooke describes the techniques for taking mushrooms and smoking hashish along with mixtures of other psychoactive plants: *Datura stramonium* and *Digitalis purpurea*. *Digitalis* is, of course, foxglove, which Dodgson referred to as 'Fairy Bells' in *Sylvie and Bruno*. Foxgloves are also known as fairy caps, and the fairy sitting on top of a mushroom in *Three Sunsets* is wearing a foxglove blossom as a cap. Blossoming foxgloves appear in three of Tenniel's illustrations in *Alice's Adventures in Wonderland*: blue caterpillar; pig baby; and cheshire cat. Tenniel's illustration of the blue caterpillar is the most significant from the viewpoint of psychoactive drugs, for it contains a magic mushroom, a narcotic smoking mixture in the hookah and a foxglove. Cooke's description of the effects of magic mushrooms as distortions in the sizes of objects, is in perfect agreement with the testimony of the blue caterpillar and the experiences of our heroine, Alice.

The day after his visit to the Bodleian, Dodgson went to the University Museum where he would have had an opportunity to see the painting of the Dodo, the extinct, flightless bird that makes such a prominent appearance in Wonderland. Three days after reading in the Bodleian, Dodgson went to London to visit the Royal Gardens at Kew, where he could have seen and learned much more about the botany of psychoactive plants. The first fruitings of *Amanita muscaria* occur in June. Thus, the train of events from the writing of 'Stolen Waters' in early May, to the singular visit to the Bodleian, an encounter with the Dodo, that was closely followed by research at Kew – establishes a dynamic pattern for Dodgson's creative imagination in the days immediately prior to this historic voyage up the Isis on 4 July 1862 with Alice Liddell and her two sisters which led to the full flowering of the drug-rich imagery of his tale of Wonderland.

Like his father before him, Dodgson made the acquaintance of pharmaceutical chemists on the faculty of the university. In the foreword to *A Tangled Tale*, Dodgson referred to the 'medicine so dexterously, but ineffectually, concealed in the jam of our early childhood'. Medicated jam, opiated treacle, drugged cakes and powerful drugs in small containers were quite commonplace elements in Victorian childhood.

Dodgson owned a library of 3,000 books. On his death most of his books were auctioned, but scholars have reconstructed the contents of his library, and 900 of the titles are known. A remarkably large proportion of his library was devoted to medicine. Ironically, Dodgson made a bequest of many of his medical books to a nephew, Bertram Collingwood, who was a student at Gonville and Caius, Cambridge. A leading scholar of Dodgson's library has written, 'Indeed if the numbers involved in the Collingwood bequest were known, the medical books might rival or exceed the mathematical books.'

Interestingly, the burning drug issue of the Victorian era was teetotalism. Dodgson was not a teetotaller. He owned several books arguing against prohibitionism. Dodgson consumed wine frequently and even sponsored wine parties at his college. He frequently offered beer to his child brides over a period of forty years of prolific hospitality to his girlfriends. Upon his death, he left behind a well-stocked liquor cabinet in his college rooms which included: eleven liquors; thirteen champagnes; five sherries and six clarets, along with six soda glasses, three tumblers, three spirit decanters, two pocket flasks and a claret jug.

Reverend Dodgson owned several general works on medicine that dealt with drugs. The author of *Health in the House* advised her readers not to force their children to take the 'soothing syrups' laced with laudanum and other preparations sold under a variety of trade names such as: 'Godfrey's Cordial'; 'Quietness'; 'Child's Preserver' or 'Syrup of Poppies'. She stated that druggists sold massive quantities of these quack remedies, and she felt it necessary to object outright to laudanum, as it was so frequently used on children during the Victorian era. Dodgson also owned, *Infant Amusements or How to Make a Nursery Happy*, which advocated boiling poppy heads, the botanical source for opium, to prepare a decoction for use in case of accidents.

Dodgson owned ten books on homoeopathy. In the nineteenth

century, many homoeopathic drugs were sold in highly concentrated form as tinctures, which came with instructions to dilute them prior to use. Tinctures of toxic plants including: Aconite; Belladonna; Cannabis; Digitalis; Dulcamara; Hellebore; Henbane; Opium and Datura were in general use in the Victorian pharmacopoeia. Many homoeopathic doctors recommended frequent doses, some as often as every fifteen minutes. Clearly, this is a scenario constantly on the brink of catastrophe, with frequent overdoses and chronic dependency for a great proportion of the population. In the nineteenth century, powerful tinctures of psychoactive and hallucinogenic drugs were prescribed for a bewildering variety of symptoms. Opium was universally prescribed as an anodyne, as well.

Dodgson abandoned his early fascination with photography to take up an avid interest in drugs and remedies, which he used as a way to meet 'pretty girls'. In September, 1879, he wrote, 'My homoeopathic remedies are coming in useful. I supplied calemula lotion for Amyatt Hull, who was suffering from blistered feet; and today I have just sent off... eight drops of nux vomica (Arsenic)... for Agnes; sick headache'.

Dodgson owned Sir Benjamin Brodie's, *Psychological Enquiries*, in which the author wrote the following passage:

> At one period opium was much in request among the inferior classes in the metropolis, and there were chemists who disposed of many boxes of opium pills on a Saturday night. Then gin became cheap; the gin-palaces arose, and opium was neglected. This was greatly to the advantage of the revenue. But was it of advantage to society? The effect of opium when taken into the stomach is not to stimulate, but to soothe the nervous system... The opium-taker is in a passive state, satisfied with his own dreamy condition while under the influence of the drug. He is useless but not mischievous. It is quite otherwise with alcoholic liquors... Opium is physically much less deleterious to the individual than gin or brandy.

Dodgson also owned W. B. Carpenter's, *Mental Physiology*, which described the psychoactive effects of many powerful drugs, stating, 'the erroneous perception of space is one of the effects of *Amanita muscaria*, an intoxicating fungus used by the Tartars', con-

firming the account of Mordecai Cooke and echoing the blue caterpillar.

Familiar with chemical operations from his academic training as
well as his practical involvement with photography, Dodgson
owned a book on technical pharmacology, Jones's *Chemical Vase
Mecum for Medical Students*. This textbook contained the formula
and colour tests for morphine, strychnine, digitaline and atropine,
all powerful psychoactive drugs. Dodgson would have had no
trouble in extracting many powerful drugs from plants with the
aid of Jones's useful book.

Stimulants and Narcotics by F. E. Anstie was the most scholarly
and technical work on drugs owned by Dodgson. The author described the effects of psychoactive drugs as 'involuntary fancy'.
This excellent text was published one year prior to Dodgson's
drug-saga, *Alice's Adventures in Wonderland*. Dodgson, who suffered from chronic headaches and insomnia, owned several practical
textbooks on these symptoms. In his 1868 poem, 'The Valley of the
Shadow of Death' he wrote:

> Within the goblet's mystic rim
> Are draughts of healing, stored for him
> Whose heart is sick, whose sight is dim,
> Who prayeth but to sleep!

One book on headache remedies that Dodgson owned prescribed
injections of Belladonna, which would have induced vivid hallucinations and delirium if he followed its advice. Another work, E. B.
Shuldham's *Headaches Their Causes and Treatment*, prescribed Aconite and Belladonna. He wrote, 'Belladonna is another fine drug for
the relief (of headaches)...(there is) occasionally more delirium,
than in aconite...There is sleeplessness alternated with fearful dreaming'. He prescribed Belladonna for menopause as well.

He owned a book written by W. H. Day, a doctor who practised
at the Samaritan Hospital for Women and Children, titled, *Headaches: Their Nature, Causes and Treatment*. For the relief of headache,
Dr Day recommended opium in small doses, but not pushed to the
point of 'narcotism'. Other powerfully psychoactive drugs suggested by Dr Day for the relief of headache include: Digitalis,
Belladonna, Amyl nitrate, Cannabis indica and Henbane.

Over a five year period, Dodgson suffered from symptoms that
have been diagnosed as migraine headaches. During these years,

he experienced two seizures that were diagnosed as 'epileptiform' attacks. A book of his, simply titled, *Fits*, by John H. Waters, suggested the use of ammonia, a highly effective and fast-acting drug as a general remedy for fits. Dodgson's migraines and seizures occurred between the years 1885 and 1891. The scholar of folklore, Selwyn Goodacre, has noticed that during this period Dodgson was under the considerable psychological strain of writing and publishing his two fairy sagas, the *Sylvie and Bruno* books. Rather than mere psychological stress, Dodgson's chronic drug dependency is a far more likely cause of his symptoms.

From 1885 to 1891, Dodgson was a frequent visitor to Outland and Fairyland via the 'eerie feeling' that he said was essential to induce his trance-like visions of these enchanting landscapes. Menella Dodgson's memorable walk with her uncle among the 'fairy rings' took place circa 1885, just when Dodgson began to strain his creative energies to the maximum in order to see fairies and to write his final fantasy sagas. In his correspondence, he wrote about the dream content in *Sylvie and Bruno*, 'The book contains no dreams, this time: what look like dreams are meant for trances after the fashion of esoteric Buddhists in which the spirit of the entranced person passes away into an actual Fairyland'.

Dodgson's two epileptiform seizures occurred five years apart in 1886 and 1891. He suffered the first convulsive attack on New Year's Day, 1886. Somehow, this seizure was audible to Edwin Morshead, who summoned his brother, who was a doctor, and a Dr Stedman. Five years later, Dodgson experienced another loss of consciousness during the morning service at Christ Church. He awoke from an 'uneasy dream' to find himself lying in a pool of his own blood in the stalls of Christ Church Cathedral. For months afterwards, he suffered from severe residual headaches, and his doctor found his digestive system to be out of order. Negative side effects of Digitalis include: convulsions; hallucinations; disagreeable dreams; lingering headaches; vertigo and gastro-intestinal disorders.

Reverend Dodgson owned another book that dealt with drugs in a rather different context from all the others; William Munk's, brilliant essay was titled simply, *Euthanasia*. Munk surveyed the history of euthanasia, mentioning the attitudes of Francis Bacon, Montaigne, Buffon and many other authorities. He referred to the use of stimulants in his discussion of the causes and treatment of delirium in the dying. He wrote, 'Opium is here worth all the rest of the materia medica'. He quoted some of the most respected sources in the history of medicine in his discussion of his preferred drug for treating the terminally ill. Thomas Sydenham was the greatest physician of the seventeenth century, and he favoured opium. Sydenham wrote, 'Of all cordials, opium is the best that has hitherto been discovered. I had nearly said that it is the only one'. Munk quoted another salient passage from Hufeland, 'Who would be a physician without opium in attendance on cancer or dropsy of the chest? How many sick has it saved from despair?' Hufeland even argued, 'Euthanasia... is the sacred duty and the highest triumph of the physician'. Munk fully discussed opium and its more potent alkaloid, morphine. He offered advice on when to administer these powerful drugs orally and when to inject them with a syringe. Opium, morphine and heroin are dangerous and deadly drugs that are of tremendous benefit to patients suffering from intractable pain. The opiates can result in death by stopping the respiration or breathing of the patient if given in too large a dose, thus their traditional use in euthanasia. They provide medical doctors who practice euthanasia with a drug that will guarantee their patients comfort and dignity in their final illnesses. Public records prove beyond any shadow of doubt that an opiate was used in combination with cocaine to euthanise King George VI.

Charles Lutwidge Dodgson developed a respiratory problem during his Christmas visit to his family home in 1897-98. After suffering with increasingly severe respiratory symptoms for about ten days, his nephew observed that, 'His breathing rapidly became hard and laborious'. On January 13, Dodgson uttered the pregnant statement of fact that is his last recorded sentence, 'Take away those pillows, I shall need them no more.' From that statement we may assume that Dodgson, a practising homoeopath and the owner of medical textbooks by Anstie and Munk, would have realised that his life was drawing to its close. From that moment of realisation, he would naturally have wished to take opium, a powerful and comforting respiratory repressant. The following day, at half past two in the afternoon, attended by one of his seven sisters who noticed that his hard breathing had suddenly ceased, Charles Lutwidge Dodgson was pronounced dead.

After his death, two boxes full of drugs and drug paraphernalia were discovered in his rooms at Christ Church. They were deemed so valuable that they were auctioned along with his other possessions.

In his brilliant coming of age poem, 'Stolen Waters', he wrote,

> I drank the juice, and straight away felt
> A fire within my brain:
> My soul within me seemed to melt
> In sweet delirious pain.

DRUGS OF LIBERATION:
From Psychiatry to Psychedelia

Antonio Melechi

The Case of Dr Johnson

In the early 1950s, Dr. Donald Johnson published two deeply paranoic booklets on the subject of hallucinogenic drugs and mental health. In the first of these, *Indian Hemp: A Social Menace* (1952), Johnson argued that the grain or extract of hemp provided the perfect means 'to discredit you personally... to remove you for some time from your affairs, and perhaps permanently from the place where you are living'[1] – in which time 'your enemy, who will have laid his plans, will be consolidating in uninterrupted fashion his control over your finances... or your wife.'[2] As far as Johnson was concerned, there were countless psychiatric patients who were nothing more than hapless victims of hemp poisoning, effectively being held hostage by the institutions in which they were sectioned. In *The Hallucinogenic Drugs* (1953), Johnson reiterated the same fears – adding LSD to the list of substances that could produce insanity in the unsuspecting victim – and called upon his fellow medical practitioners to recognise this possibility when treating the manifestly psychotic.

21

Donald Johnson's career as a drugs commentator is of particular significance to this brief history because not only did his involvement in the issue of hallucinogenic drugs anticipate the work of Aldous Huxley, but if Johnson can be believed – and there is good reason for some doubt – his writings were based on personal experience. Furthermore, Johnson's experience revealed to him not only the diabolical aspects of drug psychosis, but, like Huxley, Johnson also had intimations of another reality, of the transfigured universe invoked in the writings of the mystics, and it was this transcendental realm which Johnson struggled to address in his work.

According to Johnson, he and his wife Betty were poisoned in October 1950, shortly after they were called back to their Oxfordshire hotel, The Marlborough Arms Inn. Over the course of a weekend, the Johnsons experienced a growing and unaccountable sense of anxiety which quickly escalated into full-blown paranoia. As the hotel staff became increasingly concerned with the Johnsons' strange behaviour, husband and wife were admitted to Warneford Psychiatric Hospital in Oxford. In a matter of days, Mrs Johnson had recovered enough for her to return home to the care of relatives. Meanwhile her husband remained in a 'state of mental excitement'. At times believing himself to be undergoing clandestine training for a high ranking position in the UN or the Commonwealth, Johnson also began to suspect that he and his wife had been victims of foul play: 'I felt that I had been poisoned and continued to say so until I saw that no notice was being taken. I had no idea what the poisoning agent was: at that time I still shared the general ignorance in regard to Indian Hemp.'[3]

Soon after his discharge, Johnson set out to establish if the psychosis he had suffered over a period of four weeks could, as he suspected, have been drug-related. A visit to a Harley Street doctor and friend indicated that the symptoms he described were consistent with poisoning by a combination of hemp, opium and datura, and this satisfied him that his suspicions had been founded. Further evidence arrived in September 1951, when the *Sunday Graphic* published a series of articles which sought to alert its readership to the impending danger of the 'reefer craze' becoming 'the greatest social menace this country has known'.[4]

Convinced that hemp had been used to poison him and his wife, Johnson set out to track down his mysterious nemesis. Finding no immediate evidence to implicate his hotel staff or guests, he was quickly distracted from his enquiries by an article in *The Lancet* which reported the outbreak of mass mania in the French town of Pont Saint Esprit, where four people had died, 15 had gone insane and 200 had fallen ill. The consensus of medical opinion favoured the theory that the epidemic was most probably a form of erysipelas caused by an ergot fungus in the local bread – a throwback to the medieval outbreaks of ergotism known as St Anthony's Fire – but Johnson was struck by the similarity between his own psychosis and the outward symptoms of the mania, and in its wake he set out to investigate. From the accounts which he managed to glean from doctors and townsfolk at Pont Saint Esprit, Johnson was left in little doubt that the town had been the victim of a case of mass poisoning by hemp – which he had found to be growing in outlying rural *departments*. Returning home with this even more alarming evidence of the hazards of hemp madness, Johnson set about informing medical practitioners and the general public of the grave dangers which hallucinogenic drugs posed to the nation's sanity.

The connection between hemp and psychosis which Johnson set out to forge was not a new subject for the British. Some 60 years previously the British Army in India had conducted exhaustive research into the use of hemp amongst the native Assamese. The Indian Hemp Drugs Commission Report of 1894 asserted that: 'the excessive use of hemp drugs may, especially in cases where there is any weakness or hereditary predisposition, induce insanity. [However] It has been shown that the effect of hemp drugs in this respect has hitherto been greatly exaggerated, but that they do sometimes produce insanity seems beyond question.'[5] Though Johnson sought to establish a more emphatic link between hemp and insanity, he obscured an aspect of his hemp poisoning which had made a deep impression on him, an experience of profound consequences which he was later able to acknowledge as having changed the whole course of his life.[6]

Addressing the mystical aspects of psychosis in *Indian Hemp*, Johnson noted that 'the transcendental states described by literary *hashishiens* of the nineteenth century are not only specific to hashish, but are also closely paralleled by certain phases in the manic stage of manic-depressive insanity.'[7] As evidence of the latter, Johnson cited John Custance's *Wisdom, Madness and Folly*, an autobiographical account of manic depression in which the author describes the sense of mystical epiphany, telepathic communication and magical release experienced in moments of elation. While Johnson the would-be politician avoided explicit reference to the mystical aspects of his own psychosis, it is clear that he had himself recognised many of the experiences to which Custance made reference.

Indeed, it can be assumed that the following account – which Johnson attributed to an anonymous 'Mr A-', who suffered a 'transient form of mania for no discoverable reason'[8] – is almost certainly his own:

> I too was aware of this 'heightened sense of reality'. I was aware of an increased acuity of vision which brought all colours shining out at me with the brightness of luminous paint. I was afflicted with the rapidity of association of ideas which not only brought out in its early stages remarkable flashes of intuitive insight, but eventually became so overpowering as to burden my reasoning power. I experienced the abnormal suggestibility to which Mr. Custance refers. It was as if everything which I read and heard and saw 'meant something', was conveying a message to me....
>
> I had the same telepathic experiences in a hospital ward as he describes – the personnel of which appeared to act up, almost unconsciously to my own delusions. It was as if the 'unconscious' of everyone who surrounded me appeared to well up inside them as a result of my presence. I was supremely conscious, no longer of the polite superficialities of civilised society, but of the deep forces that motivated and rent the human society in which I was living – forces whose divergencies seemed to be my mission to harmonise....
>
> Finally, I experienced the sense of ineffable revelation as if, in the words of Mr. Custance, 'the whole pattern of one's life seemed to fall into place and make sense', which, also with him, 'I am impelled to rationalise with the idea of an infinite life beyond Time and Space in which all things are possible and all patterns complete.' For me, all the world's problems solved themselves, all sex relationships harmonised, all religions automatically synthesised – all in words which seemed to me to come from the outside, but which issued from my lips, words which should be unforgettable, but which I have unfortunately forgotten...

I lived in a transcendental state. Though a matter-of-fact person, strictly confined in my perceptions in my normal life by the ordinary laws of the physical universe, I became for a short time aware of another world that surrounds us, one of celestial and demonic forces – the world of saints and mystics and divine relations.... A world which I now appreciate exists, as for several days I lived there myself.[9]

Through the account of his alter-ego, Johnson echoes the four aspects which William James identified as characteristic of a state of mystical consciousness: Ineffability – the sense of a fundamentally incommunicable knowledge; Noetic Quality – of overpowering significance; Transciency – the unsustainable aspect of the mystical experience; Passivity – the sense of being in the presence of a higher power. In *The Varieties of Religious Experience* – a key point of reference in John Custance's autobiography – William James observed that in the 'psycopathic temperament' there is the 'love of metaphysics and mysticism which carry one's interests beyond the surface of the sensible world'.[10] Furthermore, James's experiments with nitrous oxide left him in no doubt that it was possible to artificially 'stimulate the mystical consciousness to an extraordinary degree'.[11]

Dr. Johnson's account of his other worldly adventures demonstrates how the transcendental aspects of the drug experience could be expressed and grounded in the language of psychology, a discourse that James was adamant could never simply explain away the religious experience. In this sense, Johnson's hemp experience anticipates the direction of psychiatric experimentation with hallucinogens during the course of the 1950s, which would increasingly reveal the worlds of madness and mysticism as two sides of the same coin. But Johnson's interpretation is one of a number of ways in which the drug experience has been understood by drug users and commentators. Among these other approaches, it is the framework of eastern spirituality mediated by writers such as Huxley, Watts and Leary which is commonly seen to have determined the popular reception and interpretation of psychedelic drugs.[12] This emphasis on the eastern inspired approach to psychedelics has tended to obscure the whole psychiatric context of experimentation, which in the course of the 1950s and 1960s delved into theology, spiritualism and the arts in order to examine the psychology of the psychedelic experience. Out of these dialogues emerged powerful mythologies of transcendence and liberation which informed both the medical and popular use of hallucinogens in this period. These psychedelic mythologies will be examined in this essay, with particular reference to psychiatry and anti-psychiatry in Britain.

The Psychiatric Trip

In the early 1950s, British psychiatrists began to increasingly experiment with hallucinogenic drugs, such as mescaline and LSD. Hallucinogens were not only seen as a means of mimicking and thereby exploring the psychopathology of mental illnesses, they also demonstrated a remarkable capacity to diminish the patient's resistance in therapy and accelerate the talking cure. Even cannabis, long relegated to the Extra-Pharmacopoeia, was again being used with patients demonstrating symptoms not dissimilar to those Johnson had experienced in his own psychosis.

In 1954, the St Guy's Gazette reported the successful treatment of a case of depersonalisation at the York Clinic. Cannabis tincture was administered to a young woman who had experienced an intense sense of detachment and unreality since the birth of her child:

> As the intoxication proceeded she became aware of increasing feelings of anxiety and apprehension which reached a climax at about 6 p.m., when she began quite suddenly to re-enact her labour. At this point she became emotionally excited and claimed she was going to have the baby, without apparent realization that this was a re-enactment of the past... The experience culminated in the delivery of her baby...The following morning when she awoke she had complete insight for the whole process and had regained normal contact to a remarkable extent.[13]

The cathartic release of repressed memories and emotions, known in its therapeutic application as abreaction, had been developed as a clinical technique before the war, when a catalogue of substances, including anaesthetics, opiates, cocaine, mescaline, cannabis and barbiturates, were variously administered to patients suffering from a range of mental disorders. 'Narco-analysis', as the method was known in the 1930s and 1940s, achieved most success in the treatment of neuroses, and was particularly used in wartime with those suffering from shell-shock. Two modes of treatment became connected with narco-analysis. In the first, more commonly used in the treatment of war neuroses, the patient would be administered a large intravenous dose, inducing light sleep or drug coma, particularly with insulin, and the psychiatrist would attempt to establish a hypnotic rapport with the patient as they regained consciousness. In the second method, smaller and slower intravenous injections were used to induce a feeling of well-being and openness, which the psychiatrist could exploit to fathom the genesis of the problem.

The most striking aspect of narco-analysis was its ability to stimulate the recall of withheld traumatic experiences and forgotten events from childhood, manifestly providing psychiatrists, especially the Freudian-minded, with a short-cut to the unconscious. But there were problems. While some psychiatrists claimed that therapeutically it was often enough for the patient to emotionally relive the experience connected with a neurosis, diagnosis was certainly not cure. Furthermore, the technique encountered a recurrent problem: the visions and imagery which narco-analysis prompted were apt to recur with such persistence that they effectively replaced the neurosis.

Abreaction, however, proved of little use or no value in the treatment of the profoundly psychotic. As the search for the psychogenesis of schizophrenia intensified, attention turned to the possibility of an organic basis of mental illness, and psychiatric researchers began experiments with mescaline, the active principle of *peyotl*, the Mexican dumpling cactus, as a possible window into schizophrenia. While mescaline's psychotomimetic properties had been chronicled in numerous experiments since the 1880s, it was not until the 1950s, with the work of Humphry Osmond and John Smythies, that research intimated a breakthrough into discovering a biochemistry of schizophrenia. Smythies's and Osmond's interest in mescaline began with an observation of the similarity of its chemical structure with that of adrenaline, which the body produces naturally in times of stress. Initial self-experimentation left them in no doubt that they had experienced schizophrenia, and this led them to the 'M Factor Theory', postulating that the chemistry of schizophrenia could be understood as the transformation of adrenaline into something akin to mescaline. But, more importantly, they returned from their experiences with the conviction that 'nobody is really competent to treat schizophrenia unless he has experienced the schizophrenic world himself'[14], a sentiment that would become widely held in the psychiatric community over the next twenty years.

In the same way that Havelock Ellis had half a century earlier introduced mescaline to a small coterie of writers and artists in the first British experiments with mescaline, Osmond and Smythies enlisted the services of a number of writers and philosophers whose professional sensibilities would lend themselves to articulating the bizarre and often ineffable transformations of perception and consciousness which mescaline produced. One of the first of these volunteers was Harry 'Ghost Hunter' Price, an Oxford professor of philosophy and former president of the Society for Psychical Research – of which Smythies was a past member. Price was administered .4 grammes of mescaline by his friend Dr Smythies in July 1952. Besides feeling his 'interest in physical or clock-time diminished to almost zero', the session was principally notable for Price in producing a 'heavenly or paradisiac way of seeing', with profound visual transformations which he likened to the paintings of Impressionists and Post-Impressionists.[15] After eight hours or so, when the effects of the mescaline had begun to wear off, he experienced a lasting visual hallucination, as a bedspread transformed itself into a pile of over-sized dead leaves. Price, whose own field of expertise was in the philosophy of perception, was naturally delighted by his hallucinatory experience, reporting it as the best he had ever seen. Mescaline did not, however, provide any insights into the psychic mind – the object of the experiment. There was no telepathy or clairvoyance, no precognition or introcognition, and nothing approaching ESP.

In May of the following year, Osmond introduced mescaline to his most celebrated volunteer, Aldous Huxley. Having contacted Osmond to express an interest in the research he and Smythies were conducting, Huxley had reckoned on mescaline thrusting him into a Blakeian inner world, where he would behold 'visions of many coloured geometries, of animated architectures, rich with gems and fabulously (lovely, of landscapes with heroic figures, of symbolic dramas trembling perpetually on the verge of ultimate revelation.'[16] While mescaline intensified his apprehension of colour and shade, the spectacular visions and fancies which he anticipated did not arrive; mescaline instead edged Huxley towards communion with the real and immediate universe which was transfigured before him, so that in the folds of his trousers, the legs of his chair, the books which lined his shelves, he sensed the rapture of pure existence, a sacramental vision of altered reality.

As the session progressed, Huxley took a walk with Osmond into the garden. In the afternoon sunlight, Huxley's eyes were assailed by a kaleidoscope of colour and pattern, light and shade, and his sense of wonder became infused with a feeling of terror: an intimation of what it must truly be like to be mad. From this experience, Huxley was able to concur with Osmond that mescaline had induced a type of schizophrenia:

> The schizophrenic is not only a soul unregenerate, but desperately sick into the bargain. His sickness consists in the inability to take refuge from inner and outer reality (as the sane person habitually does) in the home-made universe of common-sense...The schizophrenic is like a man permanently under the influence of mescaline, and therefore unable to shut off the experience of a reality which he is not holy enough to live with, which he cannot explain away because it is the most stubborn of primary facts, and which, because it never permits him to look at the world with merely human eyes, scares him into interpreting its unremitting strangeness, its burning intensity of significance, as the manifestations of human or even cosmic malevolence, calling for the most desperate of countermeasures, from murderous violence at one end of the scale to catanoia, or psychological suicide at the other.[17]

Published in 1954 as *The Doors of Perception*, Huxley's essay would become the single most important account of psychedelic experience – as it was soon to be coined by Osmond – and his name and reputation alone ensured a significant amount of publicity. On its publication in Britain, response was mixed. Naturally enough, the essay attracted a considerable amount of interest in bohemian and literary circles who organised their own mescaline parties.[18] At the same time, Huxley's essay incurred the wrath of theologians, such as the orientalist Zaehner, who was so disturbed by Huxley's conflation of the mescaline experience with the beatific vision that he himself volunteered to take mescaline. After being administered a dose under the supervision of Dr Smythies in December 1955, he was able to claim that 'self-transcendence of a sort did take place, but transcendence into a world of farcical meaninglessness.'[19] Huxley responded to Zaehner's heavy-handed criticisms in *Heaven and Hell*, the sequel to *The Doors of Perception*, but Zaehner's final word on the subject of psychedelic experimentation was that he 'would not wish to take the drug again, but purely on moral grounds... the more the experience fades into the past, the clearer does it seem to me that, in principle, artificial interference with consciousness, is, except for valid medical reasons, wrong.'[20]

In 1955 Huxley took mescaline on two further occasions. On the first occasion he was in the company of his long-time friend Gerald Heard, a well-known pacifist, novelist and dilettante in psychical research, who had moved to Los Angeles with Huxley at the end of the 1930s, and Al Hubbard, the eccentric president of a Vancouver uranium corporation who had been developing and popularising his own lay experiments with mescaline and LSD in a bid to reach the spirit world. This group session introduced Huxley to the social aspect of the mescaline experience, seeing it, unlike his earlier one, as a 'transcendental experience within this world and with human references'.[21] Before the end of the year, Huxley and Heard had their first experiences with LSD, courtesy of Al Hubbard. While Hubbard claimed to make psychic connection with others in the group, and Heard contact with the spirit world, Huxley experienced the same mystical transfiguration as on the first occasion with mescaline.

Confirming the potential which mescaline and LSD had in the expansion of human consciousness, these experiences also revealed to Huxley a conflict of interest and approach between those involved in the experiments. Huxley was of the mind that 'the opening of the door' by mescaline or LSD was 'too precious an opportunity, too high a privilege to be neglected for the sake of experimentation',[22] suggesting to Osmond that future research should allow the subject at least an hour of undirected time in which he or she would be left to make their own way towards the 'Clear Light'. In this respect, as Huxley acknowledged to Osmond, both he and Heard were far from ideal subjects in his or any one else's research.

The experience of having sessions conducted by different people with varied agendas, left Huxley convinced that the role of any 'Master of Ceremonies' should be wholly passive and supportive. Even the psychic experiments, which he had previously participated in with Hubbard, he now considered tiresome and childish distractions from the pursuit of personal revelation. On one point, however, he and Hubbard were of a mind. They had both in their own ways been convinced of the power of art and music in any session. While

Hubbard's bag of tricks at this time included an engraving of a child lost in a forest scene, and a pure diamond, Huxley was naturally more highbrow in his tastes, favouring the poetry of Blake, the painting of Vermeer and the music of Bach: art in which a transfiguration of the senses had been seemingly made manifest. Indeed, Huxley was so moved by listening to Bach at his first LSD session, that he wrote to Osmond shortly afterwards suggesting that if he should ever use LSD or mescaline in therapy, to 'try the effect of the B-Minor suite. More than anything I believe it will serve to lead the patient's mind (wordlessly, without any suggestion or covert bullying by doctor or parson) to the central, primordial Fact...which may serve as an antidote to mental health in the future.'[23]

While Huxley clearly had his own personal metaphysics of mescaline, he was still keen for Osmond to expand his research, and assisted with proposals to have mescaline introduced experientially to leading intellectuals. This and other similar proposals were, however, rejected. Without the funding to pursue formal mescaline research on selected artists and thinkers, Osmond restricted himself to an expanding circle of friends and acquaintances. One of these early volunteer subjects was Christopher Mayhew MP, an old friend of Osmond whom he initially contacted in 1955 with a view to having some radio coverage of his research in Britain. Instead, Mayhew suggested to the BBC that they should film him while being administered mescaline by Osmond. The BBC agreed, and in the summer of 1955 a film crew was sent to Mayhew's Surrey home, where they duly filmed Mayhew after being given .4 grammes of mescaline hydrochloride. While sitting in an armchair in his drawing room, Mayhew was intermittently asked simple questions by Osmond. Sometimes he was able to respond, at other times he was totally unreachable: lost in excursions in which he was blissfully unaware of his immediate surroundings, or adrift in profound dislocations of time, in which seconds seemed like hours. Like Huxley, Osmond and others who had experimented with mescaline, Mayhew felt he had experienced insight into the nature of the schizophrenic mind.

When the BBC deemed the footage unsuitable for coverage, Mayhew provided the following account of his experience in *The Observer*:

> I remained sane during the experiment; but there were occasions when I knew with terrible vividness what being

mad was like. The tragedy of the insane was brought home right to me – the agony of having a human heart and mind yet being hopelessly cut off from normal experience of the everyday world.

If these drugs can make normal minds abnormal so safely, how long must we wait to produce a drug which will make abnormal minds normal? For the sake of our vast and growing army of the mentally ill, research on these lines surely deserves the strongest support from governments and scientists.

And these drugs surely have exciting possibilities for the sane. Is there a kind of 'time barrier' through which science can break, as it has broken the sound barrier? Can these drugs give us fresh insight into the mysteries of human knowledge – even into the nature of reality itself.

Many people are shocked by the idea that experiences resembling religious experiences can be produced by drugs. But this fact has been well established for many years. It seems as though the same detachment from the pull of our senses which characterises religious experience can be achieved in entirely irreligious ways.[24]

In the wake of the above article, Mayhew was inundated with letters. While some readers vented their annoyance at the 'drugged antics' of such a responsible figure in public life, others volunteered their services in future experiments, but in the main letters reported experiences of a similar nature induced by yoga, meditation, anaesthetic, psychic sensitivity, bungled operations, abstract thinking and other triggers. A number of homoeopathists also pointed out that their founder, Samuel Hahnemann, had studied the effects of psychotomimetics over a century earlier, and the therapeutic value of these drugs in the homoeopathic treatment of neuroses was long recognised. On the question of the religious dimension of the mescaline experience, one Cannon was able to concede that Mayhew had experienced something akin to religious conversion, indicating that he would himself be willing to have mescaline administered to him.

For Mayhew, the experience of drug-induced schizophrenia proved of lasting significance. The insight prompted him to become actively involved in mental health issues. As a film-maker, he was instrumental in persuading the BBC and Ministry of Health to film life inside a mental hospital – checking himself in as a patient some days before the cameras arrived. This led on to more active campaigning on behalf of the mentally ill as the chair of *Mind* and other organisations. At the same time, his faith in mescaline remained undiminished, and he argued that if it was in his power he would make all psychiatrists, nursing staff and mental health workers 'artificially mad under controlled conditions, so that they could understand what it is like.'[25]

Subsequent accounts of the mescaline experience which appeared in the British broadsheets were all more or less derivative of Huxley. In *The Sunday Times*, Raymond Mortimer described the aesthetic elements of his transformed perceptions in painterly terms but with little suggestion of any significant psychological alterations. A more dramatic and mystical experience was, however, reported by Rosalind Heywood, a long-time researcher into spiritualism, telepathy and ESP:

> Even when blissful, the cosmic interweaving, impersonal, inevitable, indifferent, relentless, eternal 'beingness' of the inner world in the end grew overwhelming. I do not feel I could have survived much longer, without the protective covering of my little ego, but for the appearance of a celestial female figure. She did not seem to be linked with any particular religion. I described her as coming out of the gold, clothed in soft blue and purples, infinitely benign and compassionate... like a pearl coming into a world of diamond... She was gay with a gaiety no scherzo can even hint at and she laughed at me and said, 'You were being shown the universe before the principle of communication, which is love, has been injected into it.'[26]

Another writer who entered the debate on the religious and mystical value of psychedelic drugs was R.H. Ward. In *A Drug-taker's Notes*, Ward provides an account of a series of six LSD sessions that he undertook in 1956 under the supervision of a psychiatrist who was conducting her own experiments. Unlike Zaehner, who set out to trash the transcendental claims of Huxley, Ward expected LSD to lead him towards religious experience but he arrived at the conclusion that God was absent in his experiences, and that there was no short cut on the road to revelation. Yet, in recognising the fundamental importance of self-transcendence, it is interesting that Ward,

like James and Huxley before him, was able to assert that the schizophrenic and mystic were attempting to undertake the same 'liberation
of the soul'. In Ward's sense, the schizophrenic was a kind of near
but failed mystic, 'left supine and moribund on the psychiatrist's
couch'.[27]

While the first wave of 'professional' volunteers, such as Huxley
and Mayhew, reported various insights into the schizophrenic, mystical and creative mind, it is interesting to note that there had been
little in the way of revelations of a directly personal nature which
were manifest in therapeutic experiments. In Huxley's experiments,
his profound mystical awakening did not bring with it any psychological insights into himself. Huxley was certainly interested in this
dimension, particularly in relation to aspects of his childhood which
he barely recollected. In one session, with the psychotherapist, Laura
Archera – whom Huxley would later marry – they attempted to use
a dianetic procedure which had been used successfully by Al Hubbard
in Vancouver to recover some of these memories. In Huxley's case
the method did not yield any results. Instead he claimed he experienced 'something of incomparably greater importance: for what
came through the door was the.... direct, total awareness, from the
inside, so to say, of Love as the primary and fundamental cosmic
fact.'[28]

The Rise of LSD

Since 1947, the pharmaceutical company, Sandoz had made LSD
available to selected medical researchers. The literature which Sandoz
issued with LSD suggested that its use was two-fold: firstly to elicit
release of repressed material in patients suffering from anxiety and
obsessional neuroses; secondly to enable the psychiatrist to gain an
insight into the world of ideas and sensations of mental patients. In
this first respect, LSD provided psychiatrists with an abreactive
action which was largely lacking in the mescaline experience, and
from the early 1950s LSD began to slowly and quietly establish a
foothold in therapeutic treatment.

In Britain, the first psychiatric institution to use LSD was Powick
Hospital in Worcester, where Dr. Ronald Sandison and his colleagues began experiments in 1952. Initial research on patients

suffering from psychoneurotic problems led Dr. Sandison, the pioneer of LSD treatment in Britain, to advance the theory that LSD
exerted a 'selective action on the genes which may be the seat of
repressed memories.'[29] The first experimental study on neurotic
patients at Powick, made the following observations regarding the
LSD experience. Firstly, there was a tendency for the patient to
regress to an automatic, uninhibited and more 'primitive' type of
behaviour. Secondly, there was often a powerful release of repressed
material, frequently accompanied by crying and screaming. Thirdly,
in response to this intense upsurge of psychic materials, patients
were liable to become disturbed or violent, exaggerating the patients
neurotic symptoms into panic, which would require contact and
support from psychiatric staff. And lastly, there were some patients,
typically those who were previously inaccessible in previous treatments, who were found to resent the approaches of people around
them, and to be particularly sensitive to criticism or changes of
environment.

From these early clinical findings – far removed from the experiences reported by Huxley and other volunteers – a therapeutic
approach was developed at Powick which sought to enable the
patient to 'explore his own mind while retaining sufficient consciousness to record the experience and reproduce it afterwards.'[30]
As this meant patients would be increasingly required to provide
written records of their experiences to be used as the basis of therapeutic sessions, it followed that the model patient for LSD treatment
would be educated and literate; able to convey the rush of memories, visions and psychic transformations experienced under LSD.

Preparation for the LSD treatment at Powick required patients to
be admitted into hospital and given a gentle introduction to drug-
assisted psychotherapy under pentothal, a short-acting barbiturate
which had been used in the days of narco-analysis. The course of
LSD would then begin with a dose of 25 gamma, which would be
increased through subsequent sessions through the week until an
'adequate reaction' was obtained. After two to four weeks the patient's response to treatment would be evaluated, and, depending
on the reaction, patients would remain in hospital or continue the
weekly treatment as out-patients. In exceptional cases, when a patient responded particularly well to LSD, and where relatives were
co-operative, they were permitted to take LSD in their own homes.
Where there were marital problems of a sexual nature, husband and
wife were sometimes encouraged to take LSD together at home. All

patients were required to write a full account and interpretation of the LSD experience in the two or three days following the treatment. Drawings and pictures of 'more telling phantasies' were also encouraged.

LSD treatment typically took place in a 'simply but tastefully furnished room with even and non-stimulating colour'.[31] Mixed with distilled water, LSD would be given to the patient by a nurse who would remain by the patient over the course of the session. As the therapist was able to spend only limited time with patients, perhaps spending up to an hour at the height of the reaction, the role of the nursing staff was seen as pivotal. At Powick, the following instructions were given to nursing staff overseeing LSD treatment:

> The nurse may either be nearby or sit with the patient. Most patients need this human contact more as a necessary link with reality than as a sympathizer with their distress. Crying out, emotional weeping or outbursts of screaming or shouting may occur and should not be discouraged. The patient may desire to talk. Specific enquiries about the nature of the mental disturbance should be made only at the doctor's request but the questions may be answered as the nurse sees fit. Occasionally, patients prefer to be left alone, knowing only that the nurse is nearby. It should be borne in mind that the patient is in a heightened emotional state... and must not be taken personally.[32]

When the session had run its course, the patient would be provided with materials to describe and reflect upon the experience. In the day or evening following the treatment, the therapist would visit the patient with a view to drawing out 'additional psychic happenings' and helping them make the best of their material. Not all of the psychic material produced in these LSD experiences was, however, of intrinsic interest to the therapist. The transformations of the body-image, the changes in the material sense of surroundings, and even many of the illusions and hallucinations were not seen as having any necessary relation to the patient's unconscious.

For Sandison, *bona fide* unconscious material was seen to bear a Freudian or Jungian stamp:

To deal with the Freudian material, phantasies of inter-
course with parents, death wishes and supreme love to
parents, phantasies of conception, intra-uterine life and
birth may be cited as examples. The therapist, nurses and
other patients may also become temporarily transformed
in the patient's mind into the parents and may be asked
to play these roles by the patient. In Jungian terms, the
sense of dissociation from the body, of timelessness of an
atmosphere of ancient things. There is a common tendency for patients of European origin... to have phantasies
of being in ancient Egypt or Greece.[33]

The LSD experiences which were published in the psychiatric journals of 1950s make fascinating reading. The testimonies describe
hallucinations of snakes and spiders, fantasies of Ancient Egypt,
visions of hell, out of body experiences, and full scale abreactions of
recovered memories. The most common abreaction was that of being born. In the experience of one psychotherapist, Frank Lake, over
half his patients underwent some kind of birth trauma in the course
of LSD treatment, finding that the re-enactment of this primal drama
often brought dramatic relief to their current symptoms. Working at
the frontier of psychiatry and theology, Lake recognised the patient's notion of 'God' and 'Universe' to be intimately connected to
early infantile experience. The preternatural states experienced under LSD were seen as the return of these earlier primal emotions.
According to this approach, the mystical sense of unity and oneness
reported by patients was recognised as a re-living of the child's
relation to the mother.

While the production of unconscious material was seen as a vital
step in LSD treatment, recovery required the patient to work through
the insights that had manifested themselves under the influence of
LSD. Transference was held to be the key to successful therapy, and
this process was itself rapidly accentuated by the suggestibility of
the patient under LSD. On one level, transference required the patient to recognise and produce what was expected of him or her, and
LSD was seen to instantly produce a degree of transference usually
achieved after a couple of months of analysis. At Powick, this process was taken to its natural conclusion when patients were sometimes
recommended to read Jung's *Modern Man in Search of a Soul*, Francis
Wicke's *Inner World of Man*, and Chricton Miller's *Psycho-analysis*. Of
course, this also reflected the intellectual capacities of the patients,

which at some institutions was an important criterion in the selection of those suitable for LSD treatment.

By 1956 over 100 patients suffering from a wide variety of neurotic problems had received LSD treatment at Powick. The success rate was high, with over 60% of patients recording an improvement or total recovery. Furthermore, experimentation on a small body of schizophrenic patients gave promising signs that a combination of LSD and chlorpromazine – a neuroleptic drug – might prove a basis for treatment of psychotics who had been previously regarded as unresponsive to LSD therapy. At the same time, lessons had been learned. Firstly, LSD appeared to be of little use as an abreactive for recent traumatic events – its assumed speciality was in bringing deeply repressed or long forgotten childhood experiences into consciousness, as well as birth and pre-natal experiences. Secondly, the traditional psychiatric ward or ward side-room was clearly not a suitable setting for the treatment.

In 1958 Powick opened a purpose-built LSD unit, and in the same year began a long running experiment in permissive group therapy. Bringing together a group of ten women patients who had been ill for a number of years and failed to respond to any previous treatments, Powick's Medical Superintendent, Arthur Spencer, set about creating an environment in which traumatic childhood experiences could be re-lived in the emotional security of a family-like group. A large room was furnished in the style of a child's playroom, complete with sand pit, paddling pool, modelling clay, piano, miniature zoo and an assortment of games and cuddly toys. And there was also a record player on which light classical music was played.

With therapist and nurse consciously assuming the role of surrogate father and mother to the group, the negative emotions that would be stirred in abreaction needed to be channelled outside the group – the possibility of uncontrollable violence having made Spencer err against having male groups – and this problem was solved by the use two fully dressed adult and children tailor's dummies. These dummies were the 'bad family' who would bear the brunt of the physical rage that might flare up against parents or siblings.

Decapitation, dismemberment and other forms of violent assault were not uncommon. The principle victim of these attacks was the father dummy, who was on one occasion dragged to an adjoining toilet, where his was head shoved down the pan and the toilet flushed. Mother dummy and children were left surprisingly unscathed. As emotions ran high, feelings of love and attachment would also emerge. Often patient's would seek re-assurance from the therapist/father and nurse/mother, sitting on their knees while being consoled. The various objects and toys in the room were also subject to intense bonding, with one patient taking a fancy to a large teddy bear, from which she was subsequently inseparable. The freedom of the patients to express themselves was paramount; the nurse or therapist would only intervene when a patient appeared likely to injure themselves or others. This freedom extended to leaving the room at any time during the day, and patients would sometimes spend the best part of the day in the hospital grounds, where they could walk, pick flowers, and even swim naked in a nearby brook.

When we consider the staging of the LSD environment, the roles played by psychiatric staff and the cues issued to patients, we are clearly entering the scene of an elaborate drama with its own ritualised content.[34] The dramatic element has special relevance to group therapy because of its emphasis on action. Whereas individual therapy relied heavily on reflection, with patients written accounts being discussed in subsequent meetings with the therapist, the healing process in group therapy seemed to have shifted to the scene itself, so that therapy was taking place in real time. While a tape recorder was at hand to capture conversations, most patients objected to hearing themselves played back, one patient complaining that it was like hearing her soul speaking.

Not all LSD treatments, however, staged therapy as drama. At Marlborough Day Hospital, where research with LSD began in 1958, treatment was more sober in character. Here LSD was seen to be most effective in specific cases of neurosis and psychosomatic illness among the educationally privileged, which by 1961 was already limited to 5% of new diagnostic patients. Suitability for treatment was assessed by use of the Rorshach Test. Talking was discouraged during the session as this was seen as 'a form of defence against deep feeling and recall of repressed memories.'[35] Staff could be called when needed, and would stay with patient as and when requested. While teddy bears, mirrors, family photographs and feeding bottles were available to the patient to act out infantile feelings, treatment was much more steered to reflection. As at Powick, patients were asked to produce a report which would form the basis of an interview before the next session.

Minor cases of neurosis and anxiety were generally treated at Marlborough. One of the successful treatments recorded was the 'case of a would-be writer who succeeded in unravelling his unconscious difficulties under Lysergic Acid.'[36] The author, 'Joseph', was referred to Marlborough by his GP in 1958 suffering from 'tension, irritability and difficulty in working'. In a series of ten LSD sessions Joseph experienced a number of intense emotional experiences closely linked to his childhood. The most profound of these experiences was the feeling that he was dying, if not already dead. From this experience he felt his life to be subsequently transformed, making him, in the words of his therapist, 'a well adjusted and productive neurotic whose deep understanding of human motives is a real contribution to his fellow men.'[37]

Having had insights into their own unconscious, it was natural for patients to develop interests and faith in psychology. In Joseph's case, he realised how essential the mother-son relationship is, claiming that psychological theory on this subject was correct. In the case of a 45-year-old academic treated at Marlborough for a 'character disorder', Freudian theories were employed in a complex auto-analysis which led his therapist to suggest he had been actually overly influenced by his reading.

Despite the increasing numbers of psychiatrists and therapists using LSD in the early 1960s, it remained an essentially fringe treatment whose efficacy was questioned by the mainstream. A *Lancet* editorial from 1961 argued that 'Much more knowledge of good (and ill) effect is needed before LSD can be introduced into the mental welfare curriculum. It remains a talking point whether drug psychosis has most in common with schizophrenia, affective disorder, toxic delirious state, or extended temporal lobe aura, and it is even more doubtful how far it is therapeutically effective.'[38] Furthermore, some Jungian analysts, such as Michael Fordham, were sceptical of the value of drug-induced archetypal imagery, claiming that the burden of integrating the deluge of psychic material produced under LSD into the ego was an unmanageable task.

But LSD had certainly captured the imagination of both patients and therapists. Being commonly agreed among practitioners that self-experimentation with LSD was a necessary and valuable experience for those using it in treatment, some sceptics argued that the therapist's 'affective identification' with the LSD experience created an unhealthy dynamic. However, these notes of caution fell on deaf ears. Those who had been privy to the LSD incursions into the unconscious were rarely just impressed, they were believers. In this respect, Osmond's own fervour was unrestrained:

For myself my experience with these substances have been
the most strange, the most awesome and amongst the most
beautiful in a fortunate and varied life. These are not es-
capes but enlargements, burgeonings of reality... Those who
have had these experiences know, and those who have not
had them cannot know, and, what is more, the latter are in
no position to offer a useful explanation.[39]

A decade after Osmond's first experiments with mescaline, the
connections between the psychotic and psychedelic experience had
become well documented. As a consequence, there was a remarkable
willingness for researchers and experimenters to regard the schizophrenic and mystical experience as sides of the same coin. LSD and
mescaline had opened a window onto the private world of schizophrenia, eroding the stigma and misunderstandings which surrounded
it. As one recovered schizophrenic was reported as saying:

One of the most encouraging things that happened to me
in recent years was the discovery that I could talk to normal
people who had the experience of taking mescaline or
lysergic acid, and they would accept the things I told them
about my adventures without asking stupid questions or
withdrawing into a safe, smug world of disbelief. Schizophrenia is a lonely illness and friends are of great
importance.[40]

Laing and Anti-Psychiatry

A new and radical understanding of schizophrenia was now also
beginning to manifest itself within psychiatry, most particularly in
the work of R.D. Laing, whose early writings, *The Divided Self* (1960)
and *The Self and Others* (1961), described an internal logic in the
schizophrenic's splitting of the self, and argued against the use of
tranquillisers and electroshock to jolt the psychotic back to 'reality'.
In *The Politics of Experience* (1967), Laing's re-thinking of schizophrenia and its social labelling moved him even further in rescuing madness
from the discourse of psychiatry, reclaiming it as a form of self-
healing, and making implicit parallels with transcendental and

psychedelic experiences. While Laing's version of schizophrenia as the failure of the social lobotomy found little support within mainstream psychiatry, his politics of alterity found a ready audience in the psychedelic underground, who adopted Laing as guide for their collective journey into inner consciousness.

Laing's own introduction to LSD occurred in 1960, at the Hampstead flat of a colleague who had begun LSD experiments with patients at Shenley Hospital. Having been told to anticipate a psychotic reaction, he prepared himself for the worst, but the experience, as recorded in this unedited interview with Loveday Drugs Books, proved revelatory:

> I took it with a certain amount of anxiety but this first experience was both very remarkable, and it had, it was an experience of extraordinary familiarity, as though my ordinary experience was transitory and alienation or estrangement from more radical, more primary sort of experience which it seemed I had probably been in as a very young baby, a very young child which I had lost in adjusting to other people's social reality... And it was remarkable in all sorts of ways which have been described by all sorts of people; enhancement of multi-levels of association that one can simultaneously bring to bear in a way that one only glimpses in a usual state of consciousness. The experience of being able to travel through time in a way that the past wasn't simply something at a distance but parts of this present experience were co-present to one, one could move from one to the other and any nook and cranny to the side was opened out etc.[41]

Over the next few years, Laing's drug experimentation brought him closer and closer to the counter-culture. After his first experience with mescaline, which proved even more powerful than LSD, he introduced it to Alexander Trocchi, the Glaswegian poet, novelist and former Situationist. Laing's relationship with Trocchi took him to the heart of the 1960s drug culture. Laing's therapeutic defence of cannabis was included in Trocchi's sigma portfolio, and with Trocchi and William Burroughs, Laing began to collaborate on a book on drugs and creativity, *Drugs of the Mind*, which never progressed beyond lengthy discussion.

In 1964, Trocchi provided Laing with an introduction to Millbrook through Allen Ginsberg. Having been forced to give up his academic position at Harvard, Timothy Leary had turned his back on psychology and found religion in LSD. At Millbrook, a large estate north of New York, he headed The Castalia Foundation, which had just begun to train guides for future 'workshops' for invited luminaries and the paying public. Not looking forward to the prospect of meeting a 'dreary platitudinous British psychiatrist', Leary was bowled over by Laing the 'turned-on, wry Scottish Shaman'. As Leary recalls the meeting:

> We sat at the table, ate a sandwich, drank wine. I told him that the medical-therapeutic talk about LSD was a fake. I was interested only in the mystic aspects of the drug.
>
> He said that the only doctor who could heal was the one who understood the shamanic, witchcraft mystery of medicine... After a bit he said he knew an interesting game. Did I want to play?
>
> We took off our shoes.
>
> The point of the game is to move your hands and your body without talking.
>
> We began to spar.... Our hands changed into a dance. Paired sculpturing of air, moulded liquid forms, now moving slowly, then whirling. My eyes were riveted to his eyes. I was gone. Spun out of the kitchen at Millbrook, spun out of time. Stoned high in a Sufi ballet. We were two organisms from different planets – communicating. I was an Eskimo on an ice floe. He was a visiting explorer. We were exchanging the hard-core information about life, our tribe, the mystery. We were two animals of different species, of the same litter, from separate ages.[42]

If in Leary's opinion Laing was the most fascinating man on the planet, Laing's attitude to Leary and Millbrook is less clear. In *Bomb Culture*, Jeff Nuttall writes that Laing was impressed with IFIF – The International Foundation for Internal Freedom – which Leary and his ex-Harvard colleagues were running at Millbrook, and that Laing and Trocchi corresponded with Millbrook after his visit. In a recollection of the Millbrook meeting, over two decades later, Laing claimed that 'it was a bit sticky, we didn't have very much to talk about', and goes on to distance himself from their messianic belief in LSD as the road to salvation.[43] Yet, while Laing was certainly no

acid revolutionary, there was clearly more common ground between him and Leary than he was prepared to concede publicly.

Some months after their first meeting, Leary sent Richard Alpert
over to London to discuss LSD with Laing. Alpert and Laing took
psilocybin together – a larger dose than the less experienced Laing
had taken before – and shared a trip in which few words were
exchanged, but there was a deep sense of exploring each other's
presence. Shortly afterwards, Alpert was invited to give a talk on
LSD at the Langham Clinic, where Laing was a director. While
Alpert gave a lucid account of LSD's properties to therapists and
researchers connected to the clinic, he did not make a favourable
impression. Laing's connections with Trocchi and the drug culture
had already caused a rift between himself and Eric Graham Howe,
the clinic's founder. The Alpert talk served only to further alienate
the two, and soon afterwards Laing was asked to resign.

By the summer of 1965, Laing had severed all connections to The
Tavistock Clinic, the Institute of Psychoanalysis and mainstream
psychiatry. At his private practice at Wimpole Street, he attracted an
increasing number of fashionably troubled clients, with whom he
would sometimes share an LSD session on a Saturday afternoon;
and at Kingsley Hall, in the East End of London, Laing's version of
an anti-hospital cum residential community was taking shape.

Kingsley Hall was a more radical and anarchic version of Villa 21,
an experimental unit for schizophrenics which David Cooper – who
first coined the term anti-psychiatry – had begun at Shenley Mental
Hospital in 1962. Working within the NHS, Cooper's ward broke
down some of the divisions between 'staff' and 'patients', giving
'patients' the power to organise their own work and plan their own
activities. Building on this precedent, Kingsley Hall provided a permissive environment for its residents, allowing the healing process
to run its natural course without intervention. But Kingsley Hall was
more than just a residential community. From the very beginning it
staged exhibitions, conferences and lectures, as well as providing a
base for the Anti-University. Quickly establishing itself as an important centre of underground activity, Kingsley Hall came to embody
a type of radical lifestyle and philosophy which, according to Laing's
son Adrian, was seen to champion the search 'to find one's true and
authentic self, to let go of the pre-conceived ideas of one's false self
as imposed by the family and society at large.' To this end 'a plethora
of mind-altering substances were floating around. Most popular of
all LSD-25.'[44]

Shaman to the Underground

Since 1966, LSD had become the subject of increasingly mixed publicity. While the poet George Andrews claimed 'LSD is the only answer to the atom bomb'[45], and Paul McCartney confessed how he had discovered through LSD that 'God is everything and everywhere and everyone',[46] reports of delayed psychosis, attempted suicide and possible chromosomal damage now appeared in medical journals. Elsewhere, the MP Jonathan Aitken reported his own LSD experience, featuring 'visions of hell. Continents dripping with blood. Black men fighting brown men, fighting yellow men.'[47]

With LSD making the headlines, Laing was increasingly asked to state his thoughts on the psychedelic experience. In January 1966, Laing delivered a paper on the 'Phenomenology of Hashish, Mescaline and LSD' to psychiatrists at London Hospital, followed some months later by a paper on 'The Experience of LSD' at the ICA. In the *New Society's* report on the latter he was reported as speaking in 'mystical almost medieval language', whilst insisting that the experience should not be undertaken without due care, and, most importantly, in the presence of a guide.[48] On the subject of LSD in *Student*, Laing suggested its 'therapeutic' potential lay in its ability to open up emotional free flow, dissolve defences and make available much of the unconscious. He would not, however, be drawn to openly advocate its use. Instead he suggested that 'one ought not to believe that the regimentation of one's own biochemistry comes solely within the province of the state.'[49]

While all of Laing's public statements on the subject of LSD and other hallucinogenic drugs showed him to be a reluctant advocate of the psychedelic experience, he was known to his inner circle as an enthusiastic experimenter. By the summer of 1965 he had taken LSD on 20 or 30 occasions, overseen a hundred or more sessions, and was clearly a believer in the consciousness-expanding potential of LSD:

> ... we'll presume that the ego is a very small part of what we potentially can experience, and that in order to fit into other people's aims, that is, to social reality, our egos have become very small indeed. And the relevance of drugs is that they release the person from being as it were imprisoned inside the ego... what it seems to open out is a sort of relatively undifferentiated matrix of experience which

is perhaps comparable to the way a child experiences itself in the first few months of life, and beyond that again...call it the void or nothing or the primary clear void...Coming back from the void into the matrix is what I would call reincarnation and from the matrix experience into the ego again is what I would call re-birth...There's a tremendous need to get out of this alienated little ego here and if the people don't do it by flipping out into a psychotic state, a lot of people try to do so by means of drugs, and in fact I think they are enabling themselves to have a perfectly natural experience, I think, by means of drugs.[50]

With talk of re-incarnation, re-birth and the primary clear void, Laing was privately embracing a new order of language, abandoning psychiatry's claim to psychosis, the drug experience and other forms of altered consciousness. While Laing's fellow anti-psychiatrists Aaron Esterson and David Cooper – who together with Laing fronted the Philadelphia Association which managed Kingsley Hall – broadly shared the same belief in regression as a form of self-healing, there were differences between them. Not only did neither Cooper or Esterson share Laing's fascination with psychedelic drugs, but the more politically-minded Cooper was only interested in the transcendental in as far as it might provide an opportunity of escaping the strictures of the social world, priming the subject for radical engagement.

The publication of *The Politics of Experience* (1967) took Laing to new heights of popularity; his heady mixture of polemic and poetry fast becoming required reading for the counter-culture. Laing's thesis was that schizophrenia was not an illness but a label attached to a particular form of alienation, and his analysis of the psychiatric diagnosis and treatment of the schizophrenic experience served as a more general critique of a social system intent on producing normality. 'Pseudo-sanity', for Laing, represented the triumph of the outer over the inner, the ego over the self, in a systematic denial of genuine experience. Echoing the social theory of Herbert Marcuse, Laing argued that society was educating its children to lose themselves:

As adults we have forgotten most of our childhood, not only its contents but its flavour; as men of the world, we hardly know of the experience of the inner world: we barely remember our dreams, and make little sense of them when we do: as for our bodies, we retain just suffi- cient proprioceptive sensations to co-ordinate our movements.... unlearning is necessary for anyone before one can begin to experience the world afresh, with inno- cence, truth and love.[51]

For Laing, like many of the influential thinkers of the radical left, mystification ruled the day. Liberation was possible, but only through a radical unthinking of the known. To move beyond, to disengage one's self from one's ego, called for a revolution in the head. A prototype of this new anti-heroics was to be found in psychosis and schizophrenia:

When a person goes mad, a profound transposition of his position in relation to all domains of being occurs...The Madman is however confused... Nevertheless, he often can be to us, even through his profound wretchedness and disintegration, the hierophant of the sacred. An exile from the scene of being as we know it, he is an alien, a stranger, signalling to us from the void in which he is foundering... [Yet] Madness need not be all breakdown. It may also be breakthrough. It is potentially liberation and renewal as well as enslavement and existential death.[52]

As evidence of the curative power of the schizophrenic experience, Laing devoted one chapter of *The Politics of Experience* to an account of 'A Ten-Day Voyage' undertaken by the sculptor Jesse Watkins – a psychotic regression in which Watkins felt he had tapped into lost powers, returning from his adventure re-awakened to himself and the world. For Laing, Watkins's experience, his voyage, was not an illness to be treated, but 'a natural way of healing our own appalling state of alienation called normality'.[53]

While *The Politics of Experience* took its place on the psychedelic bookshelf, it did so without explicit reference to hallucinogens, and it was only in snatches of its prologue, *The Bird of Paradise*, where intimations of a psychedelic influence in Laing's thinking could be traced. *The Bird of Paradise* was Laing's attempt at a prose poem in the spirit of Gérard de Nerval. Contained within it are fragments of psychedelic sensations and epiphanies, ending with his famous final plea: 'If I could turn you on, If I could drive you out of your wretched mind, if I could tell you I would let you know'.

One of the many psychiatrists who were scathing in their criticism of *The Politics of Experience* was Humphry Osmond, who accused Laing of presenting a 'psychedelic model of madness'[54], wilfully confusing the psychotic and psychedelic experience. That Laing was connecting the journey of the schizophrenic with that of the 'voyager' – a term which he adopted from the American psychedelic movement – was indeed clear, but Laing was certainly not claiming that the actual experiences were anything more than comparable. Where the two experiences were connected for Laing was at the level of function: both serving as possible inroads into the transcendental. In as far as any model underpinned this re-writing of psychosis as a sacred journey, it is shamanism that appears to have been the important influence on Laing's thinking.

Laing had been fascinated with the ritual of primitive healing since the early 1960s. This interest evolved in no small measure through his friendship with Francis Huxley, whom he came into contact with in this period. As an anthropologist, Huxley had begun his studies in early 1950s in Brazil, coming into contact with the vestiges of shamanic customs in the Urubu Indians. Through his Uncle Aldous, Francis developed an interest in LSD and mescaline, and had in the late 1950s and early 1960s acted as guide in some of Osmond's experiments at Saskatchewan Hospital. From his understanding of healing ritual and drug use in shamanic culture, Huxley turned his anthropologist's eye onto the clinical and therapeutic community and observed the dramatic function of LSD therapy well before Laing's writing took its shamanic swerve. In the late 1960s Laing and Huxley played host to a visiting Brazilian shaman, which various members of the underground were invited to see in action, watching him on one occasion remove ectoplasm from someone's back without leaving any trace of entry. Indeed, it was not unknown to see Huxley and Laing themselves perform the odd spot of shamanic exorcism and voodoo ritual on willing friends.

While Laing kept his interest in the shamanic private, and was certainly not prepared to openly acknowledge this influence in his writing, it is clear that in divesting the schizophrenic experience from the language of pathology and physiology, he sought to accord the returned 'voyager' a status akin to that of the shaman in traditional cultures. In this sense, Laing was following the religious historian Mircea Eliade, who argued that:

the primitive magician, the medicine man or the shaman is not only a sick man; he is, above all, a sick man who has been cured, who has succeeded in curing himself. Often when the shaman's or medicine man's vocation is revealed through an illness or an epileptoid attack, the initiation of the candidate is equivalent to a cure.[55]

Having navigated through the geography of inner time and space, Laing suggested that the returned voyager was qualified to assume the role of guide, joining physician and priests in shepherding other voyagers back to make contact with the reality we have all long lost contact with. The most famous exponent of this philosophy at Kingsley Hall was Mary Barnes, a diagnosed schizophrenic who was allowed to act out her wish to return to an earlier version of herself under the guidance of fellow psychiatrist Joe Berke, Laing and others. In her first two years at Kingsley Hall, she was fed with a bottle, played with her faeces, and became totally dependent on her carers. By the end of 1967 she began to recognise her past as a spider's web – an hallucination commonly reported in LSD treatments – in which she was enveloped. Through painting, Mary was encouraged to break free from her past, and her monstrous spiders appeared in her first artistic efforts. As her abstract and biblically inspired finger paintings began to spread over Kinsgley Hall, much of the press and media attention which the community was receiving singled her out for special attention. In the spring of 1969 Mary had her first exhibition at Camden Arts Centre, was featured in a BBC documentary on schizophrenia and was interviewed by a number of national newspapers. In the *International Times*, which had from day one adopted Laing as its guide into inner space, Mary was placed in the mystical tradition of St Teresa, describing her as a 'remarkably sane woman' who demonstrated that 'the few sane people in our society are those who have experienced, out of breakdown, a kind of resurrection.'[56]

By 1969 Kingsley Hall was, however, coming to a close and Laing himself was preparing to spend a year out in Ceylon and India, to 'seek out situations where serious meditation was going on'.[57] With the demise of anti-psychiatry as an influential social movement came the increasing rejection of LSD by mainstream psychiatrists. A 1968 survey by the Institute for the Study of Drug Dependency showed that 4,300 patients and almost 200 volunteers had taken LSD since the early 1950s, totalling nearly 50,000 sessions in all. Furthermore the study revealed that only 41 clinicians were still using LSD, and the majority of those who had discontinued its use did so because they deemed it either ineffective or dangerous. Although the clinical rejection of LSD was clearly linked to the adverse publicity which it had received in the medical reporting of alleged chromosomal damage, psychosis and suicide, it was the demonization of LSD in the popular press which created far greater difficulties for psychotherapists and psychiatrists.

By the end of the 1960s the discourse of psychology had all but lost its claim on the psychedelic experience. The chasm that had opened up between anti-psychiatry and psychedelia was now evinced in David Cooper's belated lament that the drug culture's pursuit of the clear void was an 'historical impossibity' and 'betrayal of the revolutionary imperative'.[58] While the counter-culture still sought to transcend the ego and journey into the innermost regions of the self, the cult of regression was now only one form of retreat from the world. Psychedelia had by now evolved a new language of alterity, turning to eastern spirituality, magical arts, space, astrology, folklore and children's literature, to explore other lost worlds and create new mythologies of liberation.

Notes

1. Johnson, D. (1952) *Indian Hemp: A Social Menace*. London: Christopher Johnson, p 76.

2. *Ibid.*, p 83.

3. Johnson, D. (1953) *The Hallucinogenic Drugs*. London: Christopher Johnson, p 13.

4. Ralph, J. *Sunday Graphic*, 16 September 1951. Quoted in Johnson (1952), p 45.

5. Hemp Drugs Commission Report 1894, quoted in Andrews, G. and Vinkenoog, S. (eds) (1972) *The Book of Grass*. Harmondsworth: Penguin, p 200.

6. In 1961, at the Royal Medico-Psychological Association's conference on Hallucinogenic Drugs and their Psychotherapeutic Use, Dr Donald Johnson MP claimed that through his 'transcendental emotional state' he had been put in contact with a force ordinarily

removed from everyday life. As a consequence, he confessed that 'the whole trend of my life did happen to alter', acknowledging the influence of this experience in helping him to secure his first parliamentary seat!

7. Johnson, D. (1952) *op.cit.*, pp 69-70.
8. *Ibid.*, p 73.
9. *Ibid.*, pp 73-74.
10. James, W. (1960) *Varieties of Religious Experience*. London: Collins, p 45.
11. *Ibid.*, p 373.
12. See Lenson, D. (1995) *On Drugs*. Minnesota: University of Minnesota Press, p 143.
13. Rolls, E.J and Stafford-Clark, D. (1954) 'Depersonalisation Treated by Cannabis Indica and Psychotherapy', *Guy's Hospital Report*, 103, p 333.
14. Stevens, J. (1993) *Storming Heaven*. London: Flamingo, p 58.
15. H.H. Price (1964), 'A Mescalin Experience', *Journal of the American Society for Psychical Research*, 58, pp 3-20.
16. Huxley, A. (1985) *The Doors of Perception*. London: Granada, p 13.
17. *Ibid.*, p 46.
18. One such mescaline gathering, at the home of Enid Thompson Browne, is referred to in Vansittart, P. (1995) *In The Fifties*. London: John Murray, pp 94-96.
19. Zaehner, R.C. (1957) *Mysticism Sacred and Profane*. Oxford: Oxford University Press, Oxford, p 222.
20. *Ibid.*, p 226.
21. Horowitz, M. and Palmer, C. (eds.) (1994) *Moksha: Aldous Huxley – Writings on Psychedelics and the Visionary Experience 1931-63*. London: Flamingo, p 69.
22. *Ibid.*, p 89.
23. *Ibid.*, p 93.
24. 'An Excursion Out of Time', *The Observer*, 28 October 1956. Reprinted in Ebin, D. (ed.) (1961) *The Drug Experience*, New York: The Grove Press, pp 294-300.
25. Quoted in Crocket, R. et al (eds.) (1963) *Hallucinogenic Drugs and their Psychotherapeutic Use*. London: H.K.Lewis, p 174.
26. Quoted in Zaehner, *op.cit.*, p 209.
27. Ward, R. H. (1957) *A Drug-Taker's Notes*. London: Victor Gollancz, p 216.
28. Quoted in Horowitz, *ibid.*, p 85.
29. Sandison, R. *et al* (1954) 'The Therapeutic Value of Lysergic Acid Diethylamide in Mental Illness', *Journal of Mental Science*, 100, p 507.
30. *Ibid.*, p 493.

31. *Ibid.*, p 505.
32. *Ibid.*, p 507.
33. Sandison, R. (1960) 'Some Established Principles and Unsolved Problems arising from the use of Lysergic Acid Diethylamide in Treatment during the years 1952-1960' (unpublished paper), p 4.
34. See Francis Huxley in Crocket *et al*, *op.cit.*, pp 174-179.
35. Ling, T. and Buckman, J. (1963) *Lysergic Acid and Ritalin in the treatment of Neurosis.* London: Lambarde Press, London, p 22.
36. *Ibid.*, p 63.
37. *Ibid.*, p 63.
38. Quoted in Masters, R. E. L. and Houston, J. (1966) *Varieties of Psychedelic Experience.* London: Anthony Blond, p 319.
39. Osmond quoted in Heywood, R. (1957) *The Sixth Sense.* London: Pan Books, p 191.
40. Quoted in Cohen, S. (1970) *Drugs Of Hallucination.* London: Paladin, p 71.
41. Quoted in Laing, A. (1994) *R. D. Laing.* London: Peter Owen, pp 109-110.
42. Leary, T. (1970) *The Politics of Ecstasy.* London: Paladin, p 95.
43. Mullen, B. (1995) *Mad To Be Normal: Conversations with R. D. Laing.* London: Free Association Books, p 220.
44. Laing, A. *op.cit.*, p 108.
45. Andrews, G. (1963) *Burning Joy.* Trigram Press, London, p 33.
46. Paul McCartney quoted in Leary, *ibid.*, p 93.
47. Quoted in *International Times*, October 14-27, 1966, p 4.
48. Quoted in *New Society*, 16 June, 1966, p 5.
49. Reprinted in *International Times*, September. 6-19, 1968, p 105.
50. Unpublished interview with R.D. Laing, Loveday Drug Books, 1965.
51. Laing, R.D. (1974) *The Politics of Experience and The Bird of Paradise.* London: Penguin, London, p 22.
52. *Ibid.*, p 110.
53. *Ibid.*, p 136.
54. See Siegler, M. Osmond, H. and Mann, H. (1969) 'Laing's models of madness', *The British Journal of Psychiatry*, (115), 525, 1969. Reprinted in Boyers, R. and Orrill, R. (eds.) (1973) *Laing and Anti-Psychiatry.* London: Penguin, pp 99-122.
55. Eliade, M. (1989) *Shamanism: archaic techniques of ecstasy.* London: Arkana, p 27.
56. See *International Times*, April 25 – May 8, 1969, p 5.
57. Quoted in Mullen (1995) *ibid.*, p 236.
58. Cooper, M. (1974) *The Grammar of Living.* London: Allen Lane, p 38.

LSD THERAPY:
A Retrospective

Ronald Sandison

LSD was first produced synthetically in the laboratories of Messrs. Sandoz in Basel in 1938, during a series of chemical syntheses from ergot of rye. Some of its physiological effects on the behaviour of isolated animal organs were noted, and effectively LSD-25, as it was then known, was 'put away in a drawer'. Ergot is an interesting substance, with a long history in folklore and medicine. Albert Hofmann says of it: 'Once dreaded as a poison, in the course of time it has changed into a rich storehouse of valuable remedies'. Hofmann says of LSD:

> Yet I could not forget the relatively uninteresting LSD-25. A peculiar presentiment – the feeling that this substance could possess properties other than those established in the first investigations – induced me, 5 years after the first synthesis, to produce LSD-25 once again so that a sample could be given to the pharmacological department for further tests.[1]

Hofmann was a chemist, and, as far as I can discover, had displayed no special interest in those hallucinogenic compounds which were already known. Chief among these was mescaline, whose chemical composition is quite different from ergot. Despite his presentiment, Hofmann was in a very different position from earlier investigators into the properties of mescaline. Those men, Mooney, Prentis, Beringer and Lewin, were actively involved with ideas to do with the effects of drugs on mental processes. They were contemporary with those who were demonstrating that medicine's new acquisitions, such as ether and nitrous oxide, had mind-altering properties, and they were fascinated by their discoveries. What happened to Hofmann was apparently totally unexpected, and resulted from the accidental ingestion of a minute quantity of LSD on April 16 1943. It does not seem that Hofmann had been in any way influenced by work which for the most part had taken place in a different field half a century earlier.

Hofmann's Discovery

Hofmann's own account of the events of that and subsequent days is as follows:

> Last Friday, 16 April, I had to stop work in the laboratory in the middle of the afternoon and had to go home as I was overcome by a strange restlessness and a slight dizziness. At home I went to bed and sank into a not unpleasant intoxicated state marked by the most stimulating effect on my imagination. In this drowsy state with my eyes closed (I found the daylight unpleasantly bright) fantastic pictures of extraordinary vividness and an intense kaleidoscopic interplay of colours forced themselves upon me without interval. After about two hours this condition gradually disappeared.[2]

He continues:

> On that Friday another extraordinary substance had been used in the laboratory, d-lysergic acid diethylamide... I had just succeeded in getting the d-lysergic acid

diethylamide as a well-crystallizing tartrate, readily soluble in water. I could not, however, explain in what way I could have been affected by a sufficiently large quantity of the substance to produce the above mentioned syndrome... But I wanted to get to the bottom of this and I decided to experiment on myself with the crystallized d-lysergic acid diethylamide tartrate.[3]

It is at this point that Hofmann allies himself with those interested in the mind, in mythology and in the spiritual nature of human beings, rather than being the chemist and the physiologist. Had it not been for this intuition, foreseen when he describes his 'presentiment', he might have dismissed the whole thing. It is an interesting and ideal example of what has occurred many times in history; that the discovery is not enough. There has to be a matching process in the discoverer which gives meaning to his initial discovery. There were many variants of ergot produced in the laboratory, all as unremarkable as getting in and out of the bath was until Archimedes noticed something about it which brought a long hidden scientific law into man's consciousness. Such discoveries are often risky, as Galileo and many others found to their cost.

True scientist that he is, Hofmann wanted to 'get to the bottom of it', and a few days after the original discovery he took 250 micrograms in a watery solution. He reported on what has become known as 'Hofmann's bicycle ride', as follows:

> I asked my assistant to accompany me home as I believed it would take the same course as it did last Friday. But on the way home on my bicycle it was obvious that the symptoms were stronger than the first time. It was an effort to speak clearly and my vision was blurred and distorted like the image in a distorting mirror. I had the feeling that I was not moving although my assistant told me that we cycled at a good speed.[4]

All the manifestations of the drug's action were subjective. A doctor, called to see Hofmann as soon as he got home, 'Found the pulse weak but otherwise the bodily functions were normal'. Hofmann recalls that he could remember every detail of the experience with the greatest clarity. He wrote to Professor Stoll and Professor Rothlin about his findings, and both were astonished that so minute a quantity of LSD could have produced such a powerful effect. Displaying the same spirit of scientific enquiry that Hofmann had shown, Professor Rothlin and two of his colleagues both took LSD, but only in one-third of the dose which Hofmann had used. Even so 'the effects were still extremely impressive and quite fantastic. All doubts about the statements in my report were eliminated.'

A programme of psychological and physiological research was then set up. At first, LSD was given on a total of 49 occasions to 11 adult men and 5 women, mostly laboratory workers and students. Many measurements were made on these dedicated volunteers, and the results were written up by Stoll in 1947. Some of the observations made by the subjects foreshadowed the future possibilities of LSD in psychiatry:

> I can watch myself all the time as in a mirror and realise
> my faults and mental inadequacies.[5]

Another subject said that LSD had made her think of things 'better left forgotten'. Several wanted to 'let go' emotionally, but felt ashamed to do so. These feelings of course reflect the setting, which was a strict laboratory one, where people are supposed to behave properly.

Nevertheless, Hofmann felt urged to try LSD on some psychiatric patients. Accordingly they went to the Burgholtzli hospital where they gave LSD on 20 occasions to 3 male and 3 female schizophrenics. The results, as might be expected, were inconclusive. Hofmann did not immediately follow up this work with patients. He subsequently reported that he took part in some work which was being carried out in Czechoslovakia in 1956. This, however, was after Busch and Johnson's tentative work in the State Mental hospital at St Louis, Missouri, and our own pioneering work at Powick hospital in England.

Hofmann and his experimental subjects noticed that there were sometimes what they called 'after-reactions' to LSD, and in our own work we recorded 'flashbacks'. These sometimes occurred several months after the administration of LSD, and very exceptionally we heard of them up to two years later. Their origin is a matter of some debate. It has been said that once you have taken LSD you are never the same again, meaning that an inner world, previously unknown, has been revealed. It is this material which is the subject of therapeutic analysis. At Powick we found that nearly all our subjects were able to re-enter their 'LSD-world' with some facility. This offered another puzzle to the researchers. Lanz, Cerletti and Rothin established that, in the mouse, the half-life time of LSD in the blood is 37 minutes.[6] Assuming that this can be roughly extrapolated to human subjects, it becomes clear that the bulk of the response experienced by the subjects after a single dose of LSD occurred after the drug had been metabolised. In confirmation of this, Stoll, Rothlin and Ruschmann found that the LSD content of the brain diminishes even more rapidly than in the blood.[7] They did this by investigating the fate of carbon-labelled LSD in the animal body.

Presumably the metabolites of LSD become bound in the central nervous system, and this is a matter for present-day research. The occurrence of very late 'flashbacks', say years after the ingestion of LSD, must be questioned on physical grounds.

The Status of LSD Compared with Other Psychoactive Drugs

It became clear from the time of the earliest work on LSD that its mode of action was of an entirely different order to that of other psychoactive drugs which were being developed in the 1950s, and indeed to other drugs used in general medicine. There was no specificity in the action of LSD and its subsequent clinical use ran contrary to the search which was current at the time, for greater specificity in psychopharmacology. LSD is not a naturally occurring substance, but its action is somewhat similar to two substances occurring in nature. These are mescaline and compounds of the psilocybine group, whose properties have been known for thousands of years. They are associated with early South American and Mexican cultures. Psilocybin is derived from a particular species of mushroom, and was synthesised in Dr Hofmann's laboratory in 1958, but knowledge and use of hallucinogenic mushrooms has been widespread from early times. Those who worked with mescaline in Europe at the turn of the century realised that it had been hitherto the exclusive property, in the country of its origin, of the shamans, priests and medicine men. Likewise Wasson found that psilocybin-containing mushrooms were ritually and exclusively taken by the priest. He alone was sufficiently holy to be able to experience the god speaking through him in an authentic manner. Likewise, these early experimenters in Europe who took mescaline were able to keep the secrets of the experience to themselves, so to speak. It was as if western society held them to be the equivalent of shamans. Society needed, in the best traditions of ancient ritual, to keep its cultural heroes apart: they formed a secret society immune from public scrutiny. The royal family in Britain were the last survivors of this ancient tradition, which has only recently been abandoned in their case. It was a tradition which at one time encompassed the upper classes and most of the professional middle classes, including poets, musicians, writers and academics. The loss of power and status resulting from media intrusion into every walk of life has achieved its aim by destroying mystery. Indeed it could be said that the greatest threat to the spiritual life of humankind during the past 50 years has been the destruction of mystery. The priests and shamans of our time are not immune from this process. The response of medicine is to search for new and more powerful drugs, while the mysteries of magnetic resonance body scanning and laser surgery have replaced the elegant prescriptions of our medical forebears.

Changes in Societal Attitudes During the Last Fifty Years

I mention this change in social attitudes because an understanding of them is vital to any clear thinking about the potential of LSD as a healing agent in the closing years of the twentieth century. LSD happened to become available to doctors and psychotherapists a short time after the ending of World War Two. It was a conflict which left countless millions displaced for ever from their homes, or scarred emotionally by the fortunes of war. It also coincided with a huge impetus to the belief that everybody could have everything. After World War One Britain was going to be a land fit for heroes to live in. As everyone who survived was a hero it followed that all were entitled to participate in the good life. In the USA Henry Ford declared the model 'T' Ford as available to all. William Morris did the same in Britain, while in Germany, taking longer to recover, it required Hitler to announce the Volkswagen, the People's Car. In Britain after the World War Two everything was going to be free for everybody: health, education, social security. Nationalisation of all major industries would lead to cheap fuel and food and to the good life. I suspect that in the United States this view was also around but less openly stated; the good life for all was advertised as freedom under democracy.

The Birth of LSD Therapy

These considerations were not foremost in my mind when, in 1952, I started seriously to consider the possibility of using LSD for therapeutic purposes. In my training years I had been in analysis with a Jungian analyst and the hospital at which I received most of my training had a strong analytical tradition embracing Freud as well as Jung. When I arrived at Powick Hospital as a consultant in 1951, I found a very different state of affairs. The physical state of the hospital had been so run down by the blinkered temperament and parsimony of the previous medical superintendent that all my energies during my first year had to be directed to alleviating the daily misery of the patients. Properly trained medical and nursing staff had also to be recruited, and different attitudes towards patient care had to be taught. The nursing staff were dedicated in the extreme, but had lived in an incestuous world of restrictions for most of the twentieth century. For example, I discovered that no female patient had ever been interviewed alone by a doctor, a nurse invariably being present.

It all seemed a million miles away from the therapeutic atmosphere to which I was accustomed, but, nonetheless, much was achieved during that first year. At its conclusion, in September 1952, I decided to take a break, and joined a study tour of Switzerland organised by Dr Isabel Wilson. Thus it was, in Basel, that I had the opportunity to visit the pharmacological laboratories of Sandoz, and to hear all about their research into LSD. It was to be the first of many visits over the next 15 years. During my stay that year I visited Burgholzli Hospital, of which Professor Bleuler was at that time the medical director. This hospital had the reputation for being the finest psychiatric hospital in Europe but I cannot say that I was greatly impressed. I felt that the hospital was living on the reputation of Professor Bleuler's father, Eugen Bleuler, who had given schizophrenia its modern name and had done much to rescue the psychosis from the attitude of untreatability into which it fell in the late nineteenth century. There was an atmosphere of rigidity and a lack of warmth in the Burgholtzli from which I could not escape. When I enquired about LSD I was told that it was not believed to have any value in psychiatry. I received much the same answer to my enquiries about the use of psychotherapy in the hospital. This depressed me in view of the fact that Jung had studied at the Burgholtzli as a young physician, and that some of the observations which led to his formulation of the concept of the collective unconscious had been made there. Jung was indeed a prophet without honour in his own country.

Thanks to the worldwide scanning of medical literature undertaken by Sandoz, I came across a short paper by Anthony Busch and Warren Johnson entitled 'LSD-25 as an Aid to Psychotherapy', which had been published two years previously, in 1950. They gave the LSD in very low doses (20 to 40 micrograms) to 21 psychotic patients. They commented that they were 'impressed by the various attempts most of the patients made to establish some kind of interpersonal relationship with the personnel.' On the strength of this vague statement they proceeded to give LSD in similar doses to eight patients who were already in psychotherapy. Two of these were classified as catatonic schizophrenics and the remainder into several varieties of neurosis. They reported that these eight patients 'Had experiences which profoundly influenced the course of their progress... Some of the patients were... able to evaluate the emotional meaning of some of their symptoms, and improved.'

What happened to Busch and Johnson and the work at the St Louis State Mental Hospital I never discovered. They published no more, there was no word of them at the meetings in the US on LSD which I subsequently attended, and they never tried to communicate with me. But their tiny contribution to the literature on the therapy of psychiatric illness was the stimulus which encouraged me, as I returned to England, to think of starting to use LSD therapeutically in the UK.

Despite the environmental difficulties at Powick I managed to establish a valid programme of treatment. In this I was assisted by the late A.M. Spencer, untrained in psychodynamics but an enthusiastic student of the psyche, and John Whitelaw, a General Practitioner who was keen to work on the project. By November of the following year (1953) we were able to report on the treatment of 36 patients.[8] I was aware from the beginning that we were in the possession of a substance capable of causing profound changes in perception and of subjective mental experience. I believed from the outset that patients should be carefully selected, that the treatment should only be carried out in a setting where there were trained staff and adequate in-patient back-up, and that the nursing staff and all who came into contact with the patients before, during and after treatment, should have clear instructions about their role. At the end of our first paper I drew two conclusions which were certainly ignored by many, especially in the United States:

> 1. Our clinical impressions have convinced us that LSD *when used as an adjunct to skilled psychotherapy,* is of the greatest value in the obsessional and anxiety groups accompanied by mental tension.

> 2. *We cannot emphasise too strongly, however, that the drug does not fall into the group of 'physical' treatments and that it should only be used by experienced psychotherapists and their assistants.*[9]

In the paper we gave in detail the instructions which we issued 'for the guidance of the nursing staff.'

In parallel with that paper I published a study entitled 'Psychological Aspects of the LSD Treatment of the Neuroses' which was a detailed study of the psychodynamic material emerging under LSD, and which was the subject of therapy. In that paper I concluded:

> The patients in the hospital group are all aware that LSD is a new drug for assisting the unconscious to reveal its secrets and one has been most encouraged by the help they have given in the work of investigating its uses. Many patients have assisted at clinical meetings by describing their experiences...[10]

The LSD Culture and its Fate

The papers by Stoll[11] and Benedetti[12] in Switzerland escaped the notice the press. Likewise with Busch and Johnson[13] in the States. When we published we were still relying on the containment offered by the fact of publishing in a learned journal. But, as usually happens, the most dramatic aspects of the medical world caught the eye of the press. It latched on to the reports that some patients had vividly relived forgotten events in their childhood, and that they even felt as if they were children. Hence it gained the reputation of being the 'Alice-in-Wonderland' drug. Somehow a journalist of the day conjured up the following:

> 'This medicine', the doctor said holding out a spoonful to the young woman, 'is going to make you live over again a day in the past. You are going to be a little girl again.'[14]

I need hardly mention that we never made any prediction of any kind to our patients as to where they might go under LSD. Despite this unpromising start this journalist did advise caution:

> Although it seemed useful in uncovering repressed memories, the doctors indicate that it will never be given by any doctor merely because a patient thinks he or she would like to have it.[15]

Brave words, but the suggestion is there that this interesting, if not extraordinary experience, might be something which could improve the lot of everyone. Once we had published, LSD became available in imagination to readers in millions of homes as the wonder drug which could transform lives by freeing people from the shackles of childhood trauma.

Forty years later we are again in the grip of a culture which considers mental and physical abuse in childhood as a potent cause of later social and personal ills, and there is much truth in the assertion.

It was about this time that Charles Williams's book *Many Dimensions* was republished, the first edition having been in 1931.[16] A Persian prince arrives in Britain to protest at the theft of a stone encircled by a crown of gold. It is in the hands of a small group of businessmen. It is known that the stone possesses infinite potential and that it is infinitely divisible. The Prince warns that it is all that is left of the crown of Suleiman ben Daood, ancient King of Jerusalem. It is claimed that since Suleiman's time, 'No-one has sought to make profit from it... or if they have they and their names and all that they did utterly perished from the earth.' The Prince continues:

'You know very well that he who betrayed the Stone to you broke the trust of generations. I do not know what pleasure you find in it and for what purpose you mean to use it, unless indeed you make it a talisman for travel... I warn you that it is dangerous to all men and especially dangerous to such unbelievers as you.' The Persians called the stone the End of Desire and again the English business-men are warned, 'If the End is reached too violently it may mean chaos and madness.'

The analogy of this description to the fate, not only of LSD, but of many other 'wonder drugs' is evident. At every stage of history humankind has had a burning desire to achieve wholeness. For-merly this was to be reached by moral and religious means. In our age, more than ever before, humankind wishes 'the end of desire' through wealth, power, knowledge and sometimes religion. If we transcribe religion into spiritual knowledge, then the rise of many cultural trends, alternative religions, and the street use of cannabis and LSD, are common ways of attempting to find wholeness in western society.

However, while some say that only full self-knowledge can bring an end to this consuming hunger, others believe that God, manifest through his prophets, or, in the case of Christians, through his son, is the only way to salvation, that is, wholeness. It is of interest that Christians believe in a personal God, to the extent that Christ can enter the heart of each individual, although he remains one person. The Stone, however, was reputed to bring unhappiness and possible destruction when it was disseminated into the material world. In so doing it lost its exclusive power and so lost its mystery. To the Christian, God achieved success in the spiritual world by preserving the mystery while at the same time becoming available to all. This mystery is indestructible and the Church has been careful to build up a powerful containing culture to match the power of the word. In this century psychoanalysis and analytical psychology have de-veloped as ways in which people can find their souls. Just how this process is related to religious revelation has been the subject of much debate, especially in Jungian literature. Psychotherapy based on these two schools has survived and developed over the past hundred years in a way that no other therapy has. The question to be asked is: 'Was LSD just another of those many cures for the sickness of man's soul, or did its fall come about because, like the stone of Suleiman, its mystery had been violated?'

There may have been a short period in the early 1960s when some non-medical uses of LSD were explored which appeared to genuinely enlarge and enhance human experience. Artists and those in training for the religious life claimed that LSD helped them to enhance their vocational experiences with new insights and with greater intensity. What happened next is well described by Hofmann:

> At the beginning of the 1960s, LSD use spread with epidemic-like speed through all social classes... in the course of the inebriant mania in the United States. The rapid rise in drug use, which had its beginning in this country about twenty years ago [i.e in Switzerland about 1959] was not however a consequence of the discovery of LSD, as superficial observers often declared. Rather, it had deep-seated sociological causes: materialism, alienation from nature through industrialisation and increasing urbanisation... and lack of a religious, nurturing and meaningful philosophical foundation to life.[17]

Although the discovery of LSD cannot be made the scapegoat for the rise of drug consumption by all classes of society, it was seen by many of the 'hippy' culture as something which was predestined, that it had come like a saviour to alleviate the pain and deprivations of modern living. Such a 'saviour drug' had been foreshadowed by Huxley in *Brave New World* when he described the use of the drug Soma.

It is difficult to avoid the conclusion that North American culture at that time was badly adapted for containing a valid medical treatment within professional boundaries. It was bad enough in this country. There was a movement which felt that medicine, especially psychological medicine, should not be the sole province of doctors, but that clinical psychologists, social workers and nurses, perhaps also teachers and priests, should also play an active part in therapy. This has largely been realised in the field of psychotherapy, where today psychotherapy training is available to people from a large group of professional backgrounds. This had already happened in the USA by the late 1950s, and journalists, painters, writers and others were taking LSD and writing up their experiences, not in medical journals, but in publications open to a very wide readership. Almost all of these reports were expressed in exaggerated language and presented LSD as the saviour substance of the age. How much these publications contributed to the extraordinary rise in the distribution and non-medical consumption of LSD is hard to evaluate. Once the drug had been released to a hungry world the process was unstoppable.

In trying to assess just what happened in those years we need to look more closely at the immense underlying and unmet need for spiritual sustenance that the world experienced after World War Two. Medical and non-medical therapists, however professional they were to start with, could not escape this phenomenon. It is not surprising that some, like Timothy Leary and Richard Alpert of Harvard University, were also victims of the disease. The fact that their popularity and influence was if anything enhanced when they were disgraced and removed from their university posts is a sign of the unconscious power of the social forces at work. They have, as phenomena, some affinity with what happened in the totalitarian states before the war, and psychoanalysts would agree that the mechanism of identification with the aggressor has been played down or suppressed for political reasons.

My belief and wish was to ally the use of LSD with the analytic movement. To this end I coined the term 'Psycholytic therapy' in order to denote the sense of loosening of unconscious mechanisms. It is a phrase which has not always been understood. Hofmann thought it referred to 'the dissolution of tension or conflicts in the human psyche'. The Oxford English Dictionary was not far out:

> **Psycholytic** – applied to a drug such as LSD which can disturb or disrupt certain emotional reactions that have become fixed in the unconscious or can block normal chan-nels of response; chiefly in psycholytic therapy, therapy that combines controlled use of low dosages of such drugs with psychotherapeutic instruction for the patient and subsequent discussion.[18]

The Dictionary quotes a short statement from *Hallucinogenic Drugs and their Psychotherapeutic Use* (1963) as:

> (R. A. Sandison)... this total experience of the unconscious, brought about by the power of LSD to loosen the psyche, has led to a feeling that the hallucinogenic drugs should be renamed the psycholytic drugs. This name, which is free from the many objections attached to the word 'hallucino-genic', was adopted at Gottingen last year.[19]

The Americans, however, stuck to the term psychedelic therapy. It was proposed by Humphry Osmond in a letter to Aldous Huxley in 1956, and suggests 'making manifest or visible'. Osmond thought of LSD as a drug 'capable of enriching the mind and enlarging the vision'. Much larger doses of LSD were used in North America than in Europe, and it will be evident that Osmond's definition opens the way and indeed encourages the non-medical use of LSD which was not implicit in the term psycholytic.

My clinical work with LSD continued at Powick until 1964. In 1965, Sandoz ceased making LSD, and issued a long memorandum explaining their reasons. These reasons seemed to me to be entirely valid and in keeping with the high ethical standards which I have always associated with that company. The patent held by Sandoz had run out in 1963, and there were no barriers to less ethical manufacturers producing and distributing it from then on. In 1969 I wrote:

> We live in times which are hard to evaluate, but which have produced phenomena which are highly disturbing, especially to the middle-aged and therefore to the establishment generally. I refer particularly to such things as new social and working relationships between young and old, between management and employees, between class and class; to the challenging of old values by almost every social group; to the popularity of mind-altering drugs; to the clash between those who value predictability in human behaviour and those who do not. Much of the work of psychiatrists arises as a direct consequence of these phenomena, especially as they seem of little concern to the traditional doctor, still deeply committed to the one to one relationship between himself and his patient.[20]

And that:

> large numbers of people, mostly young, male and with high intelligence and creative ability are taking hallucinatory drugs without the medical profession being much aware of it. It is only when something goes wrong that the doctor is involved.[21]

As I explained later in the same paper, LSD had gone far beyond the relatively safe confines of medical and psychotherapeutic practice. By 1970 its use was widespread among young disaffected inhabitants of the cities. Consequently I found myself in a new role. On two occasions I was involved in major trials at the Old Bailey, one concerning a murder, and the other arson. In both cases the participants had been taking large quantities of drugs, including LSD, for weeks if not months on end. It might be said that they were on a continuous 'trip', where their judgement and grasp of reality was gravely impaired.

Development of a Medical Culture for LSD Therapy

Following the publication of our early papers on the therapeutic use of LSD a number of therapy centres using our model sprang up, both in UK and in Denmark, Holland, Germany, Czechoslovakia, and to a lesser extent in France. Many visitors came to Powick, and I was busy lecturing in various places. Nevertheless, we were feeling our way as we went along. In a paper on transference problems I quoted as follows from a patient who had a course of LSD therapy three years previously:

> In those days I think the doctors knew little more than the patients about it... sometimes I could almost think I was in a test-tube. I am sure the doctor suffered from wondering what was going to happen next and was he clever enough to deal with it.[22]

She continued, later:

> I think LSD was a wonderful opportunity and I would not have missed it for anything. I felt I had been given the chance so few people get to have contact with my innermost self, but I think also this drug can be dangerous.[23]

She was right about our uncertainty. In my work over almost fifty years I have always, consciously or unconsciously 'trusted the psyche'. There is something about the human spirit which will always point the way if you can see it, and the unconscious is no chimera; it is there, solid, massive and reliable. Sometimes, perhaps often in psychotherapy, these very qualities are what prevents it from exerting its full potential. But it is dependable.

The task, as I saw it, was to develop strategies which would harness the power of the unconscious without letting it destroy either ourselves or the patients. We were asking our patients to glimpse the infinite. Such an experience enhances one's view of oneself as finite and mortal. To make a metaphor: the higher you fly the safer must be the landing arrangements.

Our policy led us to acquire a purpose-built unit for the sole use of LSD therapy. This was designed by our team and was approved and built by the Birmingham Regional Hospital Board. I trained a team of nurses and assistant doctors, we carefully prepared our patients, we trained a team of volunteer drivers who transported the patients to and from their homes; we had a daily group meeting with the patients and staff, and a more formal group for those patients not having LSD that day once a week. We were careful not to let powerful unassimilated LSD experiences be swamped by yet more LSD treatment, preferring to pause and work through the material which had already been revealed. We carefully monitored transference and countertransference problems. There is much more which could be written on this theme, as it was, in my view, essential to the success of the therapy. The Gnostic wing of the early Christian Church failed because it had no liturgy and no Church. The LSD unit was our Church and our method was our liturgy. Like all good liturgies, it was not fixed, we refined and developed it as we went along. Gnosticism, like LSD is not dead, but the spirit and the practice of its golden age can never be recovered. The destruction of our 'Church' came in the mid-1960s. It was a fragile culture, with only a few years of history to rebuild it.

The Search for a Model to Describe
the Effects of LSD

In 1954 Denis Hill wrote:

> At the present time there are two sorts of psychiatries, one
> based upon the physical approach to psychiatric disor-
> ders, the other upon psychopathology. Although each side
> is invading more and more of the territory of the other,
> there is no common language or ground for discussion
> between them.[24]

LSD took both sides by surprise. Traditional psychiatrists elected
psychosis whereas Denis Hill's 'psychopathologists' proposed a
psychodynamic model. Initially the psychosis model won the day
and the term 'psychotomimetic' was coined, although the 'fit' with
schizophrenia was not a good one. Most drugs used in medicine
had predictable effects, LSD did not. Such drugs are usually
discarded. Here was a substance with unpredictable responses
which not only varied from person to person but were also different
from one dose to the next. It survived in clinical medicine for three
reasons: there was a fascination about its properties and their effects;
in the 1950s the press and the public were far less concerned about
drug safety than they are today; and lastly, it did not appear to offer
any danger to health. Once its street use began who knows how
many suicides, accidents and even homicides could be attributed
to the misuse of LSD.

Jung, Jungians and LSD

The psychotherapists treated LSD with great caution. Victor White
was a Dominican priest who had a deep interest in Jungian analysis,
writing several books on the interface between religion and dynamic
psychology. He was a frequent visitor to Powick Hospital where my
colleagues and I had our LSD clinic and he sometimes saw patients
who had become stuck with a religious problem. He wrote to Jung
about this saying that he had been invited to the hospital 'To talk to
the staff and to lend a hand with the religious-archetypal material

which patients were producing under the LSD drug'. Jung replied on 10 April 1954, which was about the time that our first paper on the therapeutic use of LSD appeared. Jung had read Aldous Huxley's *The Doors of Perception*, published in the same year, and he tended to equate LSD with mescaline. He wrote to White:

> Is the LSD drug mescaline? It has indeed very curious effects, *vide* Aldous Huxley – of which I know far too little. I don't know either what its psychotherapeutic value with neurotic or psychotic patients is. I only know that there is no point in wishing to know more of the collective unconscious than one gets through dreams and intuition. The more you know of it, the greater and heavier becomes your moral burden, because the unconscious contents transform themselves into your individual tasks and duties as soon as they begin to become conscious. Do you want to increase loneliness and misunderstanding? Do you want to find more and more complications and increasing responsibilities? You get enough of it. If I once could say that I had done everything I know I had to do, then perhaps I should realise a legitimate need to take mescaline. But if I should take it now, I would nor be sure at all that I had not taken it out of idle curiosity. I should hate to feel that I had touched the sphere where the paint is made which colours the world, where the light is created which makes shine the splendours of the dawn, the lines and shape of all form, the sound that fills the orbit, the thought that illuminates the darkness of the void. There are some poor impoverished creatures, perhaps, for whom mescaline would be a heaven-sent gift without a counterpoison, but I am profoundly mistrustful of the 'pure gifts of the Gods'. You pay dearly for them.[25]

Later in this very long letter he adds:

> I should indeed be obliged to you if you could let me see the material they get with LSD. It is quite awful that the alienists have caught hold of a new poison to play with, without the faintest knowledge or feeling of responsibility. It is just as if a surgeon had never learned further than to cut open his patient's belly and to leave things there.[26]

I was, perhaps fortunately, unaware of this correspondence at the time. It was important for me to find my own way through the maze. Jung had fallen into his own trap, that of voicing a prejudiced opinion without actually knowing anything about what we were actually doing with LSD. But today, I have to agree with some of what he said. There were other Jungian critics. The late Michael Fordham, the distinguished analytical psychologist, once chaired a meeting at which I delivered a paper on our work with LSD.

His comment in opening the discussion was to the effect that we were using LSD as a 'short cut' to cure, something which hard pressed psychiatrists in mental hospitals were always searching for. Jung's charge that we had opened the belly but had no idea what to do next may have applied at some centres, but we were aware of the problem and we had more faith in the unconscious as a self-regulatory organ that Jung appears to have had.

Margot Cutner was a Jungian analyst who used LSD extensively and published a well-crafted paper on her work in 1959. She writes:

> It is not begging the question to say that the phenomena observable under LSD seem to confirm, even more clearly than those observed in general analysis, Jung's idea of the psyche as a self-regulatory system, in which conscious activities function as compensatory factors in the service of striving toward wholeness.[27]

Cutner warns that the great danger of LSD therapy lies in the possibility that powerful images from the unconscious may remain unassimilated and therefore act as barriers to further personal development.

The general analytic climate of the time followed the idea that the unconscious would reveal itself in its own time, and that to 'hurry up' the process by a drug was contrary to 'nature'. I have long maintained that there are some unconscious contents, usually of a personal nature, which no amount of analysis can uncover, but which, when they appear, make sense of the patient's predicament. They may be classified as the memories 'better left forgotten' of Hofmann's subjects, but they were not in analysis, and such revelations may require long and careful handling. Very few of us are like Jung, who from his lofty position of many years' acquaintance with own unconscious, could write as he did to Victor White. Most of us are the 'poor impoverished creatures' of whom he wrote that mescal-LSD would be a 'heaven-sent gift'.

Other Models for LSD

Psychiatrists and analysts were not the only ones who needed models. Those with religious inclinations saw LSD as a substance which could bring them closer to God. Walter Pahnke gave it to theological students before Communion and noticed that some of them experienced intense feelings of religious ecstasy and of closeness to God. When LSD's street use began it was generally seen as mind-expanding. The existentialists noted those effects by which some subjects felt outside time and outside their bodies.

There were those to whom the experience was 'transcendental', 'mystical' or 'cosmic'. They clashed with those who saw genuine mysticism as only obtainable after a lifetime of work, sacrifice and prayer. Therefore it is perhaps not surprising that when Professor Zaehner, an articulate proponent of this view, took LSD, it was 'but a slight experience'. So LSD was already beginning to look like the Crown of Suleiman ben Daood, all things to all men, and a different thing to each group. As one of Hofmann's subjects said: 'I saw benzene rings everywhere but then, I am a chemist.'

The Freudians and LSD

The Freudian psychoanalysts showed more interest than the Jungians. The work of Joyce Martin throws some light on the psychoanalytic model for LSD, and also on Freudian thinking about social phenomena in the 1960s. Martin worked extensively in private practice with LSD but her only publication was entitled 'The Treatment of Twelve Male Homosexuals with LSD' (1962).[28] She worked on the classical Freudian view that homosexuals are trapped at an arrested stage of psychosexual development, and therefore that they were 'treatable'. Astonishingly, she reported that seven out of the twelve homosexuals had, after LSD treatment, become heterosexually orientated, and remained so after three and six year follow-up respectively.

The Effects of the LSD Era on its Practitioners

I have already mentioned that when I took up my appointment at Powick it was a depressed and run-down hospital. It was a big contrast to the well-organised institution run on the open-door principle with its strong team of analytically orientated psychiatrists that I had left. Powick stood out like a Victorian workhouse surviving into an age when innovation and progress were stirring everywhere. The desperate worldwide conflict of 1939-1945 had been over for a mere six years. People were struggling to find new values, new modes of self-expression, and a wholeness which would protect mankind against the perils of future conflict. The shadow cast by the bomb intensified the need for goodness and the rekindling of the human spirit.

There was an excitement about this in the 1950s. There were many changes which tend to be forgotten today. Colour came into people's homes; new materials were available; do-it-yourself was born. Powick Hospital within a few years became transformed in every department and lived what was undoubtedly its golden age. Such transformation is not achieved without pain and sometimes error. It is a story which has remained buried and may never now be fully told.

Following the publication of our first paper on LSD in 1954 and my visit to the United States in 1955, at the invitation of the American Psychiatric Association, the hospital suddenly acquired an international reputation. Visitors came from all over the world, some of whom, such as Caldwell, incorporated what they had seen into their books. My own journeys took me to many centres in England, and not a few in Europe. In Denmark I was hosted by the Danish psychoanalyst Thorkil Vanguaard, who conducted the only known comparative trial between LSD therapy and psychoanalysis. He was a frequent visitor to Powick. In the States there were two Macy Foundation conferences at Princeton and Amityville, and in Europe conferences in Rome and Gottingen. In 1961 the prestigious Royal Medico-Psychological Association of London (the forerunner of the Royal College of Psychiatrists) recognised the importance of the contribution that LSD therapy was making to psychiatry by an unprecedented departure. This was to devote the whole of one of its three-day quarterly meetings to papers and discussions on LSD. A number of distinguished speakers took part, including those from the fields of anthropology, philosophy and religion. The proceedings were edited by Richard Crocket and myself and appeared in 1964 as a hardback volume.

The culmination of LSD study in England came with the holding of the 6th International Conference in Psychotherapy in London in 1964, when a special section covering two days was devoted to the use of LSD and related substances. By that time we had already formed the Psycholytic Society: a loose group of LSD therapists who met at international events. But Rome was already falling and the society never became institutionalised. We were also hampered by the insistence of some European colleagues that only medical therapists could become members, thus excluding some who had contributed significantly to LSD therapy. But the decline and fall of LSD had already begun.

Late History of LSD: The Rise of Street Use and the Ethical Dilemma

In 1964 I moved to a new job in Southampton where for a short time I gave LSD to a small number of patients, but there was no supporting unit and I gave it up. Meanwhile most of my colleagues who had been working with LSD turned their attention to other matters, moving on, everything was changing again. The talisman that was LSD had become public property. In the Hampshire village where I lived a float appeared at the annual carnival bearing the legend 'Flower Power and LSD'. Sidney Cohen's book *The Beyond Within* was published in 1967 and exposed the dangers of the casual and unsupervised use of LSD.[29] But this had no power to stop the epidemic of street use.

In a few short years a moral dilemma had been thrust upon us which had not been expected. Once LSD had escaped from the confines of the laboratory and the consulting room it was a substance which knew no cultural or ethical boundaries. I had to ask myself whether we were responsible for the social consequences of publishing the results of our treatment. Suppose Hofmann had never discovered it. Would the world have found a substitute? It is not a valid question to ask. The events happened; there is an inevitability about the LSD era which takes it out of the world of chance. In many fields the time was one in which the consciousness of humankind was taking a great leap forward. The real progress of this century lies in the discoveries that have been made in the inner world of man. The intention of psychoanalysis was to bring order to the lives of those disordered by a chaotic world. LSD played its part in that process, and in doing so added to our knowledge of that inner world.

The other side of this movement towards order was the increasing violence and social disintegration in our society. As Jung taught, 'The greater the good the greater the evil'. Hofmann shared this dilemma. He wrote, in 1979:

> Would LSD become a blessing to humanity or a curse? This I often asked myself when I thought about my problem child.[30]

He goes on in a rather complaining way to protest that the other valuable drugs which he had introduced to medicine had behaved properly, so to speak. His Swiss sense of order had been sadly disturbed.

Just as the remnants of the Roman Empire lived on in central Europe for centuries, and the influence of that empire spread all over the world, so LSD therapy continued for some years beyond the Iron Curtain and in Germany, where, for all I know it is still being used. In 1970, two years after the Russian invasion of Czechoslovakia I visited Milan Hausner at Sadska, a few miles from Prague. I was impressed by the work he was doing in the face of Communist hostility to LSD. Whatever the reality I was assured by the Communists that there were no street drugs in the Soviet Union or in the satellite States. True or false, it allowed Hausner to continue his work. At that Conference in Prague I gave my last paper in public on the subject of LSD.

The Effects of the LSD Era
on its Practitioners: In the Clinic

The excitement of travel, of conferences, and of meeting people was matched at a different level in the LSD clinic. There the reality was more intense and the possibility of becoming drawn into the experiences which the patients were undergoing was almost irresistible to some. Consider the following 'snapshots' from a patient undergoing LSD therapy in our clinic. She was a married woman, 29 years of age, of German birth. She wrote:

> I began to see a face on the wall, it was a man with one eye and he had a moustache. He sometimes smiled at me cynically and sometimes looked very grim and threatening. I tried to connect him with something which had happened to me a long time ago. It was then that he got mixed up with Hitler and I saw nothing else but swastikas. For one brief moment it was my father's face. Then I remembered one man in particular. He was a German officer. Then I remembered the incident connected with that man.[31]

The patient goes on to describe how this officer took her to his flat one evening and seduced her. She continues:

> The thing that bothered me most under LSD was that I was being forced against my will without showing the slightest resistance. As I pondered over this Hitler appeared again and I saw the connection. He too, in a subtle way, together with his powerful personality, made me do things against my will without me resisting. Then I had a feeling of falling down deeper and deeper and yet I felt detached just as if I were watching it all happen.[32]

There followed a series of reductive and unpleasant sessions, of which the following is an example:

> There was a huge image of Hitler on the wall like a big shadow in which I could see many other hostile faces. I wanted to get away from these hostile men and tried to

hide in a corner. Then I saw skulls and crossbones on the wall and suddenly I felt the flesh falling off my bones and I was a skeleton, I think only from the waist down. I remember my teeth falling out and when I tried to bite I was biting on my gums.[33]

In the next series of treatments the degradation persisted; she saw herself, for example, as a prostitute stabbed and lying in the gutter, she became depressed and suicidal. She describes the tenth LSD treatment as follows:

There is tremendous confusion within me. There is no harmony. The muddled faces had terrific mouths and tried to swallow me up. I felt that they would swallow me up only as long as they were in a such a muddle and it was therefore necessary to find order in this confusion. I then found that there was some order insofar as there were two sides to it each opposing the other and pulling in opposite directions. I tried to find out about the two parts and discovered that they must be the good and evil in me.[34]

The patient then had a dream. In the beginning part of the dream she meets her lover and feels very happy but she is unable to make love to him. She goes on:

I tried to find out why I could not make love to him and suddenly something inside me said: 'Because you have not picked up the five stones from the bottom of the sea. You did not do it for your parents either, that is why you could not love them'. I felt as if all my problems had been solved, or at least that I now knew what I had to do.[35]

In the next LSD treatment she decided to investigate this. She wrote:

I feel I must overcome my fear and go to the bottom of the sea. Then I started going down under the water but I met alligators who were waiting for me and I could feel their teeth in my body. I went down under the water again and as I went deeper my fear grew less. I could see the stones, but they were now only four in number. It was as if the fifth had represented fear which has now gone. I came

closer and closer and suddenly it was as if I were looking
in a mirror. These four stones formed a face. I cannot
describe its ugliness and horribleness. At the same time
the face was beautiful. I could not say what piece was
ugly and what piece was beautiful, for in it were both
extremes completely merging and forming a whole. I felt
that these were my anchors and on these I had to build up
my personality. I knew too that this was the same in all of
us and everything alive. I had a feeling that what I had
just seen was part of God.[36]

It is tempting to comment on this fascinating material, but it speaks
for itself. The point I am making is that we were in the presence of
such heady stuff day in and day out. I personally worked with LSD
patients, apart from breaks for holidays, every day for 12 years. The
possibility of getting drawn into the unconscious vortices which the
patients were experiencing was considerable. Worldwide, some did.
The 1960s was such a period of social and ethical change that alone
was enough for most people to manage. At Powick we must have
treated over 500 patients in all. Some I am still in touch with, and the
nurse who, I believe, did most for our patients out of all our small,
dedicated team is still in touch with me.

Culturally, we, the LSD therapists, were a well-knit group. Most
of us had taken LSD ourselves. I recall sitting at dinner one evening
with two other LSD therapists and a fourth who was not and who
had never taken LSD. As we started to talk about how a rose looked
under LSD we became transfigured, it reminded us of other experiences under LSD when everyone felt at one with everyone else –
except for the unfortunate outsider, who could in no way share what
we were discussing and feeling. It was that culture, due to its very
nature, which we were unable to sustain. With hindsight, the reality
was that I needed a rest from LSD.

Perhaps a sense of that very same intensity partly accounted for
the silence of the British press, on April 16 1993, the fiftieth anniversary of Hofmann's discovery, about the very core of LSD, the
therapeutic years. *The Times* said that LSD was used therapeutically
but that the idea 'never really caught on in Britain'. *The Independent*
carried an interesting interview with Hofmann, but the work of
British, European and North and South American therapists received no direct mention.

1964: My Vision for the Future

My vision was that the two psychiatries that Denis Hill had written about ten years earlier should become one. In this concept I received strong support from Joel Elkes, then Professor of Psychiatry at Birmingham University, our academic base. As a result of the peculiar history of academic psychiatry in Birmingham, the university had appointed a pharmacologist rather than a psychiatrist to this chair. Like many maverick appointments it was a great success as far as psychiatry was concerned and Elkes quickly became an international figure. The university was also fortunate in having Mayer-Gross as its emeritus Professor of Psychiatry. The two were a formidable combination. Joel and his wife Charmian conducted the first large scale clinical study on largactil, generally acclaimed as a model for clinical trials. Thus it seemed natural that when Sandoz, the manufacturer of LSD, introduced the tranquilizer Melleril (Mellaril in USA), that Powick should be asked to undertake the clinical trials.

The findings of that trial are not relevant to this paper, and they were reported in 1960, but some of the footnotes to the trial, which could not be included in the published reports, supported my vision that there was an unexplored interface between pharmacotherapy and psychotherapy. For a long time, before studies at the Maudsley Hospital and at Powick had shown that deep insulin treatment was no better than placebo, only far more dangerous, I had been interested in the psychodynamics of the physical treatments. I had worked with a group of patients in the deep insulin unit at Warlingham Park Hospital where some fascinating material emerged which could only have been of interest to a psychotherapist. Some of the experiences related by patients on coming round from coma bore a close resemblance to those which I later noticed in my LSD work. Cook, as early as 1940, had written on the psychology of ECT, and there may be some justification for the idea that the real healing agent in these crude and traumatic physical treatments was related to the need of the sick person to experience an ancient passage rite in which he symbolically dies and is born again. One patient I observed in the insulin room was convinced that she had been born again 'over the end of the bed'. A birth or rebirth experience is not uncommon during LSD therapy. Some of Hofmann's subjects felt as if they were recovering from a physical illness after emerging from an LSD session: 'I feel young, fresh and beautiful – It is like being reborn.'[37]

To develop this theme further, the following are some experiences of a woman patient of 30, married with no children, while undergoing deep insulin therapy. She had always lived in a world of her own, adapting herself poorly to social situations, and disliking men. Despite this she held down a good job but she finally broke down into schizophrenia. In the first post-insulin fantasy she was dressed in yellow which she regarded as a holy colour, holding an orange in her hand which she said was a symbol of life and potential growth. God was in the sky above from whence he was raining down steel rods, so that she had to enter a house without windows made of concrete. In the second fantasy she was very small and overshadowed by a large blue cloud in which God dwelt. The steel rods were replaced by a syringe containing insulin and they have formed themselves into a rigid framework in which she has to live. It represents family obligations and social conventions. Thus far the insulin experience is forcing her into the realities of everyday life. In the third fantasy there is a table laden with good food, behind it stands a benevolent figure who gives good things to his children. She is a child and goes with her basket to receive the gifts.

Just as she is about to receive them numerous shadowy figures drive them away. She was, on coming round from the coma, saying 'Too late', based on the idea that she could never receive the food. In the final fantasy she saw a large pear-shaped structure, like a womb, above her bed into which she climbed, meeting a child there with whom she became united. In this manner she felt herself being born into the bed with the aid of a nurse who became her mother. She felt as if she was three weeks old and drinking milk instead of glucose.

Analysts also report that their patients sometimes have strong fantasy experiences. One of my patients, depressed for many years, felt during one session as if a huge block of stone had been lifted from her head. When she went outside into the London street she found that it appeared to be paved with all manner of rich jewels. Another (this was when I worked in the country) went to a small stream nearby which became the river of life in which he had to bathe to be made whole. It was a turning point in his life.

During the work on the Melleril trial we learned many things. We learned that if you gave the drug to one half of the patients in a long-stay ward the patients who did not take the drug also improved. The results also varied from ward to ward despite the fact that the different observers correlated well on the rating scales. These and similar observations could not be written into the trial report without confusing the main issue, but similar findings have been reported elsewhere.

So here we have a huge, relatively unresearched, field of enquiry where psychiatrists and psychotherapists could get together. The two psychiatries first need a common language and they will not have that until a psychodynamic training becomes obligatory for all psychiatrists in training.

In the United States the two psychiatries appear to divide between the state psychiatric institutions and private office practice. It has always been a matter of regret to me that so much of psychiatric practice pays scant attention to the mind. There is a large gap between what the public thinks psychiatrists do in the consulting room and what actually happens in a great many clinics. Balint taught many years ago that the power of the doctor lies in himself rather than in any drugs he may prescribe. Modern hi-tech medicine removes this ideal still further from reality.

Readers may ask what happened to that vision of more than 20 years ago. I moved to fresh fields in Southampton, Professor Mayer-Gross retired, Professor Joel Elkes moved to the States, others moved on, some have died. My vision of those days is still far from being realised. I would like to see some serious research done to explore the interface between those who give drugs and those who talk to their patients. Times may be changing, but there must still be only a few who do both. There are many models from the past. Pinel at the Bicetre in the 1820s is credited with having removed the chains from the lunatics in his care. How he did it was by talking to the patients and getting them to talk to each other. The first medical superintendent at Powick Hospital in the 1850s insisted that craftsmen and women should replace nurses. The discharge rate from the hospital was not equalled for a hundred years.

The Tavistock Clinic, born in the 1920s, offered psychotherapy to the shell-shocked victims of the war rather than sedatives. In 1938 at least two mental hospitals in the United Kingdom were entirely open and the use of drugs almost unknown.

At Warlingham Park Hospital I was fortunate. In general the lot of psychoanalysts working in psychiatric hospitals has not been a happy one. Exceptions must be Chestnut Lodge in the States and the Cassel Hospital in UK. The trend has been to set up separate psychotherapy departments in district hospitals, which keeps the divide between the two psychiatries intact. Psychodynamically this is splitting rather than diversity.

1997: Is There a Future for LSD Therapy?

The fiftieth anniversary of the discovery of LSD's properties passed without comment in the major psychiatric journals. In psychiatry the closure of famous hospitals and the struggles of local authorities to provide alternative care are the major preoccupations of the profession. I see no sign of this being an era of a great upsurge in creative advances, such as occurred in the 1830s, the 1920s and the 1950s. What I have written is more in the nature of an obituary notice. The potential power of LSD is still there, but, medically speaking, it has returned to its home, where, like the Stone of Suleiman and the Genie in the Bottle, it is destined to go. We know of course that the drug is still made in large quantities and circulates illegally amongst those who seek some short-term lift to their lives which will make human relations seem less difficult. That, of course, is an illusion. The experience gained and the memories of that short period of the true therapeutic use of LSD are valuable and precious. I believe that it made a real contribution to our understanding of the human psyche, and of the interaction between patient and healer. We have learned that in the field of psychopharmacology nothing is fixed or certain. The response of the human subject to every drug known to medicine is the result of an interaction between the personality and physiology of the taker, his state of mind when the drug was taken and the mental and physical state of the administrator. We have learnt that this interaction of doctor and patient is not only as important as the potency of the drug itself, but will largely determine how the patient responds to the drug. This axiom must in future underpin all psychiatric healing and have profound implications for all other branches of medicine.

There are two major players, both of them Swiss, who should have the last word. It will be remembered that Jung wrote to Victor White that, in effect, LSD could add nothing except to burden the analyst still further with unconscious material. In a letter written late in his life to Dr Betty Eisner, in 1957, he made it clear that his real anxiety was that the patients would be unable to integrate their experiences under LSD. I do not believe this to be true provided that the patient is in the care of a skilled therapist. Sadly, if we had more support from the analysts in the 1950s we might have been able to do a great deal more.

The great obstacle to any resumption of LSD therapy, in my

view, lies in the fact that we now live in a different world; we breathe different air, so to speak, from that of those remarkable times.

Albert Hofmann remains more optimistic:

> I believe that if people would learn to use LSD's vision-inducing capability more wisely, under suitable conditions, in medical practice and in conjunction with meditation, then in future this problem child would become a wonder child.[38]

Notes

1. Hofmann (1883), p 14.
2. *Ibid.*, p 15.
3. *Ibid.*
4. *Ibid.*
5. *Ibid.*
6. Lanz, Cerletti, Rothlin (1955) p 207.
7. Personal communication.
8. Sandison *et al* (1953).
9. *Ibid.*, p504.
10. Sandison (1953), p 514.
11. Stoll (1947).
12. Benedetti (1951).
13. Busch, A. K. and Johnson, W. C., (1950), pp 2-4.
14. *News Chronicle*, 1953.
15. *Ibid,*
16. Williams (1931).
17. Hofmann (1983).
18. Buchfield (ed.) (1982), p 880.
19. *Ibid.*, p.881.
20. Sandison (1969) p 224.

21. *Ibid.*, p224.
22. Personal communication
23. *Ibid.*
24. Personal communication
25. Jung (1976), p 382.
26. *Ibid.*, p 383.
27. Cutner (1959) p6.
28. Martin (1962).
29. Cohen (1967)
30. Hofmann (1983), p 30.
31. Personal communication
32. *Ibid.*
33. *Ibid.*
34. *Ibid.*
35. *Ibid.*
36. *Ibid.*
37. Hofmann (1983), p 28.
38. *Ibid.*, xiii.

Bibliography

Benedetti, G. (1951) 'Beispiel und Strukturanalischen und
   Pharmacodynamischen Untersuchung an einem Fall von
   Alkoholhalluzinose Charakterneurose und Psychoreaktiver
   Halluzinose', *Zeitschrift fur Psychotherapie Medizinische Psychologie*,
   (1) 5.
Burchfield, R.W. (ed.) (1982) *Oxford English Dictionary, supplement*, vol.
   3, Oxford: Clarenden Press.
Busch, A. K. and Johnson, W. C. (1950) 'LSD-25 as an aid to
   Psychotherapy', *Diseases of the Nervous System*, 11, 241.
Cholden, L. (ed.) (1956) *Lysergic Acid Diethylamide and Mescaline in
   Experimental Psychiatry* (Proceedings of a Round Table held at the
   Annual Meeting of the American Psychiatric Association, 1955).
   New York and London: Grune and Stratton.

Cohen, S. (1967) *The Beyond Within*. New York: Atheneum.

Cook, R. C. (1940) 'Psychological Aspects of ECT', *Journal of Mental Science*, 86, 484.

Crocket, R., Sandison, R. A., and Walk, A. (eds.) (1963) *Hallucinogenic Drugs and their Psychotherapeutic Use* (The proceedings of the Royal-Medico Psychological Association). London: H. K. Lewis.

Cutner, M. (1959) 'Analytic Work with LSD 25', *Psychiatric Quarterly*, 33, pp 715-757.

Hill, D. (1954) Personal communication.

Hofmann, A. (1983) LSD: *My Problem Child*. New York: Jeremy Tarcher.

Jung, C.G. (1976) *Letters*, Vol.2, London: Routledge.

Lanz, U., Cerletti, A., and Rothlin, E. (1955) 'The Half-life Time of LSD In the Mouse' *Helvetia. Physio. Acta*, 13.

Martin, A. J. (1962) 'The Treatment of Twelve Male Homosexuals with LSD', *Acta Psychotherapeutica* 10, pp 394-402.

Pahnke, W. (1960) 'Drugs and Mysticism'. A Thesis (Personal Communication).

Sandison, R. A., Spencer, A. M., and Whitelaw, J. D. A. (1954) 'The Therapeutic Value of Lysergic Acid Diethylamide in Mental Illness', *Journal of Mental Science*, (100), 419, pp 491-507.

Sandison, R. A. (1954) 'Psychological Aspects of the Neuroses', ibid, pp 508-515.

Sandison, R. A., and Whitelaw, J. D. A., (1957) 'Further Studies in the Therapeutic Value of Lysergic Acid Diethylamide in Mental Illness', ibid. (103) 431, pp 332-343.

Sandison, R. A., Whitelaw, E. and Currie, J. D. C. (1960) 'Clinical Trials with Melleril (TP 21) in the Treatment of Schizophrenia', *Journal of Mental Science*, (106) 443, pp 732-741.

Sandison, R. A. (1969) 'The Hallucinogenic Drugs', *Newcastle Medical Journal*, xxx, 7, 224.

Sandison, R. A. (1991) 'LSD: Its Rise, Fall and Enduring Value. A New Perspective', *Bulletin of the Albert Hofmann Foundation*, 2,1.

Scott, R. D. (1950) 'The Psychology of Insulin Coma Treatment', *British Journal of Medical Psychology*, 23, pp 15-44.

Stoll, W. A. (1947) 'Lysergsaure-diathylamid; ein Phantasticum aus der Muttercorngruppe', *Schweitzer Archiv fur Neurologie und Psychiatrie*, 60, pp 1-45 Translated by Dr. Ruth Hofmann.

Wasson, V. and Wasson, R. G. (1957) *Mushrooms, Russia and History*. New York: Pantheon Books, 2 Vols.

Williams, C. (1931) *Many Dimensions*. London: Victor Gollancz. Republished, Faber and Faber, London, 1947.

World Health Organization (1958) 'The Hallucinogenic and Ataractic Drugs', Technical Report Series, No. 152.

ACID VIRGIL:
The Michael Hollingshead Story

Antonio Melechi

After a decade spent proselytising the sacrament of LSD on both sides of the Atlantic, Michael Hollingshead, Britain's most infamous exponent of the psychedelic experience, chronicled his peripatetic career in *The Man Who Turned on the World* (1973). Reflecting on his involvement with Timothy Leary at Harvard and Millbrook, and the founding of his own World Psychedelic Centre in London, Hollingshead arrived at the conclusion that LSD had been for him little more than a preliminary to genuine self-realisation, at best an intimation of real spiritual experience.

If the pursuit of self-knowledge had, as Hollingshead claims, led him to reject LSD, such lofty ideals did not, however, inform the writing of his autobiography. Hollingshead was no more reliable as a narrator as he had been in real life, and *The Man Who Turned on the World* is as much fiction as fact, its author having embellished and reconstructed his life story beyond the claims of dramatic licence.

In the opening pages of *The Man Who Turned on the World*, Hollingshead describes how, after a conversation about LSD with Aldous Huxley, he and an English doctor friend contrived an order of LSD as a control drug in a bogus bone marrow experiment. After receiving the package, Hollingshead sets to work in his kitchen, mixing the LSD with icing sugar and measuring out exactly 5000 spoonfuls into a sixteen ounce mayonnaise jar. But in the course of preparing his 'divine concoction' Hollingshead inadvertently licks his fingers, absorbing 'about the equivalent of five heavy doses', before finding himself transported out of his body into the 'realm of the primordial', an 'ecstatic nirvana', from which he returns dazed and reeling many hours later.

In reality, Hollingshead came into the possession of a substantial quantity of LSD through John Beresford, an English doctor who had begun to use LSD in chromosomal research at a New York hospital. Hollingshead had known Beresford since the mid 1950s, when the two shared a flat in Belsize Park, London. In 1957, after finishing his medical studies, Beresford left London for New York, and a year or so after the unwelcome Hollingshead arrived unexpectedly on his doorstep. Hollingshead settled quickly. After a few months he met his wife to be, Sophie, and began to establish the British American Cultural Exchange Institute, gathering an impressive array of directors for its board, including Lord Douglas, W.H. Auden and Lionel Trilling. With offices provided by Huntingdon Hartford, a philanthrophic millionaire, Hollingshead established scholarships and courses of study at UK universities, using his considerable talents to secure funding from charitable foundations and wealthy patrons.

Shortly after the birth of his daughter in the spring of 1961, Hollingshead was given a few hundred trips worth of LSD by John Beresford, who had begun to distribute LSD amongst friends interested in conducting their own experiments. Over the next few months, Hollingshead's experiments led him to become increasingly absorbed by questions of the spiritual and philosophical significance of the LSD state. Unhappy in his marriage, Hollingshead became convinced that the LSD experience might come to disclose the nature of some vital personal truth. Consumed by questions of LSD's visionary powers, his marriage began to show signs of breakdown, and the institute's work ground to a halt. In his state of confusion, he turned to Beresford, who after enduring his demands for as long as he could, directed him in the direction of his friend Timothy Leary at Harvard University.

In October 1961, Professor Timothy Leary received a phone call from Hollingshead, who, after introducing himself as a colleague of the eminent Cambridge philosopher George Moore, suggested that they should meet to discuss an urgent matter of mutual interest. Leary, a well-respected professor of psychology, had spent almost a year conducting research into the therapeutic effects of the halluci- nogenic mushroom *psilocybe mexicana*. In that time he had played host to a number of distinguished visitors, including Allen Ginsberg, William Burroughs and Arthur Koestler, all of whom provided Leary with their own personal testimonies of 'the mushroom experience'. As Leary's interest in psilocybin became more than merely aca- demic, his research methods provoked mounting criticism from his colleagues and his position was becoming increasingly untenable. The arrival of Hollingshead with his mayonnaise jar of LSD was destined to have a cataclysmic effect on Leary, transforming the Harvard professor into the high priest and prophet of the psych- edelic movement.

Hollingshead's first meeting with Leary took place at the Harvard Faculty Club. Over lunch, Hollingshead, avoiding any mention of his alleged involvement with Professor Moore, outlined the plot of a novel he claimed to be writing about a bank clerk who discovers the art of levitation – a thinly disguised parable of his own experi- ences – but ends up estranged from his lover, lost in despondent isolation. Leaving the subject of his LSD experiences till last, Hollingshead only managed to briefly touch upon the troubling nature of his own experiences before Leary had to leave for a meet- ing. A couple of days later, Hollingshead dropped Leary a note at his office in which he explained that he was lonely, confused and ready to kill himself – and Leary was the only person that could help him.

Receiving Hollingshead's note just before he was scheduled to fly to New York, Leary arranged to have Hollingshead's wife and daugh- ter join him, and have them all installed at his home. Before returning from New York, however, Leary did some research on Hollingshead, and an associate of Huntingdon Hartford informed him that he was a 'no-good, two-bit English con-man' with a lengthy criminal record, and wanted, furthermore, by Interpol. Yet despite the warnings, Leary and his colleague George Litwin decided to let him stay on.

Hollingshead's reunion with his family proved short-lived. After a week or so his wife and daughter returned to New York – Sophie complaining to Leary that Michael was insistent that she should convince her father to cash in some savings bonds. Hollingshead now found himself a job at the Harvard book store and set about trying to have his host try some LSD. Leary, insistent that nothing could surpass his own beloved psilocybin, resisted the temptation for some weeks, until one evening when Hollingshead managed to persuade the jazz musician Maynard Ferguson and his wife Flo to join him in a trip. Coming down from his study, Leary found the Fergusons in beatific repose. Seeing them overcome by a sense of ineffable wonder, Leary decided to finally succumb to a spoonful of Hollingshead's LSD.

Hollingshead was proved right. LSD eclipsed psilocybin, and Leary emerged from his trip feeling that he had well and truly flipped into another dimension. Having introduced psilocybin to hundreds of volunteers and guided them through their experiences, it was now Leary who was lost and confused. In this state of help-lessness he turned to Hollingshead, who was transformed in Leary's eyes into the 'victim of some greater power', seeking others who could share in his profound but lonely knowledge. Not only had Hollingshead managed to break all the rules that the Harvard project had worked out for the set and setting of psychedelic experimenta-tion, he had also temporarily unhinged its founder. As Leary's colleague Dick Alpert remembers, it was five days before Leary spoke a word and some weeks before he re-appeared as a semblance of his former self.

With Hollingshead cast in this new messianic role, Leary ar-ranged for him to be employed as an assistant on the psilocybin project, combining domestic duties of looking after Leary's children with some hands on involvement in research sessions. Working alongside Dick Alpert, Ralph Metzner and other members of the academic team, Hollingshead came to play his part in two important developments over the following months. The first of these was the Harvard Concord Project, which had been administering psilocybin to inmates of the maximum security state prison, with a view to transforming aspects of their entrenched behaviour. The second was the 'Good Friday Experiment', which was to thrust the Harvard Project into the glare of national publicity. Taking place at Boston University's Marsh Chapel, the experiment sought to introduce psilocybin, in double-blind fashion, to five groups of theology stu-dents. Hollingshead acted as sitter to one of the groups that had received psilocybin. With 9 out of the 10 volunteers receiving psilocybin, reported four or more categories of mystical experience, and The Good Friday Experiment confirmed to both Leary and Hollingshead that the ultimate significance of the psychedelic expe-rience lay in a transcendental dimension, a realm which psychological theory was barely able to grasp.

In the summer of 1962, as Leary, Alpert and Metzner left Harvard for Mexico, intending to start their own psychedelic colony, Hollingshead headed for a holiday in Jamaica. As his finances dwindled, Hollingshead devised a plan to pay his way back to Europe. In a letter to Eileen Garrett, the world-famous medium and president of the Parapsychology Foundation, Hollingshead outlined the psilocybin research he had been involved in at Harvard, and called for assistance to continue his research. Garrett responded by paying to have Hollingshead fly out to stay with her in Le Piol in the south of France. After a few days Hollingshead was on his way back to London with a grant of $3000 for him to provide the foundation with a report on the Harvard-Concord Prison Project.

The scam precipitated a fall-out between Hollingshead and Leary, who having received news that Hollingshead was being funded to report on *his* project, informed Eileen Garrett that Hollingshead had only been nominally involved in the research. Discovering that Leary had asked Garrett to take him off their pay-roll, Hollingshead wrote to him, defending his apparent trickery:

> In the first place I have never conned anyone in the criminal sense. However much I enjoy giving, adding, and living this image, it is not factually true. Because I live like a gangster, i.e. on the fringe of society, it is to be expected that I shall be critically interpreted by others for whom life is one long mountain path.
>
> But I fail to understand why you should want to do so. Why it has become necessary for you to say to people that the group supported me for seven or eight months when, in reality, not only was I working at Concord on Mondays and Thursdays, but I would also help out in a number of small ways, help you run sessions, work *positively* toward your professional and private goals...
>
> I also take a very dim view of the rumour you are putting out to one and all that I suddenly became paranoid – I was, certainly, angry with the way certain events of my life had become altered in the retelling, but the evidence was real and not as you seem to have convinced yourself illusory – or that I am circulating vile rumours about little Dickie [Richard Alpert], threatened to go to the prison to get prisoners to blackmail him, etc.[1]

While it is not clear whether Hollingshead had in fact plotted to blackmail Richard Alpert (over his homosexuality), in his next letter to Leary, Hollingshead apologised for an 'egregious blunder' on his part, stating his hope that they would resume friendlier relations in the near future.

Returning to New York in January 1963, Hollingshead made his way once again to John Beresford, who had now founded his own research institute, the Agora Scientific Trust. Regarding Hollingshead as irresponsible and full of his own self-importance, Beresford was less than pleased to see him, but against his better judgement allowed him to stay temporarily at the trust's offices on 81st Street. Receiving much of its funding from Howard Teague, a Nassau millionaire, Agora had established itself as an open-ended research project which would not seek to impose any philosophical or psychological set on the LSD session. In its statement of purposes, Agora described its research as 'an investigation into the nature and potential of mind, a dynamic consideration of the range and chemistry of consciousness, [with] the utilisation of new and old techniques of intensifying and expanding the mind's apprehension of reality'. This was clearly intended as an alternative to the kind of psychedelic session which Leary was now propounding, and which Beresford saw as disempowering the subject, encouraging submission in the LSD state. According to Beresford, this attitude was responsible for the increasing number of freak-outs that were now being reported, and it was vital that initiates should be encouraged to control, shape and direct their own experience.

While Hollingshead would in *The Man Who Turned on the World* claim that he was the prime-mover behind Agora, with Beresford and Jean Houston as his co-directors, he was in fact little more than an involved spectator, playing little part in Agora's research. Instead, Hollingshead spent much of his time in New York engaged in a fantastically ambitious project to establish a Pavilion for the Mind at the World Trade Fair, intending to sell the psychedelic revolution to international captains of industry. To this end, Hollingshead established the Excelsior Trust and began fundraising in his own inimitable manner. In one of his privately run sessions at Agora, Hollingshead attempted to guide his wealthy volunteer to an understanding of the importance of his planned Pavilion for the Mind, trying to impress upon him the necessity that he make some financial contribution towards it – which he ultimately refused. On another occasion, John Beresford recalls being taken by Hollingshead on a social visit to a Wall Street broker in Long Island, where pleasantries were quickly dispensed with when Hollingshead threatened his friend with blackmail. Thwarted in his work on the Pavilion, Hollingshead left New York in the autumn of 1964, with an invitation from Leary to join him at Millbrook.

After leaving Harvard, Leary, Alpert and Metzner had formed the International Federation for Internal Freedom, campaigning for the constitutional right to psychedelically expand one's consciousness. Now installed in new headquarters, and re-named the Castalia Foundation, the psychedelic gospel was starting to spread. Absolved of his former sins, Hollingshead became a key figure at Millbrook. As well as running workshops in consciousness expansion for paying visitors, he assumed the role of guide to many of the famous names who arrived at Millbrook keen to be turned on, including the English painter Feliks Topolski, NASA scientist Steve Groff, jazz musician Charlie Mingus, and cartoonist Saul Steinberg – who returned the favour by producing a fictitious diplomatic stamp for Hollingshead's passport. A Hollingshead session typically involved readings from the *Tao Sutra* and *The Tibetan Book of the Dead*, music from Stockhausen, Bach or Miles Davis, and projected images of stars and galaxies. The session would culminate with a movement throughout the tantric scale, culminating in the final head chakra – from which Hollingshead, born Shinkfield, sometimes claimed to have taken his name.

Yet, while Hollingshead used the eastern writings to signpost a session, he was not in any sense a believer, being naturally cynical of the more earnest proponents at Millbrook. Thus, when the group became absorbed in the writings of the philosopher Gurdjieff, and took to playing self-remembering games, Hollingshead went through the motions, teasing the more earnest followers of 'Mr G'. More interested in playing his own games, Hollingshead enjoyed spiking people, or perhaps beginning a session as someone's guide and deserting them half-way through. In one session which Ralph Metzner remembers, Hollingshead tried to convince him that he had also been to the very village in Switzerland from which Metzner had just returned. In Millbrook speak, this was 'mind-fucking', wilfully confounding someone during a trip, and Hollingshead was its leading exponent. Hollingshead's imagination was, it seems, directed more towards discovering ways of breaking with set and setting. For Dick Alpert, who took charge of Millbrook after Leary and his wife left for India, Hollingshead's irresponsibility presented a real problem. As much as he enjoyed Hollingshead's bizarre sense of humour, and did not personally mind being spiked, Alpert considered him a sociopath, and as such an absolute liability.

After a year at Millbrook, Hollingshead was dispatched on a mission to London armed with half a gram of Czech acid, several hundred copies of *The Tibetan Book of the Dead* and instructions to set the scene for the arrival of Timothy Leary, who was to be introduced to a gathering of London's psychedelic converts at the Royal Albert Hall. While this was probably little more than a ruse to get him out of Millbrook, Hollingshead took his duties seriously, and before setting off for London in October 1965, he had managed to contact a potential sponsor, Desmond O'Brien, an ex-Etonian entrepreneur who was keen to develop a psychedelic centre. Within a month of his arrival, O'Brien had arranged for Hollingshead to become the leaseholder of 21 Pont Street, a luxurious Belgravia apartment which he christened the World Psychedelic Centre. Operation London was up and running. In December, Hollingshead and O'Brien were joined by Joey Mellen, an Oxford graduate who had in his own small way been introducing LSD to friends at a nearby flat in Cadogan Lane. Mellen's approach to LSD was heavily influenced by the teachings of Bart Huges, a Dutch physician who was to resurrect the practice of trepanation as a means of achieving a permanent high. Following Huges, Mellen insisted that initiates should be encouraged to take sugar and vitamin C to avoid the ego being threatened by sugarlack. While Mellen had little time for Hollingshead's mantras and mandalas, preferring not to impose any structure on the LSD session, he agreed to join the World Psychedelic Centre on the proviso that his recommendations would be made explicit to all would-be trippers.

Hollingshead threw himself into his missionary work with a feverish zeal. With only a few months to prepare for the anticipated arrival of Leary, he openly he proselytised the virtues of LSD, running tantric-inspired sessions for newcomers, while seeking a broader platform to communicate the Millbrook philosophy. In the literature which he disseminated from the centre, Hollingshead placed his own personal spin on Leary's notions of set and setting, producing what was probably Britain's first homegrown psychedelic manual, with a 12 point plan for new initiates:

1. For private sessions it is advisable to restrict the numbers present to about six; four or five is perhaps the optimum ideally and all should be well-known to all. Observance of this advice lessens the likelihood of personal antipathies, paranoias, misunderstandings arising.

2. Care should be taken that influences external to the scene itself are not allowed to intervene (telephone calls, visitors, etc.).The setting (locale, environment) is all important, and the overriding condition here should be that the atmosphere be as 'serene' and undisturbed as possible and remain so.

3. The drug effects last from 8-10 hours on normal dosage (4-5 hours with psilocybin), so that those taking part should ensure that any other engagements are fixed far enough a head to avoid being worried thereby...

4. Participants should as far as possible be adequately prepared for the session, i.e. should have been instructed in the broad theory and practice of psychedelics and have read some of the manuals or 'guide-books'; it should be remembered that apart from setting, the 'set' (the mental attitude the person brings to the session) is of prime importance.

5. The action of psychedelic drugs cannot be controlled, and attempts to do so inhibit the pleasurable results of 'letting-go'; therefore, in whatever form they should be accepted and made the most of. A relaxed and non-apprehensive attitude is of paramount importance: external 'game' attitudes should not be allowed to supervene, and the subject should take this opportunity of escaping – temporarily- from these and disregard such as he may see (or imagines he sees) manifested in another participant.

6. At least one experienced person (guide; guru), in whom the rest all have confidence, should be present throughout. Knowing from experience the scheme and cycle of events and their nature, the guide should be able to re-assure participants who become distressed or worried by a temporary unpleasantness of vision or feeling. It must be remembered that while, normally agreeable, even beautiful sensations predominate, they are not

consistently guaranteed. Their very depth and intensity must give rise to occasional feelings (if only due to their unfamiliarity) of non-comprehension and disquiet.

7. Should someone become actively uncomfortable and frightened (a circumstance the writer feels impossible given the conditions outlined, and that the person concerned has not previously had a history of psychotic illness), the drug effects can be aborted by administration of 25-50 milligrams of Chlorpromazine (intramuscularly).

8. Apart from ensuring a comfortable and non-disturbed atmosphere, the session 'guide' should provide, as possible, such environmental aids as pleasant lighting, music, colourful well-designed and interesting objects, pictures and materials.

9. The guide may talk to or hold the hand of one who may be temporarily unsettled, either to emphasise the harmless nature of the imagined trouble and its beneficial aspects, lend confidence or distract his attention in any way to more agreeable areas; he should not attempt to verbalise and intellectualise, during the session, the particular source of such 'worries'. Participants should be sure that verbal or physical contacts they make are welcomed, and as such they are part of a contract agreed upon before the commencement of the session: ideally it is suggested that the first few hours be conducted without conversation, though with music, poetry-readings, etc.

10. At the commencement of the session all should take their dosages simultaneously; for psychological reasons these should be measured and given in the presence of all and (with due reference to the directions below) be in the same amounts.

11. Though it will be found that most of the period is spent sitting and lying down – physically relaxing – it is quite consistent with a successful experience for the subject to walk at will. He should, however – certainly during a first session – confine himself to the room in which it is taking place or areas immediately adjoining; it is probable that a new 'voyager' will not, in fact, feel inclined to move far afield – the multiplicity of new sensations and phenomena will fully absorb his energy and attention.

12. As more knowledge is gained of the general effects of the drugs and resultant conditions, and these become more easily recognised and understood, new experiences and pleasures, and benefits may be obtained by exploring specific areas. For example, a person may devote an whole session to certain activities, such as visits to concerts, films, art galleries, or to walking in parts or streets.[2]

In other pamphlets, Hollingshead claimed the support of Alexander Trocchi and William Burroughs as active collaborators, attempting particularly to gain support through the use of Trocchi's name. While Hollingshead was at Millbrook, he and Trocchi had begun an amusing exchange of letters, and Trocchi was looking forward to finally meeting Hollingshead when he came to London. After meeting Hollingshead, Trocchi introduced him to Burroughs, Roland Penrose and a number of other people who could help him in his venture, but quickly regretted doing so, finding Hollingshead to be unscrupulous in the way he claimed to have the support of people in his work. In the case of William Burroughs, not only had Burroughs gone on record expressing his antipathy towards both LSD and psilocybin, he had told Hollingshead about his feelings about psychedelics on a visit to Pont Street with Trocchi.

In Roland Penrose, artist and director of the ICA, Hollingshead spotted a means of securing the ICA as a venue for a series of workshops in Consciousness Expansion, to be run between Leary, Metzner and himself. When Trocchi discovered how Hollingshead was using himself and Burroughs to canvas support, he wrote to Penrose warning him of Hollingshead:

> Over the past two months I have received literature originating in Pont Street in which he [Hollingshead] seems to claim the wholehearted support of a number of persons, I fear, he has not always been quite frank with. Indeed, very soon after his arrival, and just after I had mentioned him to you, I found him less than scrupulous in certain ways which involved principles that were and still are, in my mind, vital. I told him positively that in view of our differences I (and any person who knew what sigma was all about) could no longer collaborate with him. His response, the undercurrent of violence ('last warning!' etc.) was alarming... It is for this kind of reason that I feel

bound, in spite of great misgivings (sincerely, I have no
wish to injure Michael) to caution you.[3]

As news of Pont Street spread through the local Chelsea set, the likes
of Paul McCartney, Roman Polanski, Donovan, Eric Clapton, The
Rolling Stones and many of the underground's prime movers passed
through its doors. But, in his amphetamine-fuelled fervour,
Hollingshead had reverted to his old tricks, spiking unsuspecting
visitors at the World Psychedelic Centre and abusing the suggestibility of people under LSD, particularly women. Word of
Hollingshead's activities travelled quickly on the psychedelic grape-
vine, and the poet George Andrews wrote to him from Tangiers
expressing concern at the freak-outs and bad trips that he had heard
about. Hollingshead carried on regardless. After one mass spiking
which involved two undercover policemen, Pont Street was exposed in the *Sunday People* in March 1966 and a bust soon followed.

Charged for possession of almost an ounce of hashish,
Hollingshead elected to defend himself in court. His performance,
under the influence of LSD, did not advance his cause, and in May
he was given a 21 month prison sentence. The activities of the World
Psychedelic Centre served to bring LSD to the attention of Scotland
Yard, and in the wake of the Pont Street bust the Drugs Squad
turned their attention to some of its regular visitors, arresting the
writer John Esam for unlawful possession and sale of LSD and DMT.
As there were no specific provisions for either of these substances
under the existing Dangerous Drugs Act, the Esam trial proved a
vital test-case. While he was eventually found to be not guilty,
Parliament had by the end of the year expanded current controls to
include LSD, DMT and mescaline. For those that had been quietly
experimenting with psychedelics before the World Psychedelic Centre opened its doors, Hollingshead was held personally responsible
for blowing the scene, and his imprisonment met with little sympa-
thy.

Prison did not, however, completely deter Hollingshead from
proselytising LSD. After being visited at Wormwood Scrubs by Dick
Alpert and Owsley, chief supplier of LSD to the American underground, Hollingshead was left a substantial quantity of LSD. While
he generally refrained from turning on fellow inmates, he made a
notable exception in the case of the spy George Blake, with whom
he had long discussions about LSD. Serving a 43 year sentence for
espionage, Blake was a figure Hollingshead could identify with –

having in his own way spent most of his adult life using his charm and guile to hustle and exploit. In Blake's cell, Hollingshead guided a session which took a surreal but not entirely unexpected turn when the spy accused him of being a secret service agent, claiming that the LSD he had been given was in fact a truth drug. As he became subject to threats from Blake, a baffled Hollingshead tried to calm him down. While he was no stranger to such mishaps at Millbrook – having on one occasion disarmed Arthur Kleps, would-be leader of the Neo-American Boohoo Church, when he started brandishing his gun during an LSD session – Hollingshead's options were now rather limited. Eventually succeeding in calming Blake's fears, Hollingshead managed to steer him towards a period of calm reflection towards the end of his session, with Blake confiding to him that he would not be able to bear his imprisonment for much longer. A few weeks later, Blake had escaped by scaling one of the perimeter walls.

After four months at Wormwood Scrubs, Hollingshead was transferred to an open prison at Leyhill in the Gloucestershire countryside, where a growing number of psychedelic inmates were in residence. It was during his time at Leyhill that Hollingshead received a draft manuscript of Leary's autobiography, *High Priest*, in which his influence was given due acknowledgement:

> It has been five years since that first trip with Michael Hollingshead. I have never forgotten it. Nor has it been possible for me to return to the life I was leading before that session. I have never recovered from that shattering ontological confrontation. I have never been able to take myself, my mind and the social world around me as seriously...Since that first session with Michael I was never able to commit myself to the game of Harvard or rehabilitation. Not even to the game of proselytising for LSD itself... Before this LSD session with Michael I had taken psilocybin over a hundred times. But in each case I was the one who was directing the session and giving out sacramental drugs. Michael was the first person to guide me and propel me out of my mind... And who is Michael with his half-bald head and his angelic gross face, pink-veined from alcohol, chain-smoking Camel cigarettes?[4]

While Hollingshead was happy to be billed as the man who had turned-on Timothy Leary, he took issue with the Leary's description of his face being 'pink-veined' from alcohol, and suggested a revised version, casting himself in an altogether more alluring light: 'with his half-bald head and angelic gross face, sunlit and tranquil, inclining its axle slowly to the waning sea unrippled, far below: a face in which nothing replies, whose silences are one more meditation for the rose.'[5]

At the end of the summer, Hollingshead was released from Leyhill and headed for cooler climes and open spaces in Norway. Renting a small farm near Lillehammer, Hollingshead wrote poetry and set about translating Norse sagas. After a few months of this self-imposed isolation, Hollingshead was ready for action, and in January decided to return to Boston. Discovering that many of his former cohorts had now settled down to academic posts and left psychedelics behind, Hollingshead used his contacts to secure him a post as trainee librarian at Harvard University Library, working as an assistant curator of Scandinavian acquisitions. But regular employment did not suit the itinerant Hollingshead. After a few weeks he resigned his post and accepted an invitation to join Leary out in San Francisco.

Since the collapse of Millbrook, Leary had lived in Berkeley, having been adopted as the godfather of the Brotherhood of Eternal Love, a group of evangelical hippies who supplied LSD to the West Coast. After a couple of months in Berkeley, Hollingshead, Leary and his wife, Rosemary, joined the Brotherhood for the summer on their 300 acre ranch near the San Bernardino Forest. During his stay, Hollingshead worked with Leary on a filmscript based loosely around life with Brotherhood, pitched in with the work that needed to be done on the ranch outbuildings and dipped in to the supply of Orange Sunshine (high quality LSD) which the Brotherhood were distributing to much of the West Coast. Every full moon the Brotherhood staged an LSD session based on an Indian Peyote ceremony, during which the psychedelic fraternity would dance around the fire, bursting into incoherent babble, or, turning skywards, try to commune with the many UFOs which had been spotted in the skies above the ranch.

By the end of the summer, Hollingshead's enthusiasm for communal life was beginning to wane. Leaving the Brotherhood, he set off for the South Pacific, spending a brief spell in Tonga before heading back to New York. The plan was to head East and join the hippy trail in Nepal, where he would approach an acquaintance from Harvard, Narayan Shrester, and float his idea of starting a poetry magazine. To finance his travels, Hollingshead worked in New York on a video on Tripping to the Moon, and in July 1969, as Apollo 11 blasted into orbit, Hollingshead arrived in Katmandu.

Having been recently promoted to the position of private secretary to the Crown Prince, Shrester was able to arrange a full year's visa for Hollingshead and introduce him to people who could help him in his venture. But before he could publish the magazine, it was necessary to receive official permission from the Prime Minister, and it took three months for Hollingshead to finally meet him in person and have the necessary documentation stamped. Soon after the publication of the first edition of *Flow*, Hollingshead was approached by Kristof, a young English traveller and poet, who was keen to contribute to his magazine. Impressed by both Kristof's poetry and his knowledge of Sanskrit, Hollingshead asked him to co-edit the second edition and assume the responsibility of organising the translation of some of Nepal's leading poets.

Some months after editing the second edition of Flow, Hollingshead left Nepal. During a brief stay in London, Hollingshead amassed a group of young, impressionable followers, to which he was happy to play the role of a psychedelic pied piper, leading them to the small Scottish island of Cumbrae to establish the Pure Land Ashram, a hippy commune based in the grounds of Cumbrae cathedral. In the summer of 1972, Kristof re-joined Hollingshead in Cumbrae, and the ashram began to transform itself into the Free High Church of Cumbrae, adopting the sacrament of the full moon trip and bestowing titles upon its members. Ordination to the church involved the smoking of one whole chillum and the chanting of a litany based on hallucinogenic plants, after which new initiates were duly presented with a certificate of membership. At Hollingshead's instigation, the church adopted the rule that any one of its members could become Pope if they were able to produce seven different hallucinogenic sacraments – a feat which was never realised. Also, friends of the church willing to make sacramental donations could have their generosity rewarded by being bestowed an honorary title of their choosing. But for all its spoof theology the church did have something of a serious side to it, namely the Full Moon Trip, which was undertaken with absolute seriousness. Before the Full Moon Trip, three full days would be spent in preparation: the house being cleaned from top to bottom, and the inevitable wrangles of communal living resolved to the satisfaction of everyone concerned. On the evening of the session the inner circle of ten or so members would gather in the main room, with one person in abstention to handle unexpected visitors and unforeseen problems. By way of an altar, Sailor Sam would turn his Jesus-tattooed back to the gathering and Hollingshead would begin the session with the I-Ching, which would continue until most of the group became lost in their own personal thoughts.

While the dean of the cathedral was seemingly happy to turn a blind eye to the ashram, the bishop pressed for eviction. Forced to leave Cumbrae, Hollingshead and his followers moved to the West Coast of Scotland, where Hollingshead worked on his idea to build a computerised version of the I-Ching. After interesting a computer company, Hollingshead sold the project to the Richard de Marco Gallery in Edinburgh. As ever, Hollingshead was the ideas man. Now the exhibition was secured Kristof and others took on the responsibility of staging 'Changes 72', which Hollingshead had devised as a series of rooms through which the visitor was to be guided. In the first room, forms were to be filled. Then the questions asked of the I-Ching were passed on to the computer room, where their processing would begin. In the third room, the I-Ching's reading was represented in sound and vision, this leading on to a mock ancient temple in which Hollingshead and others played the parts of wise old sages, interpreting the readings. In his exhibition programme, Hollingshead wrote of 'Changes' as an instrument of the 'decision revolution' which would remove all occasions for regret, and of himself: 'prophet of the acid explosion, mentor to Leary, and first to escape the Great Brain Robbery to Nepal. There and back again to the Ashram in Cumbrae, from whence evicted in the name of God and Law. But above all glad to have done it, and to have been outside when the rain started to fall.'[6]

From Edinburgh, Hollingshead and his young acolytes made their way to London, installing themselves in the home of Kristof's girlfriend, Elizabeth Davies. The plan was for Kristof and himself to work on his memoirs, with a view to sharing the £500 advance which the publishers Blond and Briggs had offered. Over the next nine months, Hollingshead dictated recollections of his life since his first LSD trip, and Kristof organised material that Hollingshead had amassed in four large suitcases, helping to transcribe some of the recordings. While working on the autobiography, Hollingshead helped Kristof to establish his own Polytantric Church in an old gas works building in Kentish Town, home to a large squatting community. Hollingshead's ability to manipulate and engineer situations, through what he liked to call a *tactique*, came into evidence after the Polytantric's stash of cannabis was stolen by a local gang headed by Scotch Alex, a volatile character feared by many of the local squatters. After arranging to meet with Scotch Alex, Hollingshead offered him the gift of a pipe, while explaining the Polytantric's predicament. Diplomacy was followed by rehabilitation, when Hollingshead engineered a publicity event in which Scotch Alex was to take the starring role, being filmed alongside the DJ Dave Lee Travis in a 'Plant a Tree in 73' video. After his community service, Alex was a changed man, presenting no threat to the local squatters.

After nine months of work on the book, Hollingshead completed the final edit of *The Man Who Turned on the World* and collected the advance. Shortly afterwards, Kristof discovered him one afternoon packing his bags at Elizabeth Davies's home, to be informed that he had he would not be receiving his half of the advance as he had used it to buy his air ticket to the New York, where he was planning to visit his daughter. Naturally disillusioned with their leader, Kristof and other members of the church rejected LSD as part of the sacrament, and by way of symbolic revenge upon their fallen leader turned to psilocybin as their new sacrament.

While the writing of *The Man Who Turned on the World* provided an opportunity for Hollingshead to re-invent his past, casting himself as an innocent pilgrim on a psychedelic journey of self-discovery, Hollingshead was also keen to pass on the benefit of his considerable experience on the question of the value and significance of the LSD, concluding that:

> LSD is not the key to a new metaphysics of being or a politics of ecstasy. The pure light of the acid session is not this – it may even be the apotheosis of distractions, the ultimate and most dangerous temptation.[7]

While Hollingshead still maintained that LSD was able to provide a window on to 'eternity', through which 'the absolute is manifest in every appearance and relationship', he was now a half-hearted champion of psychedelics, insisting that LSD had in his case provided him with little more than an inkling of what real self-exploration would amount to. Indeed, if Hollingshead had cared to labour the point, the real story behind the *The Man Who Turned on the World* would have provided him with a poweful testament to the spiritual and moral limitations of the the LSD experience.

[Michael Hollingshead died in the early 1980s. The circumstances surrounding his death are at best vague and confusing. According to different reports, he may have either overdosed in London, been killed by drug dealers in Bolivia or suffered a burst ulcer at the Rio Carnival.]

Notes

1. Quoted in Leary, T. (1968) *High Priest*, Cleveland: New American Library, pp 240-242.
2. Hollingshead, M. (1965) 'An Introduction to the Field of Consciousness Expansion with an Outline of the Effects of Psychedelic Drugs' (unpublished manuscript), pp 3-5.
3. Letter to Roland Penrose, 30 January 1966.
4. Leary, *op. cit.*, pp 256-257.
5. *Ibid.*, p 258.
6. 'Changes 72', a promotional leaflet produced by the Richard De Marco Gallery.
7. Hollingshead, M. (1973) *The Man Who Turned on the World*. London: Blond and Briggs, pp 9-10.

TROCCHI ON DRUGS

Alexander Trocchi

Introduced by Andrew Wilson

In 1964 the writer Alexander Trocchi embarked on the idea of producing a comprehensive study of the uses and effects of drugs under the title of Drugs of the Mind. *Trocchi was well qualified to undertake such a project. In 1950 he left Scotland for Paris where, between 1952 and 1955, he edited the literary journal* Merlin. *In 1954 he met Guy-Ernest Debord who, from 1956 credited him as a member of the* Lettriste Internationale *and, later, as a founder-member (in his absence) of the* Situationniste Internationale *(SI). It was a number of Algerians, also in this avant-garde milieu, that Trocchi credited with introducing him to the use of hashish and opium, and then heroin. In 1956 he left Paris for America where he wrote* Cain's Book *(published in 1960). This* roman à clef *describes in graphic detail his heroin addiction as a fight within the language of alienation. In September 1960 he was arrested for contravening New York's drug laws (he was accused of supplying drugs to a minor) but succeeded in jumping bail and escaped, arriving in London the following year.*

Shortly after arriving in London, and certainly by 1962, he was back in regular contact with Debord who made him a member of the SI's Central

Council. Later, in August 1962, Trocchi also met William Burroughs, for the first time, at the Writers' Conference organised by John Calder for the Edinburgh Festival. At this event Trocchi described himself as a 'Cosmonaut of Inner Space', to which he also added that 'Modern art begins with the destruction of the object. All vital creation is at the other side of nihilism. It begins after Nietzsche and after Dada.' Taken together, these two statements provide a useful frame for an understanding of counter-cultural activity in London in the early 1960s and the privileged position that drugs acquired within that world. Speed, violence, engagement and the negation of any artistic or other categorisation, provided the leitmotif for a generation that enacted a retreat from the word as much as from the object: a creation of a new time and new space. It was this meeting with William Burroughs, his involvement with the SI and his use of heroin that determined his creation of Project Sigma, as a means of taking over the world through the destruction of alienation.

William Burroughs saw words as agents of systems of control that had to be cut-up, dislocated and subverted. To both Trocchi and Burroughs time had given way to the demands of space. The demands of being a 'Cosmonaut of Inner Space' forged a new grammar and language that was in Trocchi's terms 'meta-categorical' and avowedly non-Aristotelian; he had additionally stated in Edinburgh that 'to free themselves from the conventional object and thus pass freely beyond non-categories, the twentieth century artist finally destroyed the object.' Present Time became a place without defining objects, a space in which intersections could be mapped and where new horizons could be sought. The charting of the intersection points was, for Trocchi as Burroughs, characterised by a fissuring of the wordscape. In Edinburgh he had explained how he aimed to continue 'writing, stumbling across tundras of unmeaning, planting words like bloody flags in my wake. Loose ends, things unrelated, shifts, night journeys, cities arrived at and left, meetings, desertions, betrayals, all manner of unions, triumphs, defeats.' This listing of his subject matter made clear his own stance as someone who, alienated from the norms of society, intended to subvert these norms as a 'a member of a new underground.' Trocchi's espousal of drugs, and especially heroin, was a way of offering a definition of alienation that could also offer possibilities for the formation of a new writing, a new art and, especially, of a new society. Outer Space, the determined structuring of life, could be deconstructed and overturned by the voyage through Inner Space. From 1963 he identified this voyage with Project Sigma – whose aims were close to the SI – in providing the motivation and means for a 'meta-categorical revolution', for the 'Invisible Insurrection of a million minds', a 'Spontaneous University', a 'Coup du Monde.'

From the beginning Trocchi made the identification between Project Sigma and his use of heroin and by 1964 had conceived of Drugs of the Mind. In June 1964 he wrote to Burroughs with news that Sigma had 'connected with some off-beat psychiatrists who will collaborate in our drugs and mind laboratory (one of the aspects of the Spontaneous U)... I am meeting them... to talk about a large premises for Sigma.' These anti-psychiatrists – R.D. Laing, David Cooper, Aaron Esterson, Leon Redler and, later, Joe Berke – had founded The Philadelphia Foundation, and the curative ambience of its centre for Treatment and Research was recognised by Trocchi to be close, in the removal of fixed boundaries and identities, both to the creative meta-categorical ambience of '(r)evolt' found in Sigma's Spontaneous University, as well as to his Inner Space-Outer Space dialectic of alienation.

Drugs of the Mind was, therefore, to be produced as a Sigma Project. A contract was prepared with Heinemann and the editors were to be Alex Trocchi, Charles Hatcher and William Burroughs. An outline had previously been prepared and sent to John Calder and to Weidenfeld and Nicholson who, though interested, were both unable to meet the terms demanded. Shortly after the contract was agreed with Heinemann, Hatcher was replaced by R.D. Laing. It is uncertain why the book never materialised. Suffice it to say that the book was re-packaged in 1970 for Aldus with Trocchi as the primary author along with the aid and assistance of various associates. Trocchi was late in sending his text and by April 1971 had breached his contract so that, by August 1971, a substitute writer (Sandra Shulman) was suggested, with Trocchi being retained to contribute an introduction or afterword. Trocchi later intended that the work which he had already done on this book would itself be re-packaged to form one section of an autobiography/collected writings/ memoir. This was also never completed, let alone published. Despite all this a large number of notes, drafts and transcripts of taped discussions exist in Trocchi's personal papers that relate to Drugs of the Mind. Although a large number of these transcripts date from November 1970 some are transcriptions of earlier tapes from 1964. The edited excerpt that follows has been extracted from a transcript of Tape 12 (c. 1970) and is a distillation of earlier tapes, with some of the passages resembling more worked-up drafts of the book. An earlier version of one section has already been published as 'Notes from a Diary of a Cure, 1965' in Alexander Trocchi, Invisible Insurrection of a Million Minds: A Trocchi Reader (ed. Andrew Scott, Polygon: Edinburgh 1991), this had been extracted from the Trocchi collection in the John M. Olin Library (Washington University, St Louis, Missouri) and had been previously unpublished.

Like Burroughs, Trocchi's preferred drug was heroin. Nevertheless, at some point while in America in the late 1950s, he and his wife Lyn took LSD under the supervision of the psychotherapist Oscar Janiger – Lyn Trocchi's report of this experience is also published here (unfortunately Alex Trocchi's report does not appear to have survived) – and Trocchi continued to experiment with cannabis and LSD. Trocchi's position within the London underground of the early 1960s was such that he had become a central figure within an emerging drug culture. Trocchi was in contact with Leary's Castalia Foundation and Hollingshead's World Psychedelic Centre at Pont Street, and he penned an occasional column for the Inter-national Times, *appointing himself as 'Junkie to the Queen.' He gained notoriety for shooting-up on American NBC television (recorded in Lon-don) in 1963 and was interviewed alongside William Burroughs by Dan Farson in 1964 for Associated Rediffusion. Trocchi was a also a leading proponent of the case for decriminalisation and staunch critic of Lord Brain's Interdepartmental Committee on Drug Addiction (1965).*

Trocchi's Project Sigma, of which Drugs of the Mind *was an integral part, was utopian and grandiose in its aims, and as a result largely unwork-able and unrealistic in practice. It is perhaps unsurprising that the book was never published. Trocchi, among others, was attempting to search and evolve a new language of expression and action in which the object might be erased in favour of a more political and social idea of engagement as a means of bringing about change. The idea of a finished text or object was anathema; perhaps* Drugs of the Mind *could only have existed in Inner Space.*

This book would not be a true book if, at the beginning, I were not to remark upon the excellent properties of that drug, amongst oth-ers, without fear or favour, as they say, like the dedicated subversive I am.

Start again.

New beginnings are always good fun.

Each time I sit down to take up where I left off, I am in a certain mood whose symptoms I recognise: a quickening of the pulse, a shortness of breath, a tingling in the abdomen. I have usually rid myself of any impulse to go out into the world, often availing myself of one drug or another, or of a few of them at the same time. Heroin, hashish, cocaine, LSD... whatever it is at hand, and whatever I think I need. Now I have no fear of such things, insofar as they are predictable. It is I who am not predictable, and that is something to do with myself, not something to do with the drug.

The attitude of men is so hysterical, I find it difficult to get all the evidence. New beginnings are always good fun, but each time you are there, the flow ceases when the electricity in the nerve complex attains its freezing point, and there is only stone in the head, the sacred bloody groove. I have needed drugs to abolish within myself the impulse to get to my feet, leave the room, and to go into the world and act and do, go and assert my rights over those of others, or alongside them, or over the external world. For it is not people I come up against. It is insanity.

I take drugs. For many reasons. One reason, or rationalisation: to learn something of the outer reaches of my mind. At least, that was my original idea. I wanted to escape out of the prison of my mind's language. But drugs are only a small part of my technics and tackle at the seam of the historical process! Last century it was still possible to explore the world. Well, there are still places to explore, but there is also *inner* space. I knew that Coleridge had written *Kubla Khan* under the influence of opium, and that I agreed the poem was one of the greatest in the language, that after Baudelaire, and possibly long before, drugs could no longer simply be dismissed as 'pernicious'. His essay on *Les Paradis Artificiels* is another masterpiece. After that I obtained Cocteau's book, another masterpiece:

> *Il est domage qu'auleur de perfectionner de la intoxication, la medicin ne c'est pas des rendre l'opium inoffensif.*

> (Translation: It is a pity that instead of perfecting the method of disintoxication, medicine doesn't try to render opium inoffensive.)

He wrote that in 1929, but few took him seriously. I did. Not then, but after the war, when the old clouds began to appear on the horizon. It was Baudelaire's considered opinion that hashish was a more dangerous drug than opium. This I found surprising until I myself became habituated to them both. For opium is 'habit-forming' in a sense in which hashish is not. The addict undergoes withdrawal symptoms if his crutch is kicked out from under him suddenly.

Sometimes I thought I was in search of an identity. *Sordid story of a drug addict* in poor taste, described by a little fart in Atlanta,

Georgia, as a journal of my sordid half-existence, onward! At other times I felt that was what others wished to impose on me, and that an identity was precisely what I was concerned to evade... 'junkie' was not my term. It was imposed upon me. I can say, and even if I am lying, my act does not provoke in me any positive physical discomfort... it is late one winter's evening, I am alone in a small room in an unfashionable part of London, quite close to a yellow black canal... that a thought which occurred to me many years ago and has recurred from time to time ever since, came to me a moment ago, an hour ago; that the more closely I focused attention on what was not external to me, the more elusive, transparent, negligible did the object of my attention become. I didn't seem to be there at all. I was the invisible catalyst of a complex process of experience, utterly dependent for such ambiguous existence as was his upon external relations. And yet, that his most intimate act was a reaction of an eternal prisoner, endowed with an infinite capacity for suffering.

What that has to do with it is perhaps not clear, but you can smoke or eat hashish for a hundred days and a hundred nights, and set off on a sailing holiday on the hundred and first without fearing pains of withdrawal. There are none. Except that it is a great pity to be without hashish at any time, indeed. It is all in the mind, as they say.

But Baudelaire was not one to be 'afraid of addictions'. He had felt the battering ram of the absolute at the doors of his soul. Apart from its propensity to hook, opium is a very neutral drug; beyond the delightful sense of relaxation it can impose upon the user, the ecstatic intensity in *being*, and the resultant cool, it opens no doors, neither into heaven nor hell. Hashish, on the contrary, is an hallucinogen. It can provoke a shift in the structure of experience. Under hashish, when one learns its ways – in 1965... and even more so in 1970... a most hazardous enterprise, for the puritan pies in England's skies – one can explore new worlds, the way of hashish can be the way of empathy; temporarily at least one can achieve the undivided state of the *ensoit*, penetrate the being of the fanatic, and of the stone. But with practice and theoretically, experimentally. Through hashish I have been able to live in an absolute poly-relational present: all relations in this state are tentative, hypothetical... no certainty beyond the sudden utter certainty of the moment is imaginable. The state of mind, too, can be a critical one; razor-like, one finds oneself sensitive to the slightest equivocation in a man's demeanour. At the same time, one is female in one's lust to be impregnated, tentatively

Christ-like in one's ability to comprehend. On a more thickly sensual level, one lusts to become the very flesh of the other, to confound oneself with, to participate in... to some extent, some of the halluci- nogens allow one to participate in an experience of this kind.

In spite of the contemporary drug hysteria, or because of it, we should scream from the rooftops that drugs are amongst the greatest blessings of our times! They will be for the study of the human soul what the microscope has been for biochemistry, what the various scopes have been for science. Under hashish it can sometimes be difficult to sustain a thought; the mind can be like a grasshopper. I find heroin useful to give me the passivity to give myself over to thought. Then I am able to sustain a flow. That I should need heroin is possibly a weakness, but then it was not I who boasted of being strong. The hashish carries one like a sleepwalker, into many pas- tures... all experimental, all hypothetical, and at times, when one is most intensely under its influence, one can explore a sense of panic, confronted by the absurdity of every alternative. All sense of objec- tivity is annihilated, and one is overtaken by the despair of being utterly disorientated. And then, knowing the drug, trusting the drug, able to relax under the drug, one can suddenly become one's body and return gradually, through sex perhaps, to consciousness, where one is again in control and without panic. But it is certain that I have found heroin useful to give me the passivity, or the relaxation, necessary. The perennial in parenthesis.

The man who can give himself over to the experience in this way, who can as it were *freewheel* on occasion, is of necessity a relativist at his best moments. He knows what it is to be a fanatic, and survives to reject him. The man of imagination will at some time or other have been with his body back in the primeval slime of evolu- tion. He has empathetic experience of what it is to be a vegetable, a blob of slime. This is to explore certain outer reaches and return. It is a kind of spiritual sewage system. It's not the horse, I have said in the past, it is the pale rider. It is not the drug, one might say, it is what the drug does to *you*. Alan Watts has said, 'Mystical insight is no more in the chemical itself than biological knowledge is in the microscope. A door is opened in the mind.' When you come down, that door is still open, at least if you can return in imagination. You have to have known what ecstasy is in order to know what you want to accomplish, without drugs if possible. But then... without drugs? without muscle? without air? We all use certain chemical changes; we bring about chemical changes in a hundred and one ways, not the least by reading the *Daily Express*. If you can attain a certain neural state with pot, you can attain the state without pot, theoretically. But sometimes it's nice to have the mechanical switch there... a shortcut. At such times as you are not inwardly calm enough to adopt the play posture, the effect of the drug can be to abolish everything except the consciously chosen object of your attention. You are intensely aware of that. It takes on a significance in and for itself, that was not available in the normal act of attention, for better or for worse, relative to your attention. Things take on that exciting 'mystical' quality, the Wordsworthian 'Wonder at everyday things' that they have for young children, which they no longer possess for most adults, whose vision is highly selective. We see only what our mind, for practical purposes, allows us to see. Pot, as it were, abolishes the utilitarian criterion of relevance for a short time, and carries us into sensual experience, undifferentiated and empathetically.

Ordinarily our thinking is slick and mechanical, geared to stock conventional categories, commanding stock conventional responses: the effect of hashish can be to allow a man to come to sense perception in a fresh and structurally innocent way. And so, a piece of broken plaster, picked at random from the ruin of a building... for example... becomes under the eye of the hashish smoker the repository of an aesthetic secret just as vivid and individual as the secret in the sculptured grain of a Japanese *Netsuki*, with its intricate carving out of some lustrous semi-precious material. Just as vivid and individual, though perhaps not so warm, as the soft thigh of one's lover.

A line of thought can sprout out of some subsidiary clause in the sentence under construction, drawing the mind along after it, and out of all relation to the original probable design... grammatical, substantial design... into a bright and variegated jungle of improbability. Proust made a distinction between two kinds of memory, Beckett talked about it in his essay on Proust. The process of the mind under pot is related to the unconscious; a vital kind of synthetic, concrete unconscious memory. The mind is nevertheless capable of wonderful thrusts of analysis though the basic posture of the mind is not analytical, but synthetic, and in one sense of the word, poetic. And if it is thought that drugs are needed by a man to escape men, it may be so. But one must stand at some distance to see at all: it is a pretty horrible world if a Jew has to go to Auschwitz, and if a junkie has to kick himself to death in a cell.

But it is not the drug. The drug simply removes the metaphysical props, annihilates the governor, and allows us to see, as it were, 'raw'. That is why it is possible for someone who is sitting in a room with people who are smoking pot to get a contact high. This unanalytical posture is infectious. That is why pot and the other hallucinogens are such useful technical substances for use in social experiment.

Ninth day of October, or first day of Beachhead Established: Diary of a Cure, Cocteau, no. I refuse to regard it in this way, and I believe that Cocteau did likewise, despite the publisher's subtitle? To do so would be to accept the conventional hysteria surrounding the subject as meaningful response. About six weeks ago, with the pressure of events, the intensity of my interest and involvement therein, I found I was using what, under non-experimental conditions, was an excessive amount of heroin and cocaine. With no effective physiological supervision, I began to feel that my consumption of these drugs was irresponsible, dangerous, and perhaps potentially fatal!

Meanwhile, it has always seemed to me a good idea to be in general in control of one's addictions, whatever they are. I knew I was out of control, relatively. Moreover, it seemed to me that if I could get my relation to these drugs under control I should be in a far better position to demand that my own rich experiences in these matters be taken into account, in public deliberations; for example, some future Brain Committee finding. I had always felt that heroin, or indeed any other drug, wasn't intrinsically unmanageable. I wanted, not to stop using the opiates for ever and ever, but to use them wisely and well, and not to be their *unconscious* victim. That would no doubt mean: occasionally. It had always seemed to me that absolute prohibition was every bit as limiting and dangerous as addiction.

So I decided to leave town and set myself up at the seaside with drugs for about twenty-four hours after arrival at normal consumption that is heroin – ten to twenty grains *per diem*, plus cocaine – two to seven grains *per diem*, carrying in all my notes for *The Long Book*, etcetera, and plenty of hallucinogens and various substitutes (various drugs, which used in conjunction with one another, would serve to re-establish the normal chemical balance of my metabolism, without, on withdrawal of heroin, provoking withdrawal symptoms: that is to say, methadone (or physephone), apomorphine, phentozine, daptazol, etcetera) to break the back of my habit and attain a state such as that I could take it or leave it in the future... that is, heroin...

cocaine is not habit-forming, in the sense of producing withdrawal symptoms following abstinence. There are no such symptoms with cocaine any more than there are such symptoms with hashish or any of the hallucinogens. This does not mean to say that one can not get into a daily habit of consuming hashish, simply that one can make a decision to move away from the situation in which one is oneself in some other important business perhaps. And indeed, much of the trouble that is attributed to drugs should really be attributed to boredom.

This evening, rather later than I had anticipated, this beachhead was established in Herne Bay, Kent. 'Later than anticipated '... that is, later in terms of my projected regimen: I no longer have twenty four hours' normal supply, on the contrary, counting the pills now, where I sit overlooking the sea (overhearing, I should say, for it is dark outside and the curtains are already drawn), I find I have, 9 PM, 28 x 1/6th grain tabs, which is rather less than five grains, or a very thin twelve hours, and instead of cocaine (I have none any longer), I have a very small dose of liquid dexedrine. So tomorrow with the dawn, other things being equal, I shall begin the experiment with LSD, 150 micrograms, and we shall see what we shall see, indeed, no doubt, too soon.

11 PM, 24!

10/10/65, 12.46 AM, 21! How can I use 21 pills to bring myself down from a consumption of approximately 100 a day? (There is here the sign of the cross, as in Catholic prayer books, etcetera) The symbol, I find is contained in the blue silk Mandarin's cloak I have donned tonight. I feel it should give a air of formality to these desperate proceedings. Hysteria in a Mandarin's garments? On verra.

Tomorrow, or rather, today: lysergic acid.

12 Noon. Up a little over a hour. The sun is somewhere and gives a pink tinge to the clouds. A few blue patches... the North Sea is brown and grey.... there are eleven pills left. We shall take a cup of Horlicks and then, to begin with, 150 micrograms of LSD. Perhaps then, I shall get things in a clearer perspective. I can't say I am not worried, vaguely, about the end of my stock of heroin. But, on the other hand. I cannot say I am very worried: I am not. I am old enough, and, I hope, wise enough, not to make any wild predictions, and I have been through it all before. Overlooking a flat brown sea. A good place to be? Under the circumstances, for me? Take LSD. (From which bank, eh?)

4.30 PM. Got the car going, means of escape to hand, there is one grain of heroin left, has been there last four hours. I feel if I can keep that grain, there, in the bottle, under the Buddha, all will yet be well. For while the grain remains, there is no need for desperation. There is no heart laid waste with black despair. Thus, I have donned the blue robe of the Mandarin and I await deliverance, propped high in my bed, overlooking the grey sea. No terror will fail to beat at my battered door.

Yesterday in town, while we (this was a young girlfriend of mine, Nicola, whom I had decided it would be a good idea to go away with while undergoing this painful transition) were exploring, a woman who owned the bookstore came into my life. In the window we had seen a copy of CAIN'S BOOK marked twenty shillings.

'Whose author will soon be dead,' the woman said.

Said the author, 'That is most interesting, madam.'

'He will soon be dead because he's a drug-addict!' the woman said.

We left the shop, laughing, and rather stunned. Several minutes later, a small girl, bearing CAIN'S BOOK, accosts me in the street. 'Can I have your signature in this book, please, sir!'

I wrote: 'I who am about to die salute you!' and went to bed in my blue Mandarin robe, overlooking the grey sea and the sad slate sea.

6.10 PM. *L tombe*. The last fix taken. That is, it no longer beckons from over there, etcetera. I feel wonderful. But now, here I am, entirely without heroin, and not yet making my move towards London. Well, we shall see.

21/12/65. *Paris*. This morning Gabriel left for England. Before he went, he made me a present of a complete opium smoker's outfit: ivory stem, bowl, assorted needles, lamp, wicks and enough opium to last an addict for a month – Marcel, owner of *Les Petits Pavés*, the bar-restaurant in the *rue Bernard-Palissy*, old fried of G's and hero of the Resistance (*héro de la Résistance, Chevalier de la légion d' Honneur*, etcetera), though I think he likes me enough, was *most* disapproving. He has evidently been trying to get G to give him a similar gift for years. I can understand his feelings: it is a princely gift in Europe, 1965.

We should not allow the Americans to persuade us that our seven-year-olds need go in fear and trembling at the thought that they may turn on to junk! In this area what we have most to fear is fear itself. Fear, together with ignorance and the general need to find someone else to blame for 'the state of the world' etcetera.

First of all let's really have a look at the state of the world (as it concerns drugs). Perhaps our seven-year-olds don't need a fix because their fathers are not (a) at war in Indo-China, (b) necessarily wearing short hair, (c) or long, (d) and because such experienced investigators as Dr R.D. Laing, Mr William Burroughs and the present author, are presently concerning themselves with a sense of urgency to match the situation. Who knows, the future may be in the hands of the hashish smokers. A grid, a field of force, spreading, a psychological infection, in pads all over, wherever the preponderant life-style is *hashishin*. These cells of hashish experience can become co-conscious participants in a global surracial strategy. No formal explicit alliance is necessary: on the contrary, no badges. On a semi-conscious level the grid exists already as a marvellously complex process of so-to-speak electric light bulbs , which can be turned on in mutual recognition by means of various tactical symbols – click click click click – in phun cities wherever and whenever they exist, from San Francisco to Katmandu. As Kropotkin said a long time ago now: 'The future is in the hands of free associations and not of centralised governments.' Whose future? Let it be ours.

The Woodstock phenomenon, the great young happening together, causes great uneasiness in establishment circles, as well it might. For, as well, it is a foreboding of things to come, when the young come together in their hundreds of thousands, and simply exclude the conventional world and its organised violence. The establishment answers with drug probes by police and dogs, *agents provocateurs* attempting through violence (the only violence at the various phun cities is police violence), trying with a kind of cold hysteria through arrests, to bring back the minds of the young back under the sway of the great confidence trick of yesterday's law and order.

You're breaking the law! You *must* be breaking the law! What's that you're smoking? Mongolian parsley? Break it up! Cover your shame, like us.

In uniform and in disguise they haunt the lawless precincts of phun city and the measure of their impotence is the piddling number of arrests they dare to make, which arrests constitute the only disturbance of the peace, and how obvious this is becoming. Drugs and the law. I have to write on the insolence of the law insofar as it makes me act against my own best interests. Insofar as a law makes a man act against his own best interests, that law is politically insolent. It is against political insolence that I shall fight. I shall fight with every weapon available, and using every scientific and artistic technique available. We are fighting for men's minds. We are fighting for mind and spirit and body, against the various paralyses of the spirit which will refuse a man experience on the equivocal grounds that experience will corrupt him (and through him, others). It seems to some of us that most of us are so utterly corrupt already that practically any experiment is better than none. And in my own experience, voyages into inner space through drugs can be every bit as exciting and meaningful as the voyages of the ancient explorers were to their contemporaries and descendants.

Would it be true to say that in the United States, funds for research are in effect allocated by the drug police?

The junkie's security, depending as it does, upon a sufficient and regular supply of heroin, is threatened by any new legal limits to his consumption. (Compare the junkie scene with the Spanish Inquisition.)

Paris, 1952. I was twenty-seven years of age. I looked into the mirror. The central panel of these panels of the cheap wardrobe in the third floor room in an hotel in *rue de Vernieuil*. That was originally a street of tradesmen's entrances and backed onto the stately and illustrious mansions of the *rue de l'Université* in the seventh arrondisement, the arrondisement in which the *Quai d'Orsay* is located. I remember writing on a piece of paper: drink, drugs, sex. I crossed out drink, I put a question mark after drugs, and I put a tick after sex.

I am involved in a revolution whose implications go far beyond the legalisation of this or that drug. When we are successful in shifting some of the conventional sediment from vital places, such reforms as the rationalisation of the public attitude and the law towards drugs will be carried out from the top.

One effect of the hashish I have just smoked is to take me very intensely into the texture of the work I am involved in. But I cannot always choose the work I am involved in under hashish. That is to say there is a certain quality of a state of mind. It allows me to live most dramatically in the present moment, a habit of mind which eludes me under 'natural' conditions: thus I find some of the correlative disadvantages outweighed by this capacity for focussing attention. Under hashish, I know that what I have to do is relax and allow my attention to be directed towards whatever it is I have decided to do.

I have been talking to Lyn about structuring things to allow her to take an active interest in this programme on drugs. Who better, when you come to think of it, to give the woman's point of view? But if, for example, the other party is not in control, is perhaps anxious, this anxiety can be quickly transmitted to one's own state of mind, unless one is solidly based. Sometimes, to bring my attention back on to, say, a writing job, I find I can escape from the nervousness of which I spoke by applying my attention, for example, to painting. In painting I can try to exploit even my nervousness: paint laid quickly and nervously, as painters know, can represent an inspired passage. It was under hashish that I first learned to have confidence in my own ability to paint, to sculpt.

Of course, the so-called problem of drugs is bound up with attitudes towards leisure and other economic facts. Crime. Actually, crime statistics are sagging ominously. As Burroughs says, 'Sad old turnkeys mutter through empty cells, Desperate for arrests, police prowl the streets like paranoid dogs...' So the narcotics criminal is invented. He breaks the law to get the money to break the law. To buy his forbidden drug, etcetera. It's a treadmill, doctor. That buncha zombies! We gotta get them outta here and onta the streets and inta statistics! You take this farm in Kentucky, the Manslayer used to say, I'm against it!

On television a few nights ago somebody posed the question, 'Is there not a danger drug-taking will become the 'in' thing?' It *is* the 'in' thing. Thus, we must plan and investigate in a tolerant, objective way. To leave the outcome of this historical process to the hysteria of headlines and the reactions of Members of Parliament to that conglomeration of ignorant headlines would be fatal.

The hashish smoker and his wondrous sculpted pipe – bewitched: a gift of god. 'What we in the East turn into the fabric of heaven, you in the West turn into the hangman's rope. You would have shown more delicacy to have preferred sisal to hemp,' said the Sultan.

'Assassin!' screamed the indignant British lexicographer, adding to his Dictionary of Definitions even more definite prohibitions. And, triumphantly, seeking to prove his spurious moral point by definition, 'Y'know what the word assassin really means?'

'Hey, sirrah!' quoth our hashish smoker, 'By what insolent authority do you seek to impose your narrow moral prohibitions upon me?'

What excites one is not the drug, but what the drug makes available to experience. For example, a critic might say, 'You've had pot!' As though that made one anything but more critical and quick to sense an evasion. Man is always perfectable, because he is never perfect? Man is perfectable in the sense that a work of art is perfectable. Man's perfection consists in the infinite possibility of perfecting his imperfections.... and the doing is the point. There is a point at which any machine is perfect. This is to be related to a tactical use of drugs in the tentative changing of states of mind.

Experience Under LSD-25

Lyn Trocchi

The night before my husband and I appeared for the lysergic acid experiment we had both taken heroin. We had not sufficient time to 'come down' from the heroin when we woke at 7.00 the following morning, but with the help of black coffee and benzedrine we were nearly 'normal' by the time we reached your office at 9.00. We were given the drug at 9.20 and I noticed no reaction to the LSD until about one hour later. Shortly after I arrived, however, after taking my dosage, I felt a touch of nausea and asked Mrs Janiger where the bathroom was. I explained that I felt sick and she assured me that there was no danger of my vomiting. However my system did not respond to her assurance and I went to the bathroom where I vomited, a hangover from the heroin 'high'. As my husband has stated in his report, neither he nor I are in any way addicted to heroin. I have used it on only three occasions.

Having read reports of experiences under LSD and talked to several people who had taken the drug, I was primed for certain reactions and concentrated in the beginning on the visual aspect. My first visual 'hallucination' came at about 10.20 as I sat with my hands covering my eyes. A series of faces and bodies, like paintings of weird pieces of sculpture, began to appear and dissolve into their own centres, a continuous stream of them each disappearing and being replaced before I had been able to note any details. The figures were mostly grotesque, but there was no uneasiness on my part; they were simply interesting, I had no desire to open my eyes to escape them, I was isolated from them. I remember one image in particular, which made me laugh out loud, of a sculptured nude (female) with the body of a young beautiful girl and the face of a hag with one protruding side tooth from which a stream of water was spurting.

I opened my eyes and began to stare at a student's lamp with a red bowl. The lamp became slowly distorted and twisted towards me before my eyes. I looked away and when I looked back the lamp was its usual shape, but as I stared it began to take the same twisted form.

Another girl in the room, also under LSD, had been describing her various sensations for some time, whereas I had just begun to respond to the drug and felt no desire to communicate my feelings. I shared one reaction with her, though – the seriousness of the others in the room (or so it seemed), especially of those who had not taken LSD, struck me as ridiculous and I was prompted to giggle at odd times when others were talking. When I mentioned that I was 'jealous' of the other girl because she was getting 'higher', I was told by my husband and by Mrs Janiger that I shouldn't compare my reaction to others. I was abashed by this and wanted to explain that I hadn't meant it seriously, but could not discuss it further. For a short time after that I felt a sense of inferiority and said nothing for fear of making a fool of myself. This feeling disappeared soon.

I gazed at an impressionistic painting of Senator Kennedy on the cover of a *Time Magazine* which was lying on the floor. Soon one eye of the otherwise undistorted picture began to bulge and redden, growing larger than the other eye, and, the iris at an odd angle, like a 'mad' eye. I asked my husband if the eye looked unusual to him and he said only slightly. I knew that the eye did not *actually* look as it did to me at that time, but throughout the day the eye appeared distorted each time I glanced at the *Time* cover.

Tactile experiences followed my first visual perceptions. My fingers tingled and felt wooden. At one point it seemed that my whole lower leg was wooden and numb to the touch. My buttocks, as I sat, seemed sometimes like a weight of stone. None of these sensations were unpleasant. At all times throughout my 'high' I functioned as a schizoid personality, the one who watched and the one who experienced or acted, both aware of the other.

ALTERED SOUNDS

Sheila Whiteley

Fill Your Tea Pot...

Psychedelia grew from varied roots, with California being the main plant pot. Acid rock had first emerged in the summer of 1965 in the Red Dog Saloon in Nevada. Pioneered by the Charlatans, the fusion of rock 'n' roll, crude light shows and LSD laid the foundation for what was to be known as the 'frisco scene. Initially centred at the Longshoreman's Hall, and fronted by Chet Helms of the Family Dog, the fusion of loud, improvised music with dance and LSD attracted a cult audience drawn from a growing hippy community. By late 1965 two venues had been established: the Avalon Ballroom under Chet Helms and the Fillmore under the promotion of Bill Graham.

It would be misleading, however, to suggest that acid rock was a single musical phenomenon, and while dance was a critical aspect of the 'frisco scene, the emergence of such groups as Jefferson Airplane, the Warlocks (subsequently the Grateful Dead) and Big Brother and the Holding Company, established an alliance with the California folk movement. Musicians were equally attracted to San Francisco from Los Angeles (Love, Kaleidoscope and the Leaves),

Texas (Steve Miller) and the East Coast, (Paul Butterfield's Blues Band, Lovin' Spoonful and the Blues Project). At the same time, San Francisco saw the emergence of such groups as Country Joe and the Fish, Moby Grape and the Quicksilver Messenger Service. As Richard Neville wrote in 1971, 'All the relevant sounds seemed somehow associated with acid and universal love. The Beatles, Donovan, Cream, Jefferson Airplane, Quicksilver Messenger Service, The Grateful Dead, The Doors, Country Joe and the Fish all celebrated the acid experience and revived our faith in each other.'[1]

The celebration of acid and its association with psychedelic rock was fundamental to counter-cultural philosophy. Since its synthesis during the late 1930s by the Swiss chemist Dr Albert Hofmann, many who came across LSD were convinced of its potential to alter the state of human consciousness. The chief exponent of the LSD experiment in the USA, Dr Timothy Leary, was dismissed from his post in the psychology department of Harvard University in 1962 and went on to propound the philosophy of the psychedelic revolution, advocating music as a guide to keep you 'on track' during the hallucinogenic state. The slogan 'turn on, tune in, drop out' was adopted by a trail of converts.

Since the drug was not made illegal by Congress until 6 October, 1966, it was used by the hippies of Haight-Ashbury who reputedly added quantities of the liquid drug into dustbinfuls of soft drink and distributed it at gatherings known variously as 'acid tests', 'trips festivals', 'be-ins' and 'freak outs'. These gatherings were unofficial experiments into the effects of LSD and incorporated light shows, music and poetry readings. Participants were encouraged to wear colourful clothes, to dance, to sing, wear body make-up and pursue as many different stimuli as possible. The climax of Ken Kesey's famous acid tests, 'The Human Be-In', which was held on 14 January, 1967 at the Golden Gate Park, San Francisco, was advertised as a gathering of the tribes. Twenty thousand people converged for a free concert of poetry and music to an accompaniment of free LSD; the Grateful Dead were a main attraction.

Whilst there was no single manifesto which summed up the aims of the counter-culture, underground magazines emphasised:

(a) the spread of an ego-dissolving delirium wherein a tribal telepathic understanding could grow up among men.

and the need to:

(b) re-ignite an overwhelming sense of wonderment at the Universe, to cultivate aesthetic perception in the face of utilitarian perception, to reinstate the metalled road as a silken ribbon and the hydraulic waterfall as a galaxy of light.

(c) expand the range of human consciousness.

(d) institute an international tribe or class outside the destructive system of the nations.

(e) to release forces into the prevailing culture that would dislocate society, untie its stablizing knots of morality, punctuality, servility and property.[2]

The expansion of human consciousness, the re-igniting of the sense of wonderment at the universe, the perception of a hydraulic water-fall as a galaxy of light and the release of forces into the prevailing culture that would dislocate society appears, initially, of its time. Yet the emphasis on tribal identity and its associations with the shaman-istic, the metaphysical and the hallucinogenic was more a re-discovery of such Indian legends as 'The Kingdom of Mescal' which tells the story of a boy who longs to get beyond the appearance of reality. This Central American legend stresses that hallucinogenics are not a simple escape remedy, but rather provide a means to spiritual transformation by extending the consciousness, opening the closed doors of the self, and increasing the richness of the soul. It is a symbolic journey into self-realisation, where the tongue forms no more words, where the heart and the mind are one, and where there is a sense of wonder at the brilliance of the absolute which is en-hanced through synaesthesia as, for example, raindrops resonate with the colour of sound.

During the 1960s, experimentation with mescaline brought with it insights into both the beauty and the dangers associated with tripping, most specifically that mind-altering drugs work on exist-ing mind-sets, which can include the nightmarish visions described in, for example, William Burroughs's *The Soft Machine* (1961). Equally significant was the emphasis on support, that mind-altering drugs can plunge the user into a Dostoievskian maelstrom of emotional experiences. The need for a knowledgeable 'guide' who could lead the initiate through the trip was important to users of both mescaline and LSD. It is significant, also, that music was considered equally integral to the enhancement of hallucinogenic experience. In particular, the musician-listener rapport was heightened by an emphasis on shared experience which, in the sixties, was reflected in the lyrics and constructed through musical techniques which emphasised an electronic mutation of sound and shifting textures of timbral colours, so providing a metaphor for the enhanced awareness of colour and temporal disorganisation associated with LSD. Associations with the metaphysical were generally structured through an adoption of Eastern scales, drones, shifting metres, chant-like singing, and particular instrumentation to include, for example, sitar, tambouras, dilruba and tabla.[3]

The emphasis on altered states of consciousness through the hallucinogenic experience was integral to such West Coast bands as The Grateful Dead, and Sly and the Family Stone. Here, the sense of disassociation with mainstream society was also reflected in the construction of a tribal family, extended groupings of like-minded people committed to peace, love and creativity. The emphasis on different conceptions of time and space, the urge to 'Break On Through To The Other Side' was equally reflected in The Doors, a group who had taken their name from Aldous Huxley's *The Doors of Perception*. Focused and popularised by such festivals as 'The Human Be-In' and the Monterey Festival of June 1967, where Paul McCartney, Donovan and Mick Jagger were on the Board of Directors and Brian Jones acted as guest MC, the counter-culture, acid rock and its associations spread rapidly. In 1967 The Beatles released 'Strawberry Fields Forever', Donovan 'Mellow Yellow' and 'Sunshine Superman', the Jimi Hendrix Experience 'Purple Haze' and 'The Wind Cries Mary', Procul Harum 'A Whiter Shade of Pale' and Pink Floyd 'See Emily Play'. Significant LPs included the Beatles's *Sgt. Pepper's Lonely Hearts Club Band*, the Rolling Stones's *Their Satanic Majesties Request*, the Jimi Hendrix Experience's *Are You Experienced* and Pink Floyd's *Piper at the Gates of Dawn*. Exactly one month after the release of *Sgt. Pepper*, the famous editorial by Rees-Mogg 'Who Breaks a Butterfly on a Wheel' appeared in *The Times*. Some three weeks later, the same paper published an advertisement advocating the legalisation of marijuana, to which the Beatles were signatories. As Richard Neville wrote in 1971, 'From Berlin to Berkeley, from Zurich to Notting Hill, movement members exchange a gut solidarity, sharing common aspirations, inspirations, strategy, style, mood and vocabulary.'[4]

This sense of 'gut solidarity' was particularly prevalent at John Hopkins's UFO Club, London, where Pink Floyd were the resident band. In October, 1966 the band had performed regularly at the London Free School's Sound/Light Workshop where Joel and Toni Brown (from Tim Leary's Millbrook Institute) first projected slides over the music and where they developed the idea of a light show to accompany the music. On October 15, the *International Times* was launched in the London Roundhouse and Pink Floyd played to an audience of 2,000 people with moving liquid slides projected over themselves and the audience. The event was covered by the *Sunday Times* which commented on the group's throbbing music and the bizarre coloured shapes which flashed on to a screen behind the band.[5] Brief interviews were recorded, including one from Roger Waters who described their music as 'co-operative anarchy... a complete realisation of the aims of psychedelia'.

UFO, however, was to become the main venue for Floyd's performances, 'the place where Jimi Hendrix could jam with the Soft Machine before a discerning and stoned audience... where the Pink Floyd perfected their sound before an audience that was right in there with them, living and feeling every note'.[6] The success of Pink Floyd had gone hand in hand with the general momentum of the underground hippy movement (comparable to the Beatles's earlier rise to prominence with the Merseybeat scene). They appeared regularly at UFO (the underground's headquarters) and were the highlight of almost all the major events, such as the 14-hour technicolour festival. Such was their popularity in 1967 (and perhaps a reflection of the general spirit of the period) that the rather cynical underground movement remained faithful despite the fact that Floyd moved into the charts with their two single releases 'Arnold Layne' and 'See Emily Play'.

At this point in time, Syd Barrett was the dominant force behind the Floyd and almost the sole writer/composer. He had coined the name for the band and named their first album (August 1967) *Piper at the Gates of Dawn* (taken from Kenneth Grahame's *The Wind in the Willows* – popular underground reading). Ten of the eleven songs were either composed by, or in collaboration with, Barrett. However, even though he was the most potent force within the band, and despite their considerable success, his erratic behaviour, due to constant abuse of LSD, made him increasingly hard to work with. It became evident during the band's first US tour later that year that Barrett's stage behaviour (e.g. staring at the stage lighting whilst mindlessly strumming a single chord for whole songs) was doing the band no favours. Thus, in the following February (1968) David Gilmour, who ironically gave Barrett his first guitar lessons, joined the band and within a few weeks Barrett was asked to leave.

Piper at the Gates of Dawn was cut early in 1967 and the tracks thematically represent the interests of the underground at the time in their focus on science fiction, astrology, mythologies and alternative explanations, the Tarot and Tolkien. The majority of the songs are surrealistic but 'Astronomy Domine' and 'Interstellar Overdrive' reflect on the worlds beyond earth to become, in retrospect, the musical base from which the Barrett-less Floyd began.

The introduction to 'Astronomy Domine' begins with distanced voices, sounds taken from recordings from NASA, and a monotonous bleeping tone. Departure, arrival and the names of planets suggest imminent lift-off, but even without the verbal clues the effect is one of distance and space, voices announcing take-off to the world of the unknown. A rhythmically unchanging bass note works like a throbbing undertone, gradually increasing in volume against the morse-like bleeps. Nick Mason's drum entry then signals the bass line which is also used as the main riff for 'Interstellar Overdrive'.

The vocal line to the chorus is based on the final B/Bb of the bass entry and has a distant, detached quality. There is little vocal inflection, rather the effect is of a disembodied incantation. This is achieved by the echo-effect on the vocal line and the gently moving organ chords. Sudden splashes of sound on the cymbals punctuate every fourth bar, highlighting both sound and silence in the ten-bar vocal phrase. The effect is of floating, with both the vocal melodic line and the supporting guitar and organ chords moving slowly to create a mood of solemnity. Subtle changes of colour are effected by the unpredictable four chord harmonic sequence (E/Eb/G/A) which underpins most of the piece and which provides a musical metaphor for the exploration of new realities within the context of space rock: 'Lime and limpid green, a second scene, a fight between the blue you once knew...'

The first planet sequence (Jupiter and Saturn, Oberon, Miranda and Titania) has a gentle underlying dissonance between the E major supporting organ-guitar chord and the reiterated C# of the vocal. The momentary shift to F major, which is unrelated to the overall harmonic context, suggests a certain naivety, when set against the hypnotic effect of the repetitive cell-like phrase in the vocal. The effect, however, is like a meteoric flash of pure colour, which contrasts with the palette-like mix of the surrounding chords and electronic effects.

'Neptune, Titan, Stars can frighten' marks a change in mood as the vocal line moves to a solid dotted minim beat over a restless bass guitar before the piercing instrumental chromatic descent. The dynamic intensity of the passage propels the listener onward through space, the cymbal clashes moving the chord sequences forward as they punctuate first alternate bars, then every bar, before the more spaced-out effect of the pulsating tied minims. The sensation is of shifting gears. Initially a feeling of speed is effected over the guitar tremoloes over the continuous throb of the bass. The slowed-down harmonic movement then has the effect of partial braking before the final echoing cymbal crash. A wavering A/G# on the organ continues for four bars before the entry of a pulsating high E natural on guitar which then changes to E flat as the listener is propelled deeper into space, evoked by the use of white sound and electronic effects. Barrett then glissandos down for a solo break. Initially this is based on high alternating sustained notes which are bent up, and sliding glissandi, fed through an echo box, before a lazy tripping sequence. This is followed by echoing strums across the chords which are distanced by the use of overlay and echo. Underneath the organ holds the supporting harmonies, while the bass guitar continues the three in a bar throbbing pulse.

The instrumental continues with increasing intensity as the basic chord structure (E/Eb/G/A) is overlaid with electronically generated noise. In the context of space, the connotations are explorative: the bricolage of instrumentals, pre-recorded effects and improvised solo lines create an aural experience of the cosmos through an emphasis on timbre and colour, whilst the established logic of the chord sequence provides an underlying sense of control. Distanced voices, white noise and increasing electronic effects then move the listener deeper into space before the vocal entry. This picks up on the rhythm of the 'Neptune, Titan' phrase of the first chorus, the 'flicker, flicker, flicker, blam' coloured by an echoing 'pow' and hissing white sound which preface the questioning 'Scare Dan Dare Who's There?' and the second entry of the tremolo descending chord sequence.

Finally, the coda takes up the initial lines of the verse: 'lime and limpid green' tying the imagery to the sounds of space itself, the sounds which 'surround the icy waters underground'. Based on an A droneover a sinuous organ line the vocals evoke the never-ending dimension of space itself before the final resolution of 'the trip'. Here a change to the established chord sequence suggests a musical metaphor for changing consciousness. Instead of E/Eb/G/A, the first sixteen bars are based on D minor/F major. This is answered by twenty bars on D major/D minor/F major with the final entry on D major bringing a sense of overall control in its resolution on a perfect cadence.

Whilst Pink Floyd stressed that they were not a psychedelic group *per se*, they drew attention to the need to know that particular forms of music, such as their own space rock, were played when 'tripping'. Syd Barrett had suggested that 'Astonomy Domine' was a description of an acid trip taken whilst composing the song, whilst Roger Waters stressed the importance of the light show, the visual context which underpinned the 'other-worldliness' and beauty of the space rock experience. 'Space Rock', as the name implies, refers to the sense of being 'spaced out', 'tripping', and is musically constructed through layers of sound, kaleidoscopic colours, unpredictable and sometimes disorienting effects which create a dramatic realisation of movement through time and space, and which are analogous to the extra-ordinariness of hallucinogenic experience. Within 'Astronomy Domine' the electronic mutation of sound, the huge overwhelming textures, the sinuous tripping of the lead guitar and organ around the harmonic riff and the incantatory, mesmeric effect of Pete Jenner's voice as he intones the names of stars and galaxies through a megaphone, resonate with the state of mind when tripping. In particular, the dip shapes in the guitar solo create a strong feeling of floating around the beat and this is reinforced by the lazy meandering around the notes, again suggestive of tripping where the fixed point takes on a new reality. The chord sequence, itself, moves against any sense of formal organisation and, apart from the pause, which separates the two parts of the song to create a feeling of stopped time, and the final cadence, there is no real resolution. Rather there is a disorientation of the norm and a total absorption within the sound itself to effect a musical metaphor for being spaced out, the escape from a rational time sense. In live performance, the electronically generated sound effects and the long improvisatory passages resonated with stroboscopic lighting to effect a feeling analogous to the effect of LSD: the 'piling up of new sensations', the associations with changed perceptions and colour.

'Tune In and Turn On the Acid-House'

The emphasis on changed perceptions associated with the increasing importance of textural and timbral colour in psychedelic rock was facilitated by advances in the 'technicalisation' of music and a growing awareness that synthesisers, such as the revolutionary RCA and the MOOG, could be creative compositional tools. Synthesis facilitated atmospheric textures and multi-layered spatial compositions where the sound could travel rather than staying at a constant distance. Components of sound could also be adjusted in tempo to effect a 'sound parts' timbre, whilst tape-splicing provided the means to access and creatively deploy sound rhythms.[7]

The concept of 'splitting up sound' and the fragmentation of recorded material is closely related to sampling which originated in the 1950s in 'musique concrete'. Here, analog tape recorders facilitated the cutting and splicing of tapes to form a bricolage of audio material. The first American example was composed in 1952 by John Cage and entitled 'The William's Mix'. Other influential compositions included 'La Poeme Electronique' by Varese, 'Concret PH' by Iannis Xenakis and 'Gesang der Junglinge' and 'Kontakte' by Stockhausen. Their influence on popular music was largely technological and psychedelic rock, in particular, made use of tape techniques and studio effects as evidenced in, for example, 'Astronomy Domine'. More significant to the development of House and Ambient were the minimalist composers such as Terry Riley and Steve Reich whose use of tape recorders, in such compositions as 'Rainbow in Curved Air' and 'Electric Counterpoint' respectively, accessed the potential of musical repetition, where the constant reiteration of a harmonic/rhythmic cell induced a hypnotic effect analogous to contemporary Trance.[8]

Conceptually, the shift from analog to digital is one of facilitation rather than style. With sampling, the transformations of the original material are achieved by the manipulation of binary values as opposed to the cutting-up of analog tape. Today, the manipulation of recorded material, editing the start/end of the sample, repeating (looping), reverse, LFO (low frequency oscillation) and velocity sensitivity are integral to both House and Ambient. In particular, repetition as a compositional device, has become integral to popular music from the late 1970s through to the 1990s. The theme of 'Still Walking' by Throbbing Gristle, for example, is created by low frequency oscillation which produces rhythm – holding down one note on a keyboard, whilst adjusting other parameters, to produce a swirling effect.

Whilst the throbbing intensity of Acid House suggests, initially, a radical change in the direction of popular music in that its motor-like repetitions and abandonment of song structures for extended forms are geared exclusively towards dance, the trance-inducing effects and 'a fascination for the primitive hygiene and metronome rhythms of German electronic dance'[9] are not without precedent. The delay machine, as popularised by Pink Floyd, had demonstrated how technology can produce more extensive repetition in music. Can's 'Aumgn' from *Tago Mago* (1971) is but one example which illustrates how repetition, as a compositional device, effectively becomes the core of composition.

The incorporation of 'the lysergic mood' into House has been attributed to the emergence of 'Detroit Techno' which combined Chicago sound (disco and Euro-electronic). It is also suggested that Genesis P. Orridge and his team formulated the acid house experience through the use of surrealism, combining repetitive reversed reverb on vocals and using vocal and synthesised loops to produce such hypnotic and danceable tracks as 'Jack the Tab'. The drug related experience of dance and Ecstasy, LSD and amphetamines becomes more overt in 'Liquid Eyeliner' where snippets of music, derived from such varied forms as classical and disco, are strung together to create a disorienting bricolage which enhances psychedelic experience.

As discussed in 'Astronomy Domine', Pink Floyd's use of, what may be termed, disorienting or psychedelic harmony (the repetitive E/Eb/G/A) is taken to extremes in Acid House. Here, the principal approach to creating a chord progression is by the unpremeditated selection of major or minor triads to form sequences. The effect is one of harmonic instability which is often intensified by combining the original sequence with a different progression to effect a confusing clash of harmony. 'Anasthasia' by T99, for example, effects a sense of disorientation by starting the sampled theme at a different place, so altering the rhythmic configuration. 'Total Confusion' by Nebula II demonstrates how textural density can be created by an amalgamation of samples of varied timbral characteristics. Glissando effects are also important and effect a swirling sound which is analogous to the giddy experiences encountered when dancing on Ecstasy.

The effect of 'psychedelic harmony' with its unpredictable patterns and textural density is intensified by complex rhythm structures. The majority of early drum machines had quantizing which effectively 'corrects' mistakes, uniforming notes into the characteristic semi-quaver structure of dance. At the same time, the layering of samples, e.g. a vocal sample over a dance rhythm, produces often a polyrhythm whilst delay machines facilitate the triplet patterns over duple figures favoured by Dub reggae.

Sampling and looping are also fundamental to Acid House. Here, sampling machines in the context of an entirely digital environment means that, via MIDI, samples can be triggered by virtually any MIDI compatible keyboard. This has facilitated the repetitive use of samples over sequenced material, the production of different effects through the length of moment of key pressure (such as the stuttering effect characteristic of DJ mixing). Keyboard themes and bass loops provide a basic outline where, for example, a four bar phrase can be repeated within an overall texture consisting of drop-ins and drop-outs demonstrating the connection between the production techniques of dub-reggae and in hip-hop and the entrance/exit of 'scratch-in' grooves.[10]

The Sky Moves Sideways

Whilst the increasing tempo of acid house, the prevalent use of sub-bass and the use of anthem sections in the middles of hardcore tracks can be attributed largely to the replacement of hallucinogenic drugs by Ecstasy and amphetamines, for those who could not sustain high-energy dancing or who wanted to relax and chill out, the emergence of Ambient provided a unique and essential musical experience. The absence of heavy drums induced relaxation whilst the textures and electronic bleeps maintained a psychedelic quality which was in tune with 'coming down' from the 'E' related experience of Ecstasy and Energy.

As Alex Patterson of the Orb points out:

> Ambient music had to happen. Perhaps a year ago no-one would have predicted that DJs would soon splice together

ambient or new age music's subliminal, minimal
soundscapes (e.g. Brian Eno), newly rehabilitated Progressive Rock experimentalists (Pink Floyd, Tangerine
Dream) cocooning soundtracks like 'Betty Blue' and
House's colimatic beats. But it makes perfect sense... they
are two converging paths to ecstasy.[11]

Other bands expressed the continuing importance of the
metaphysical:

The Shaman has always been the agent of evolution, bringing people forward. (The Shamen)

It's the way that all three elements... mind, body and
soul... act together... it's like a strong feeling, a seventh
sense giving you a strong emotional resonance. It's a real
state of being. (The Shamen)

At this juncture there is an increasing sense of déjà-vu as
hallucinogenics are once again cited for their potential to access
altered states of consciousness:

psychedelic plants help to dissolve boundaries... and help
us to witness... the ruination of the earth, the poisoning of
the seas... two thousand years of dominator culture, based
on monotheism, hatred of nature, suppression of the female. (The Shamen)

Is it, then, that the 1990s have simply found a new way of expressing
the old messages of the counter-cultural manifestoes? Is it a return
to the old Gong philosophy 'You never blow your trip forever', the
idea that music can provide insights into various mystical experiences, that it can provide a way of experiencing mind expansion
rather than having to read about it, or be told? Is it simply a revival
of an 'ostensibly daft hippy fantasy'?

It is suggested that the parallels between psychedelic space rock,
ambient and trance are rooted in an underlying philosophy based on
an expanded sense of time which is homologous with both hallucinogenic experience and musical form. At a simplistic level, this is
reflected in the length of tracks. As a reflection of alternative experience, however, the extended compositions resonate more with

different conceptions of time and space and changes in sensory perception. Pink Floyd's 'Set the Controls for the Heart of the Sun' and 'Ummagumma', for example, explore the nature of time and the inner world of thoughts and feelings through extended spatial compositions. Like 'Astronomy Domine', 'Set the Controls...' has a melodic and rhythmic simplicity and an irresistible sense of movement which is generated initially by the bass and picked up by the drums and organ. Again the piece features barely audible whispered words and occasional sinuous runs on the organ. This time, however, there are no lyrics apart from the repeated title line, and the piece, above all, is mysterious. The first of the three 'movements' is based on spaced-out organ chords and gentle discords to evoke a mood of uncertainty and contrast with the second movement which is more rhythmically energetic. The third and final movement starts with what sounds like a diminishing explosion which moves towards grandiose organ chords, an orchestral chorus and strings to end with two minutes of serene beauty.

The concept of spatial exploration through subtle and gradual build-ups in texture, the sampling of speech and sound effects are equally present in such tracks as 'Little Fluffy Clouds' by the Orb. Unlike Floyd, where lyrical content generally contributes to the overall feel of their music, 'Little Fluffy Clouds' simply uses a snippet of an interview with American singer Rickie Lee Jones to focus the listener's attention. This removal of the lyrics is largely influenced by House – good dance music doesn't need meaningful lyrics, so why should good dance chill-out music? The full line from the interview runs (in answer to the question 'what were the skies like when you were young?'):

> They run on forever, we lived in Arizona and the skies always had little fluffy clouds in, and when it would rain it would all turn... They were alone and clear and there were lots of stars at night. They were beautiful, the most beautiful skies as a matter of fact. The sunsets were purple and red and yellow and on fire and clouds would catch the colour everywhere. That was neat 'cos I used to look at them all the time when I was little – you don't see that.

The words have a dreamy, childlike quality which is re-inforced by the sonorous and relaxed tone of Rickie Lee Jones's voice. It is also important to note the level in the mix – often the music almost swamps the words, but not quite, inferring that whilst the voice is important, it should not be associated with the lead line in a song. Emphasis is laid on the rhythmic effect of words, using various abstract phrases ('that was unique', 'you don't see that') as cadence points in the music to underline their meaning, fitting, whilst not really making complete sense in themselves.

The words are played in full over the introduction to the piece to establish the mood of the music, which has a similar feeling of dream 'upness'. This technique has certain parallels with such tracks as 'Astronomy Domine', and 'Great Gig in the Sky' (from *Dark Side of the Moon*) where snippets of speech establish an underlying mood: 'I am not afraid of dying...' etc, so enhancing the song's message and feel. The quote from Rickie Lee Jones also contains a lot of imagery, vivid colours which maintain a psychedelic feel, essential to coming down from, for example, Ecstasy, itself a mild hallucinogenic. Here, there are definite parallels with Miles' description of live performances of 'Astronomy Domine': 'After a whole night of frolicking and festivities and acid came the celebration of dawn... Syd's eyes blazed as his notes soared up into the strengthening light... then came the rebirth of energy.'[12]

The basic structure of the 'Little Fluffy Clouds' is simple. The main focus of the track is the excerpt from the interview which is stated in full at the beginning of the song and as the second build up begins. Elsewhere in the music, the words work sonically, evoking atmosphere. In particular the phrase 'Little Fluffy Clouds', is used in three distinct build ups, where the different parts of the rhythm section and motifs layer on top of each other. These build ups run from bars 1-36, 37-60 and 61-84. Motif 1, is heard at the beginning of the track. It uses a flat, full analogue synth sound with a slow filter (high pass) that cycles over 4 bars. This has a kind of droning effect and the ever changing filter gives a rolling, flowing sound. This compositional tool is also used to great effect in 'Shine On You Crazy Diamond, part 2' on Floyd's *Wish You Were Here*. Here, a droning guitar note playing quaver triplets with a wah wah on it (a very similar effect to filtering) sets the basic level on to which the various layers of the soundscape are piled. The use of the drone creates an anticipatory sound, a feeling of expectation which is realised in the contrasting second motif.

Texturally, the second motif is much lighter, being a sort of soft synth flute sound, and is underpinned by complicated delay patterns. The perceived harmony of the track also changes. Motif 1 is fairly harmonically ambiguous, playing the song in not quite a major or minor key – probably tending towards the minor as there is a C natural in the second half of the riff. In contrast, motif 2 uses a C sharp which gives the piece a definite major feel. At one point motifs 1 and 2 play together for two and a half bars. The effect is to create another 'wave' in the music – shifting between minor and major feels as the rest of the piece builds around these changing riffs and the vocal excerpt. Again, this use of textural change is similar to the long build up in 'Shine On Your Crazy Diamond, Part 2' where heavily effected slide guitar and a similarly effected mono synth sound exchange 8 or 16 bar sections that gradually rise in intensity. The area of pitch that is used for the solos gradually increases with each section although the basic melodic shape remains the same. Like the use of changing sections in the Orb track, this use of different textures creates subtle changing patterns to effect a sense of 'waves within waves'.

Motif three is a simple three note pattern played, then played again, displaced by one semiquaver. The cycle length is one box this time instead of four, and this creates a smaller wave within the rising waves of music. The sound used for the third motif is also in contrast to the sound used for motif 1. This is necessitated by the fact that whenever motif 3 appears it is over the top of motif 1 and, as such, the sounds need to occupy different areas of the soundscape. Motif 3 has quite a complex timbre, rather like a synthesized bell with the attack taken off. The total effect is uplifting, floating marshmallow music.

'Little Fluffy Clouds' is the first track on The Orb's *Adventures Beyond the Ultraworld*, a sound journey through space. The journey moves from 'Earth' (track two) and concludes, at the end of disc two, with the track 'A huge ever growing pulsating brain that rules from the centre of the ultraworld'. The concept of a journey, the repetitive sampled rhythms and the extensive use of a Dytronics Cyclosonic Panner, which makes sound move in three dimensions, induces a hypnotic spacey feel comparable, in effect, to Roger Water's quadrophonic sound events where sound travelled in a circle so enabling a sense of being surrounded by music. However, with the exception of the blatant 'Back Side of the Moon' and the inclusion of a photo of Battersea Power Station on the inside cover of the album which is evocative of *Animals*, the connections with Pink Floyd are subtle. The use of questions and statements in *Dark Side of the Moon*, (the 'mad for fucking years, I've always been mad', 'I'm not afraid of dying', 'It's one of those things that never go out of fashion') establish a precedent for the 'What were the skies like when you were young?' of 'Little Fluffy Clouds'. Similarly, the Orb's 'Towers of Dub' from their album *Live '93* has parallels with 'On the Run', with both tracks using a hi-hat tape loop to establish the groove, and 'Shine on Your Crazy Diamond' which uses one main key or tonality throughout its twelve minutes plus of playing time, a common feature of contemporary Ambient.

The key to the similarities in compositional processes used in both the Orb and Pink Floyd lies primarily in the music's intention and a comparable pre-occupation with themes, such as time and space. Both styles are written for audiences using psychedelic drugs. The desired sound is spacious, with lifting and changing textures and a smooth transition between soundscapes: a sense of continuity ensures that there are no abrupt sudden changes to disturb the tripping listener.

The beginning section of Pink Floyd's 'Shine On You Crazy Diamond, Part 2' is again a good example of this. The effected guitar and synth play in different sections, but the area of sound they occupy is the same and provides a sense of focus. They only combine right at the end of the section when the piece has built to a heady climax and when a similarity in sounds would be too confusing if played in two different parts. This demonstrates the importance of the actual sound textures (and therefore the engineering) on both genres.

Despite the shared emphasis on an expanded time sense and textural structuring (trancy timbres over a solid groove), it could be argued that the Orb have more in common with New Age than psychedelic space rock in that their use of sampled sounds of waves and the sea, and soft ambient pads, suggests meditation and relaxation. It is also apparent that whilst 'Little Fluffy Clouds' shares a sense of hypnotic repetition and atmospheric texturing, the emphasis on guitar, which characterises the Floyd sound is missing. 'Astronomy Domine', 'Dark Side of the Moon' and 'Wish You Were Here' all feature long passages of improvisation which are rooted in rock. In contrast, and with the exception of Steve Hillage who occasionally plays guitar with The Orb, there is little or no direct recording of a manually played instrument in the majority of early ambient groups. Future Sound of London or Aphex Twin, for example, process every sound source through sampling, sequencing, synthesis or effects units. Whilst this can be attributed largely to the evolvement of Ambient from Acid House, newer bands such as BLO provide links with Ginger Baker, drummer with progressive power trio Cream, and evoke memories of Jimi Hendrix in their tripped-out guitar solos. Dead Flowers and Porcupine Tree have also taken on board the progressive inclinations of the rave scene, building them into a rock context. As *Hi Fi News* point out, 'This is what Syd Barrett would be doing if he had survived into the era of sampling, digital processing and push button SFX.'

Albums such as Porcupine Tree's *Moonloop* and *Voyage 34* suggest direct parallels with Pink Floyd, not only in the use of guitar, but equally in the structuring of the music experience. *Moonloop* ranges from soft melodic psychedelic progressive textures through ambient improvisation to a highly charged finale. *Voyage 34*, described on the album sleeve as 'a post rave space wave to the Dark Side of the Moon', is again evocative of Pink Floyd. The music covers both sides of the 12" record and the entire first side is strongly psychedelic in its shifting textures, dark timbres and acid-like interjections on keyboard. The music accompanies and provides musical metaphors for Brian's gradual transformation as he embarks on his 34th trip or voyage, having ingested a sugar lump spiked with acid. Each section of the 'experience' is focused by a spoken statement. Manic laughter, distanced vocals and swirling textures suggest a withdrawal into the self, and are underpinned by a incantatory and pounding drum rhythm but 'Brian's mood is changing and he orders his friends into another room... he sits on the floor, talking to himself.' The mood shifts and lighter atmospheric sounds, over a repetitive high-hat drum loop, move towards a total absorption in the sound as 'Brian is unable to snap his fingers and terminate the trip'. Initially, unvoiced female vocals suggest a state of euphoria comparable to that of Clare Torry in 'Great Gig in the Sky', but 'joy turns to fear'. The soundscape darkens, and Steve Wilson moves into a progressive guitar solo, reminiscent of Dave Gilmour in its vibrant tone and sinuous scalic figures, before the music spirals downwards into a looped swirling vortex of sound. 'Brian's rocky journey ended 12 hours after it had begun. He was shattered by it.' The swirling textures continue as the narrator informs us that 'this young man never had a bummer in 33 trips... but in voyage 34 he finally met himself coming down an up staircase. The encounter was crushing.'

Side Two of the record picks up on the swirling synthesised organ sounds. There is a dark rumbling over which the commentator suggests that 'the LSD trip is a pilgrimage far out beyond your normal mind into that risky and revelatory territory which has been explored for thousands of years by mystics, visionaries and philosophers.' Sampled sounds reminiscent of water drops overlay the continuous dark textures. Distanced and barely intelligible snippets of phrases suggest both a sense of introspection and a lack of communication with the outside world. Throughout the track sampled extracts, of what sounds like Timothy Leary, reflect on the number of young Americans who have tripped, 'who have made it part of their lives, who have heralded the start of a new indigenous religion.' The track then moves to a dance-like groove overlaid with snippets of conversation, the 'it was groovy' working as a trigger to a continuous hi-hat loop, swirling organ sounds which come in and out of focus and which are underpinned by an assertive drum line, and another guitar solo. Like 'Astronomy Domine', the effect is to move the listener deeper into space. The aural effect is primarily that of swirling textures against a remorseless drum solo which finally gives way to the original chilled-out dance groove. Here music and experience come together as the sampled female voice resonates with the freely flowing rhythm and seamless guitar in a final affirmation of the LSD experience: 'It was like a caress. You could really feel the hot, the cold... really groovy... your body is part of a groove'. This is characterised once again by a soaring Gilmour-like solo to provide a musical metaphor for both the extra-ordinariness and the positive sense of enhancement associated with a 'good' trip. The track ends with intense and swirling chords on organ, high register guitar and a sampled 'is this, is this, is this...' overlaid by 'really necessary...' which finally resolves on the statement 'Is this trip really necessary?' to become one of many questions which are printed on the back of the album, which include: 'How should Porcupine Tree be used?'; 'Does Porcupine Tree cause hallucinations?'; 'What are the five levels of Voyage 34?'

'Voyage 34', with its sampled extracts of Timothy Leary, provides a comparable example to many late sixties psychedelic tracks in its implicit suggestion of the need for guidance for first time users of LSD:

> The underlying personality, mood, attitudes, expectations and setting in which the drug is taken have proven to be far more important as determinants of the LSD experience than with drugs such as alcohol, marijuana, barbiturates,

or amphetamines... Because of the intensity and complex-
ity of the experience, it can... be disorganising and
upsetting.[13]

Gong, whose guitarist Steve Hillage was to influence much of the
Orb's output, disseminated their commitment to LSD and 'Gong
mythology' with such albums as *Flying Teapot*, *Angels Egg* and *You*
(1973 and 1974). On the surface, the albums are little more than an
'ostensibly daft hippy fantasy' as Allan puts it. Further insight,
however, reveals parallels with various mystical schools of thought
and eastern philosophies concerned with spiritual awareness and
higher states of being and communications. Like Brian of 'Voyage
34', the story follows an everyman figure, Zero, and his adventures
on a journey/trip to Planet Gong, which represents the ideal world
whilst under the influence of 'the magic potion'. Integral to the plot
is Radio Gnome Invisible, described as a 'telepathic pirate radio
transmitter direct from Planet Gong'. When he asks 'if you want to
know how you can tune into the vibes of the planet, nobody else can
tell you, everybody got their own way to do it', parallels can once
again be drawn with such contemporary bands as the Earcandy
('Time is Just a State of Mind') which mixes stoned humour with
psychedelic space rock, or Madragora's 'While the Green Man Sleeps'
with its hallucinogenic mix of Amazonian and Martian landscapes.

It would appear, then, that there is a strong sense of shared
identity between the sixties hippy philosophy and that of nineties
alternative culture. Similarities are present in the music, the influence of the drug experience (LSD/Ecstasy), an awareness of the
destruction and ruination of the earth and the poisoning of the seas.
New Age Travellers share the hippy philosophy of alternative family groupings and the freedom to opt out of mainstream society,
whilst free festivals and raves provide the space both to trip out and
experience a range of house and ambient bands. Publications, such
as the *Freak Emporium* provide guidance to a range of psychedelic
music, magazines and books, whilst *Bush Telegraph* provides features on cannabis and the dream mechanism, homoeopathy and
growing hemp in the UK. Collective experience, music and drugs
appear, once again, to provide the means whereby young people can
explore the politics of consciousness, to set up an alternative lifestyle.

Notes

1. Neville, R. (1971) *Play Power*. London: Paladin, p 79.
2. As suggested by Nuttall, J. (1970) *Bomb Culture*. London: Paladin, p 249.
3. Musical techniques associated with psychedelic experience include:
   - an overall emphasis on timbral colour (blurred, bright, tinkly, overlapping, associated with the intensification of colour and shape experienced when tripping).
   - upward movement in pitch (and the comparison with an hallucinogenic high).
   - characteristic use of harmonies (lurching, oscillating and the relationship to changing focus).
   - sudden surges of rhythm (and the associations with an acid 'rush') and/or a feel of floating around the beat (suggestive of a state of tripping where the fixed point takes on a new reality).
   - shifting textural relationships (foreground/background, collages and soundscapes which suggest a disorientation of more conventionalised musical structures and which focus a total sense of absorption with/within the sound itself. These techniques provide a musical analogy for the enhancement of awareness, the potentially new synthesis of ideas and thought relationships which can result from hallucinogens).

   Whilst the associations between LSD and psychedelic rock suggest an inner coherence, the fact that psychedelic coding was interpreted by reference to hallucinogenic experience and that this, in turn, was then pinned on to the music lead ultimately to a dilution of the form through commercialisation (e.g. the Flowerpot Men, 'Let's Go to San Francisco'). At the same time, certain techniques (such as Pink Floyd's use of synthesised sound textures) have become formative influences upon such 1990s ambient groups as the Orb and Ozric Tentacles, where soundscaping and layered sound textures effect a sense of ecstatic trance.

   See Whiteley, S. 'Psychedelic "Acid" Rock', *Encyclopedia of Popular Music*, Cambridge University Press (forthcoming).
4. Neville, *op. cit.*, p 14.
5. On October 31, 1966 Pink Floyd, together with Pete Jenner and Andrew King, set up Blackhill Enterprises as a six-way partnership to manage the group. In November they enlisted Joe Gannon to handle their lights. His slides were based on the underlying

rhythm in the music and as his hands waved over the micro-switches, different colours flashed to provide a direct link between the visual and aural effect.

See Whiteley, S. (1992) *The Space Between The Notes*. London: Routledge, pp 28-9.

6. Miles (1980) *Pink Floyd*. London: Omnibus Press. As the pages are not numbered this reference occurs under the heading '11 October, 1966'.

7. Stockhausen identified four criteria for his electronic compositions in his 1971 London lecture:

    (i)   Unified time structuring – the composition of rhythm by tape-splicing. Here, a rhythmic loop is speeded up until a continuous pattern occurs. By speeding it up more, a low tone is heard which rises in pitch. At this point, the rhythm itself is no longer heard, rather a specific timbre, a spectrum, which is determined by the composition of its component parts and which is an effect of the original rhythm.

    (ii) The splitting of sound – Stockhausen's composition 'Kontakte' illustrates 'the splitting of the sound' which is based on the principle of 'decomposed' sound. e.g. 'Owww' becomes 'Ow' and 'ww', and 'Kontakte' becomes 'Kon-tak-te'. Components of sound can be adjusted in tempo, thus altering the sound – or sound parts timbre.

    (iii) Multi-layered spatial composition – Whereby a sound no longer remains at a constant distance but can move around the listener. Stockhausen built a spatial dimension into his compositions by creating up to six layers of sound at different levels.

    (iv) The quality of tone and noise – If the degree of aperiodicity of any given sound can be controlled, and controlled in a particular way, then any constant sound can be transformed into a noise.

    Maconie, R. (1989) *Stockhausen on Music*. London: Marion Boyars Publishing Ltd.

8. Trance is slow build up music, heavily overlaid, minimalistic (often based on one rhythmic cell), with stepped dynamics which constantly build up, but without a sense of climax. The use of, for example, a particular riff for thirty or more bars, drone-like at times, focuses the sense of being 'entranced' with a particular sound or sound event and, as such, there is a relationship to drug experience (put into a state of rapture, ecstasy) Trance is very often

a hybrid form, e.g. ambient trance. In this instance, the music would be heavier than ambient but would focus comparable techniques such as soundscaping and textural colours. The growing depersonalisation of Trance has lead to a 'stripping down' to the 'pure' form, to the bare essentials of the analogue synth, the Roland TR909 kick drum and hi hats. All aspects of the music – basslines, pads, stabs and rhythmic patterns, 'sound effects' and lead instruments – are now generated from this sound source.

Whiteley, *op.cit.*

9.   Oldfield, P. and Reynolds, S., 'Acid Over' in Reynolds, S. (1992) *Blissed Out*. London: Serpent's Tail.

10. I would like to acknowledge and thank my student, Glen Sharp for his permission to use material from his 1994 Dissertation 'In The House'.

11. Logan, A. 'A Journey Through Ambience', *Outlook*, September/ October, 1993.

12. Miles, op.cit., 30 April, 1967.

13. Fort, J. (1969) *The Pleasure Seekers: The Drug Crisis, Youth and Society*. New York: Grove Press, p 130.

BACK TO EDEN:
Innocence, Indolence and Pastoralism in Psychedelic Music, 1966-1996

Simon Reynolds

Its roots may lie in the rural blues and country music of the American South, but in Britain, rock was the sound of the city. Rock was the blues electrified, wired on the hypertension of urban life. In the mid-1960s, it was in revolt against nature: rock was 'noise pollution'. It didn't have a lot to do with hedgerows and haystacks, with the peace and quiet of the countryside.

'Mod' was the apotheosis of rock's mid-1960s urbanism. Mod stood for modernist; appropriately, the mods not only embraced but amplified the neuroses of late twentieth-century capitalist life – its obsession with surfaces and commodity fetishism, its rapid turnover of styles and rampant consumerism. Mod lifestyle accentuated the anti-natural rhythm of industrial life, with its strict demarcation between work and leisure. The dead-end drudgery of Monday to Friday 9 to 5 alternated with the explosive release of the mods' sleep-defying, speed-fuelled 48 hour weekends. The Easybeats's classic song 'Friday On My Mind' crystallises the vibe of the mid-1960s: anticipation, a headlong *rush* into the future's neon glare.

Pills had everything to do with mod: amphetamine is the urban, twentieth-century drug. In *The Speed Culture*, Lester Grinspoon and Peter Hedblom argue that 'the amphetamine abuser, especially the "speed freak"... is a gross caricature of many of the pathological, ultimately destructive features of the society that produced him.'[1] If speed is the ultimate conformist drug, it's no wonder that the counterculture fastened on marijuana – a drug that slows things down, promotes contemplation and communion rather than freneticism and competitivity – in order to facilitate their secession from straight society. West Coast hippies organised a 'Speed Kills' campaign, aghast at the way amphetamine wreaked havoc on Haigh-Ashbury's love 'n' peace vibe; The Who sang of 'smoking Mother Nature'. (To this day, hemp-legalisation activists distinguish the natural, 'God-given' nature of marijuana from synthetic mind-altering 'chemicals'.)

Within two years of the birth of mod, rock's site of fantasy would shift from the city centre to 'getting it together in the country'. Early-to-mid 1960s British rock was about the 'mannish boy', about breaking free of the mother's realm, domesticity, good behaviour. Psychedelia, on the other hand, was the culture of the mother's boy, who longed to come to rest in the arms of Mother Nature. Mod's lust for action, its restless craving for kicks and kineticism, was replaced by psychedelia's cult of passivity, indolence and sleep. Amphetamine-induced insomnia (in the 1930s, the pharmaceutical had been prescribed as a cure for narcolepsy), gave way to the dreamy dissipation of LSD. Together, all these changes constituted a shift in rock's yin/yang ratio, away from hyper-masculinity to a more feminine, androgynous orientation.

Mod was a male-dominated subculture: since amphetamines suppressed sexual drives and boosted narcissism, boys dressed to impress other boys; girls were marginal. With psychedelia, ego-dissolution replaced ego-mania. Where speed encouraged a sharp sense of detachment and definition from one's environment, LSD broke down the defences, blurred the borders between self and world. White R&B's violent assertion of manhood gave way to childlike androgyny. Innocence was in, and 'experience' meant something altogether more spiritual than carnal. While mod had looked to the spotless formica future, hippy rock harked back to lost golden ages: hence its love of Edwardiana and Medievalism.

Perhaps it's no coincidence that the mods were obsessed with Italian streamlined style, from suits to mopeds. After all, the Italian Futurists despised tranquillity, resisted slumber and worshipped speed. Rejecting Romanticism's quest for the lost state of grace in Nature's bosom, F.T. Marinetti decried 'nostalgia', 'the picturesque', 'the imprecise, rusticity, wild solitude', and vowed to desecrate 'the holy green silence' with the thunder of war and industry.[2]

In contrast to mod's futurist masculinism, psychedelia revived the concerns of Romanticism (Rimbaud's pursuit of synaesthesia through 'a systematic derangement of all the senses') and of Dada (Hugo Ball's sound poetry, which imitated the babbling nonsense and voluptuous echolalia of baby talk). Like these ancestors, psychedelia mistrusted masculine logic, proposed the cultivation of 'feminine' flow, receptivity and cyclical time (The Byrds' 'She Don't Care About Time'), and believed that industrial/urban existence was synonymous with living death.

Mother Nature's Son

'O, Mother, when shall I be blessed by joining your blissful company?'
- Quintessence, sleevenotes to *In Blissful Company*, 1969

As the LSD began to kick in, pastoralism erupted amidst mod's urban landscape – literally, with the London park settings of songs like John's Children's 'A Midsummer's Night Scene' and the Small Faces's 'Itchycoo Park'. John's Children's first song, 'Smashed Blocked', had described love's disorientation in the language of amphetamine psychosis ('blocked' being mod slang for being hyped on pills). But by 1967, the band were posing for photos naked in a meadow, their private parts obscured by garlands of flowers. 'A Midsummer's Night Scene' starts with the chant 'petals and flowers' over an ominous heavily-distorted bassline, then hurls the listener into a Dionysian whirl of feedback and pagan imagery: glowering heatwave intensity, mad-eyed girls ripping up flowers and dervish-whirling the Rites of Pan.

'A Midsummer Night's Scene' was co-written by Marc Bolan. Prior to his brief stint in John's Children, Bolan was a well-known mod stylist who'd been quoted in *Town* magazine talking about his large collection of expensive suits. By the time he left John's Children, Bolan was a fully-fledged flower child with his own acoustic folk-blues band, Tyrannosaurus Rex. On albums like *Prophets, Seers and Sages, The Angels of the Ages* (1968), *My People Were Fair and Had Sky in Their Hair* (1968), *Unicorn* (1969) and *A Beard of Stars* (1970), he sang tall Tolkienesque tales that blended magical mystery, kosmic sci-fi fantasy, and rustic paganism. Bolan was not alone in his faery fancies: 1967 was the year of the man-child minstrel who mixed nursery rhyme artlessness, English whimsy, and fantasies of olden times.

Donovan, all prissy diction, beardless face, and curly locks, was a harmless homegrown version of Dylan who quickly became an enduring symbol of the sheer innocuousness of flower power. Songs like 'Mellow Yellow' and 'Jennifer Juniper' took psychedelia's Fotherington-Thomas 'hello clouds, hello trees' tendencies to the outer limits of twee, while 'Hurdy Gurdy Man' (1968) evoked the sinister, superstitious side of rustic life. Then there was Steve Winwood, who followed the classic mod-to-hippy trajectory, going from the horny adolescent R&B of the Spencer Davis Group to Traffic, one of the first psychedelic bands to embrace 'getting it together in the country'. Traffic moved into a Berkshire cottage in the summer of 1967 to record their debut album *Mr Fantasy*. Their most famous song, 'Hole In My Shoe', combined bucolic bliss with fantastical imagery borrowed from classic children's writers like C. S. Lewis, E. Nesbitt and Lewis Carroll; a stoned hippy wanders through dew-stippled grass whose moisture seeps into his footwear, then a child's voice breathlessly describes being transported on the back of an albatross to a cloud-kingdom 'where happiness reigned' eternally.

When it comes to pastoralism/infantilism, though, the group who did it first and took it furthest were the Incredible String Band. On the cover of their most famous album, *The Hangman's Beautiful Daughter*, the duo of Robin Williamson and Mike Heron nestle amidst the moss-covered trees of an English copse, surrounded by fellow members of their commune, adults and children dressed in raggle-taggle Medieval garb. The Incredible String Band's music was as rag-and-bobtail as their clothes, a blend of folk, blues and Indian raga. Albums like *The 5000 Spirits or the Layers of the Onion* (1967) *The Hangman's Beautiful Daughter* (1967), and *Wee Tam* (1968) inhabit a strange and wonderful never-neverland where English folklore and children's fairy-tales mingle with Zen Buddhism.

The Incredible String Band's worldview was pantheistic. In a 1967 interview, Williamson declared: 'Everything is a miracle. It's all magic and we are really here on earth to wonder at all these beautiful things. Our records are no more wonderful or no more magical than a lump of earth.'[3] And so 'Air' is a hymn to – you guessed it – air, Heron marvelling at the intimate way it can penetrate his body and 'kiss my blood'. This mystical pantheism bleeds into a children's storybook anthropomorphism in 'The Hedgehog's Song', where Heron is educated in affairs of the heart by a creature of the field, or in 'Little Cloud', where he befriends a cloud (a happy one, who refuses to cry, i.e. rain). This genial relationship with Nature takes on an ecological slant in 'Mercy I Cry City', where Heron dreams of 'quiet pastures' where he can escape the city's pollution and hypertension. What connects the pastoralism, the cult-of-childhood, and the pantheism is a profound nostalgia. In 'Job's Tears', Williamson dreams of returning to an 'old golden land' where worry and loneliness are banished. In the present, this wonderland can only be reached in dreams. The Incredible String Band took psychedelia's cult of slumber further than most, in songs like 'Chinese White' (where Heron sings of laying down to sleep with his arms 'around the rainbow') and 'Nightfall' (in which Williamson longs for the embrace of 'night's daughters'). In 'No Sleep Blues' he's agonised by 'delirium nosleepum'.

Psychedelia's conflation of sleep and innocence was captured in the name of a little-known band, Virgin Sleep. The best of their few recorded songs is the enchanting 'Secret' (1968). Like the Incredible String Band, Virgin Sleep take the anthropomorphism of *The Wind in the Willows* and *Winnie the Pooh* and give it a mystical twist. The song offers a new definition of 'hip', in the imagery of A.A. Milne rather than Colin MacInnes: the field mouse, toad and swan know 'what's goin' on', and the place to be isn't mod nightclubs like the Flamingo or Marquee but the woodland glade where the singer takes tea with a teddy bear. The singer hears the 'Secret' whispering through the hedgerows, but he's sworn to silence – he's down with Mother Nature.

Another minor classic of British psychedelia, Tintern Abbey's 'Beeside' (1967), also makes the indolence/innocence connection. Here, it's a creature of the field, a busy bee, who's misguided, and a human who hips him to the true meaning of flower power: 'people pick them, you lick them, just for love'. Singer David MacTavish contemplates the bee's toil and tells him to mellow out. Like Wordsworth, whose poem gives the band their name, Tintern Abbey believe that indolence feminises man, promoting receptivity and 'wise passiveness'. The state of grace comes when man is de-activated and drowsy, succumbs to what Wordsworth calls 'that serene and blessed mood' in which 'we are laid asleep/In body, and become a living soul'. Tintern Abbey's music recreates Romanticism's primal scene, the bower of bliss – groves and glades 'where the male is captured, seduced and infantilised', according to Camille Paglia, stranded in 'a limbo of lush pleasures but stultifying passivity'.[4] 'Beeside' is all synaesthesia, clouds of phased cymbal scintillating like pollen caught in midsummer sunshine. Into this idyll materialises 'a virgin of humble origin', a mystic girl-sprite whose caresses are sacraments of love that magically return to the singer his *own* virginity.

The Soft Machine were another British hippy band who proposed indolence as the route to enlightenment in songs like 'Why Are We Sleeping?' (about a man drowning in his dreams) and 'As Long As He Lies Perfectly Still'. 'Heaven on Earth, he'll get there soon', they sing of a beach bum who's 'waiting for something that's already there': nirvana.

For the hippies, laziness was next to godliness. In the Beatles's 'Mother Nature's Son' (*The Beatles*, 1968), Paul McCartney blends with the scenery and sings a 'lazy song' in a meadow of daisies. 'I'm Only Sleeping', from *Revolver* (1966) is a manifesto of quietism and passivity, a flagrant flouting of the reality-principle. 'When I'm in the middle of a dream/Stay in bed, float upstream,' croons John Lennon amidst an oneiric haze of backwards-guitar. 'Please don't wake me... I'm only sleeping'. Slumber is 'uterine regression', says Norman O. Brown in *Love's Body*.[5] *Revolver* ends with the near-nihilistic Zen hymn 'Tomorrow Never Knows': 'turn off your mind, relax and float downstream... surrender to the void'. Indolence and disengagement bestow blessed exemption from a world gone crazy; will-power and the contoured ego dissolve in an incandescent 'chaosmos' of processed guitar and treated, sped-up vocals.

Younger Than Yesterday

Unlike the British groups, many Americans went straight from folk to acid rock with no period of urban blues. The Byrds's pastoralism blossomed in their 1967 album *Younger Than Yesterday*. The title came from Dylan's 'My Back Pages', which the Byrds covered on the album. In the song, the protagonist outgrows his adolescent unrest and relearns the openness and simple wisdom of a child. In 'Mind Gardens', an orchard on a hill is David Crosby's metaphor for the self. In order to protect it from the harsh elements, he walls it in, but his over-zealous fortification blocks out the nourishing sunlight, and the 'Mind Gardens' start to wilt. Just before they perish, he comes to his senses and demolishes the wall, opening himself up to the world; otherwise 'it would have died, safely, securely'. Something similar takes place in the poignant 'Everybody's Been Burned', where emotional scars threaten to harden into an impenetrable psychic epidermis until the hero realises that risking anguish is necessary in order to stay open to rapture. In both songs, the band's music is a rippling, iridescent braid of modal folk and Indian raga chords, a pure evocation of the 'flow' that the Byrds worshipped.

On 1968's *The Notorious Byrd Brothers*, 'Goin' Back' embraces the goalless play of childhood and rejects adulthood as a barren, fun-free zone, where there's 'no more trees to climb'. Psychedelia is an enervated, unmotivated suspension ('Dolphin Smile', where the singer's 'floating free, aimlessly'), or it's sleep ('Draft Morning' goes one better than the Beatles' 'I'm Only Sleeping': here, the protagonist has to abandon his bed and dreams and wake up to reality – his duty to kill for his country). Throughout, the Byrds' vocals are an effete, susurrating murmur, as distant from the blaring self-assertion of pre-psychedelic rock as is imaginable.

Fantasies of a lost Arcadia pervaded the music of West Coast acid rock. Following the Alice-In-Wonderland-as-psychedelic-prophet analogy in 'White Rabbit', Jefferson Airplane's 'The Ballad Of You and Me and Pooneil' (from *After Bathing at Baxters*, 1967) was a vision of childhood bliss, in which Winnie the Pooh and Fred Neil (one of the band's folk music heroes) were merged as a single playmate. In Moby Grape's 'Lazy Me' (from their 1967 eponymous debut), psychedelia's cult of immobility reaches the brink of terminal entropy (the singer vows he'll 'lay here...decay here'), while the Zen (im)passivity of 'Indifference' verges on a kind of vegetative nihilism. The Grateful Dead's *Aoxomoxoa* (1969) teems with imagery of garden-dreamers. Among the first of the San Francisco groups to leave the city for rural Marin County was Quicksilver Messenger Service, whose name and second album, *Happy Trails* (1969), harked back to a time when America was a virgin wilderness. The cover of *Shady Grove* (1970) depicts a leafy bower dappled with green sunlight, where a nineteenth-century maiden sits on a knoll, in the company of a squirrel and a frog squatting on a toadstool; on the back sleeve, you can see a horse and buggy, indicating her ecologically sound means of getting there. The title track and songs like 'Flashing Lonesome' reject the city's smog and neon glare for the countryside, where a man knows who he is, when he's 'out with the trees'.

This was the touchstone yearning of the era – finding a path 'back into the garden', as expressed most famously in Joni Mitchell's 'Woodstock'. But unlike the British bands, US psychedelia could tap into the traditional American cult of the wilderness. Lamentations for the loss of the frontier and wide open spaces were squarely in the grain of American culture, from Thomas Jefferson and the anti-urbanism of the late nineteenth-century Populist movement to poets like Walt Whitman. The American hippy culture could present their revolt as a return to roots and the true American dream: they were distancing themselves from cold war consumerism because it was a betrayal of the original vision of what America was supposed to be about.

In Britain, psychedelia's pastoralism evolved into folk-rock. The most important folk-rock band were Fairport Convention, who used British folklore as a way of allegorising the impasses and struggles of the present, just as The Band did with American history. The lesser lights of UK folk-rock included Steeleye Span, Caravan, Tudor Lodge, Renaissance, Trees and Dulcimer. They generally looked like hippies gone to (hay)seed, all straggly beards, lank locks riddled with split-ends, moleskin waistcoats, voluminous mock-medieval blouses, a riot of moss-green, peat-brown and hessian hues. Perhaps more generic than most were Forest, whose *The Full Circle* (1970) managed to combine medievalism ('Hawk the Hawker', 'The Midnight Hanging of a Runaway Serf'), visions of heavenly glades ('Bluebell Dance'), odes to mystery girls ('Gypsy Girl & Rambleaway') *and* laments to lost innocence ('Autumn Childhood').

In America, the counterculture's pastoralism survived into the 1970s, with the country-tinged soft-rock of Crosby, Stills & Nash, the Eagles, and America. Burnt-out hippies found in folk and country music a tenor of desolation and fatalism that fitted well with the aftermath of the 1960s. A song that perfectly captures the poignancy of the lost Summer of Love is ex-Byrd Gene Clark's 'Lady of the North' (from *No Other*, 1974). Its setting is the meadow-heaven that was psychedelia's classic backdrop but now is only a tantalising memory. 'The earth was like a pillow', allowing Clark and his sweetheart to drift in dreams. Gravity, anxiety, conflict are all banished; 'trials never entered/any conversation'. But as the cycle of seasons turns, winter brings this sunkissed idyll to an end. Clark's mournful reverie culminates in some truly transcendental lead guitar: skyquake peals and tremors, the tears of a cloud.

Neil Young's 'Cortez the Killer' (*Zuma*, 1975) is a blues requiem for the bygone Eden of the late 1960s. The song begins with Young imagining Cortez's arrival in the Mexico of the Aztecs, and his conquest and devastation of Montezuma's empire. Then the song abruptly switches from this gilded evocation of a lost pre-Columbian utopia to a more personal lament for a lost lover. 'I know she's living there', sings Young; he knows she still loves him, but he can't find his way back to the paradise they shared and he shattered. Cortez's 'rape' of Montezuma's civilisation becomes an allegory for Young's having wrecked a relationship. In his imagination, the lost kingdom and the lost love intertwine as symbols of the fall from Eden.

Agony in the Garden

For, nothing spake to me but the fair Face
Of Hev'n' and Earth, when yet I could not speak:
I did my Bliss, when I did Silence, break
                    – Thomas Traherne, 'Dumness'

Of all the artists to emerge in the psychedelic era and its aftermath, Van Morrison and Pink Floyd are the most fixated in their nostalgia for Eden. Morrison's *Astral Weeks* was recorded in 1968, and seems to have captured the dawning sense that the moment was already passing. His songs obsessively reiterate Arcadian imagery: 'the barefoot virgin child'; wandering through gardens opalescent with misty rain; quenching a thirsty soul from pure spring water; being draped in 'silence easy'. And just as Morrison's poetry exalts opalescence and fluidity, his voice and music embody these qualities. His scat-soul singing is a brook of babble; the music is a bubbling, winding stream of folk, jazz, blues and soul, all whorls and eddies, scintillation and sunspots under the eyelashes.

The album is a vision, both exultant and tormented, of paradise lost and maybe, just maybe, regained. The first song, 'Astral Weeks', sees Morrison drifting through 'the slipstream' and 'viaducts of your dreams'. He's swimming in dreamtime. He yearns to be anointed with kisses on the eyes, born again. In 'Sweet Thing', Morrison is, like the Byrds, 'younger than yesterday'; he vows that never will he 'grow so old again'. In this heaven-on-earth, nothing needs to be interpreted, meaning is fully present in every word, deceit impossible. Everyone speaks a pure 'Inarticulate Speech of the Heart' (as he titled a later album). In 'Beside You', Morrison aches for the absolute proximity, the alienation-free bliss of pure intimacy, which perhaps is only ever experienced at the mother's breast or in the all-enveloping suspension of the womb. He longs to 'never ever wonder why', to return to that realm where doubt and dread are banished.

M. Mark has written that the 'acknowledgment of unalterable homelessness and the struggle against it' are the essence of Van Morrison's greatest work.[6] But on subsequent albums, as he makes a home sweet home for himself, marrying a flower-child and moving first to Woodstock and then to California, the edge of *Astral Weeks* is gradually softened. 1970's *Moondance* is an altogether mellower affair. 'And It Stoned Me' refers not to dope but the stupefaction of satisfaction, a feeling 'just like going home'. *Tupelo Honey* (1971) is sickly and suffocating in its dozy complacency. On the cover, Morrison has found the heavenly arbour that so haunted his imagination: he's strolling down a leafy bridle path, with his wife Janet Planet beside him riding a white horse. Morrison is starting to look a little chubby on all that home-cooking. 'Old Old Woodstock' dwells sentimentally on the image of his wife waiting patiently on the kitchen doorstep, presumably with something nice and hot in the oven. 'I Wanna Roo You' sees the Morrisons cocooned in their snow-bound cottage: while he strums his guitar, she's busy in the kitchen. Snug and smug, they're happy that they 'ain't going no-where'.

On subsequent albums, Morrison's spiritual concerns resurge; he plunges deeper 'Into the Mystic', looking for some kind of faith that'll allow him to feel at peace everywhere and ransacking the work of mystics, seers and poets for clues. His mid-1970s albums are haunted by a dream of Caledonia, 'an ancient land which sounds like home to him, a land where his ancestors made a brand new start, and where bagpipes gave birth to the blues', as M. Mark put it.[7] Caledonia has the same mythic function in Morrison's cosmology that Zion or Africa has for the Rastafarians, or the 'old, golden land' did for the Incredible String Band: it's a lost kingdom where alienation is abolished and all men are brothers. On *Saint Dominic's Preview* (1972) 'Gypsy' reconciles homesickness and wanderlust, with the old adage that, for the soul gypsy, anywhere he hangs his hat is home. *Veedon Fleece* (1974) concerns a quest for the holy grail, although no one has ever truly fathomed Morrison's symbolism. In 'You Don't Pull No Punches, But You Don't Push the River', Morrison is impatiently waiting to be engulfed in the cosmic stream, returned to his true element. 'Cul De Sac' is more placid, imagining domestic serenity as a backwater from the turmoil of life. These obsessions with revelation, redemption, rebirth and rest continue through Van Morrison's albums to the present. His songs have become more overtly Christian and gospel-tinged in the 1980s and 1990s with albums like *Avalon Sunset, Enlightenment, Hymns to the Silence, Too Long In Exile*, and today Morrison communicates little but a plump, spiritually replete serenity.

Childhood's End

Pink Floyd were one of the groups that defined psychedelia – musically (with their kaleidoscopic flux of sound) and thematically (through their obsession with 'Childhood's End', their pastoralism). Pink Floyd's singer and original guiding light, Syd Barrett, was the key figure in the shift from the macho frontmen of mid-1960s R&B, to the androgynous Peter Pan figures of psychedelia. Barrett certainly fit the mother's boy profile. His father died when he was fourteen and thereafter he developed an unusually close relationship with his mother. (Remarkably, Roger Waters, the other key figure in Pink Floyd, lost his father shortly after his birth and also fell under the sway of a 'domineering' mother.) In a 1974 tribute in *NME*, Nick Kent speculated that Barrett's mental instability was related to sinister Oedipal factors: 'I fear one has to stride manfully blindfolded into a rather more Freudian landscape, leading us to the opinion of many of the people who I talked to who claimed that Syd's dilemma stretched back to certain childhood traumas. The youngest of a family of eight, heavily affected by the sudden death of his father..., spoilt by a strong-willed mother who may or may not have imposed a strange distinction between the dictates of fantasy and reality...'[8] Taking monstrous amounts of LSD pushed the already unstable Barrett over the edge into a psychotic breakdown; he left Floyd and eventually went back to live with his mum, forever...

All of which may explain the Barrett-era Pink Floyd's idealisation of childhood. Their early single, 'See Emily Play' (1967), is a chaste, rapturous vision of floating on a river forever; Barrett's fey, nursery-rhyme intonations a startling break with the manly rasp of white blues. The debut album, *The Piper at the Gates of Dawn* (1967), took its title from the seventh and most mystical chapter of Kenneth Grahame's classic children's book *The Wind in the Willows*. Water Rat and Mole undergo a visionary encounter with the nature-god Pan, having been drawn upstream by the tantalising, primordial pipings of his mysterious music. 'Rapt, transported, trembling [the Rat] was possessed in all his senses by this new divine thing that caught up his senseless soul and swung and dandled it, a powerless but happy infant in a strong sustaining grasp'.[9] Grahame's imagery at once echoes Niezstche's writings on the Dionysian spirit of music in *The Birth of Tragedy*, and seems to prophesise the wombadelic tumult of Floyd's cosmic rock.

In the album's 'Matilda Mother', Barrett is a child imploring his mother to read another chapter of his bedtime fairy-tale. The mother's voice turns the 'scribbly lines' into magic, unlocking the door into a mystic wonderland where 'everything shines'. Children become nostalgic at a surprisingly early age: their fantasies of 'the olden days' conceal a yearning to go back to that fantastical no-place from which we've all been banished by the reality-principle. So Barrett renounces realism and longs for fairy-tales. In 'Flaming', Barrett plays the part of a sprite or wood-nymph, an invisible creature with magical powers of teleportation; one verse he's taking a nap on the clouds, the next he's idling 'in the foggy dew'. Elsewhere on the album, there's a dream of pure love untarnished by sexuality in 'Bike', where Barrett, with the boundless generosity of a child, offers to give his sweetheart 'anything, everything', and makes friends with a mouse called Gerald.

By the second album, *A Saucerful of Secrets* (1968), Barrett was already halfway out of the group, but Pink Floyd were still overwhelmingly shaped by his vision. Rick Wright's 'Remember A Day' is pure nostalgia for the halcyon daze of infancy, with its easy spirit of play. In 'See-Saw', a brother and sister frolic happily without a care in the world or a thought for tomorrow. Syd Barrett carried on in this vein midway between twee and psychotic, sickly and sicko, in his erratic solo career. His 1970 albums *The Madcap Laughs* and *Barrett* are full of chaste, childlike love songs, all honey and cream and 'Baby Lemonade'; love here is closer to the toddler's fantasy of owning a sweetshop than the carnality of adult desire.

Without Barrett, Pink Floyd drifted off into an unproblematic serenity. Control-freak Roger Waters shifted the band's orientation from Barrett's Dionysian intensity towards an Apollonian placidity (all those Icarus-complex songs like 'Set the Controls for the Heart of the Sun' and 'Let There Be More Light'). Once a chaotic flux, the Floyd's sound was now closer to a cathedral: awe-inspiring but orderly. But nostalgia was still the dominant emotion. On *Ummagumma* (1969), 'Granchester Meadows' returns to the endless Indian summer of childhood. Waters' pallid, pious vocal and meandering acoustic guitar mingle with the sound of larksong, splashing ducks and humming bees. He's in the city, but he's 'basking' in the memory of that 'bygone afternoon' when he lay in the heat-hazy meadow beside a river.

The Floyd's pastoralism blossoms on *Atom Heart Mother* (1970), with its cover image of a cow placidly grazing in a pasture. The title originally came from a newspaper headline about a pregnant mother who'd been given an atomic-powered pacemaker; drummer Nick Mason explained that the cover explored the connection 'between the cow...and the earth mother, the heart of the earth'.[10] The album itself continued this rather pompous symbolism: the whole of the first side was taken up with the 'Atom Heart Mother Suite', a sort of cosmic regression symphony. It begins with the mock-classical 'Father's Shout': stern and stately horns that comport themselves with the terrible, puffed-up dignity of the patriarchal order, mingled with the thunder of war and the revving of engines. 'Breast Milky' is a glimpse of the lost maternal idyll of nurture and nourishment. It's a poignant blues, all plangent violin, slide guitar, and a female voice, angelic and wordless. The Christian mystics often used imagery of suckling and 'spiritual milk' to describe their experiences. 'Breast Milky' recalls Saint Francois de Sales' description of the beatific 'orison of quietude', in which 'the soul is like a little child still at the breast'.[11] With 'Mother Fore', the voice becomes a billowing choir, at first soft and tender, then turning eerie and swelling into a cosmic threnody. 'Funky Dung' starts as an ambling, slick blues, then devolves into Dadaist phonetic poetry, all nonsense syllables and gurgles, like babytalk turned to opera. 'Mind Your Throats Please' regresses still further, into total chromatic cacophony. It's as though we've descended from babyhood, through the womb, the ovum, the chromosone and DNA strand, right back to the subatomic 'white light' level of consciousness that is the final destination of the LSD trip (according to Timothy Leary's *The Politics of Ecstasy*). Finally, 'Remergence' is the return to reality and distinct, contoured form: the main theme of the suite returns, an aching bluesy guitar figure that mourns the lost utopia, but is resigned to its loss.

Elsewhere on *Atom Heart Mother*, 'Fat Old Sun' is all heat-baked, opulent indolence, sepia-tinged with regret as the summer afternoon turns to dusk; the lyrics evoke the smell of grass, church bells chiming in the distance, children's laughter floating on the breeze. Other Floyd albums from the late 1960s and early 1970s are similarly elegiac, in particular the two soundtrack albums *More* (1969) and *Obscured By Clouds* (1972). *More* was from a movie about druggy bohemians on the Meditteranean island of Ibiza, and featured the song 'Childhood's End'; *Obscured By Clouds*, as its title suggests, is another requiem for summer and an evocation of paradise lost.

DreamPop

The upstarts of punk *reviled* Pink Floyd, officially because of their pompous conceptualism and musical grandiosity, but at a deeper level, because of their bucolic quietude. Punk returned to the moment just before hippy, the urban uptightness of mod; it even revived the mods' drug of choice, amphetamine sulphate. But by the 1990s, Pink Floyd's blurry sound and androgynous aura was resurrected by a mini-movement of British neo-psychedelic bands known as 'shoegazers' or 'dreampop'. These bands resurrected many of Floyd-style psychedelia's imagery and effects: transcendental imagery; chaste, devotional love songs, bled of explicit carnal longing and fixated instead on a rapture of the gaze; blurry guitars, heavily treated with effects, and eschewing riffs in favour of a droning, swarming tumult. The dreampop bands were clearly influenced by more recent indie innovators such as My Bloody Valentine and Cocteau Twins, but one group did cite Pink Floyd as an influence: Slowdive.

Slowdive's first single, 'Avalyn', made a girl's name out of the mythical idyllic realm of Avalon, echoing prog rock's obsession with the olden days of Albion. Other songs revived the pastoral reveries of 1967 – 'Catch The Breeze', 'Morningrise'. Slowdive's sound – diaphonous, like sunlight weakly piercing mist – was psychedelia filtered through Brian Eno's ambience. On the EP, *Holding Our Breath* (1991), they even covered Syd Barrett's 'Golden Hair', a late 1960s Medieval fantasy, with Syd as an entranced courtly lover calling up to a maiden in a tower. Slowdive accentuate the Gothic atmosphere, singer Rachel Goswell intoning the lyrics like a Gregorian chant echoing through the cloisters of a monastery.

Another dreampop band regressed even further back than Barrett's nursery: all the way to the womb. Pale Saints' 'Mother Might' took its title from Swinburne's 'Atalanta In Calydon': 'For there is nothing terribler to men/Than the sweet face of mothers, and the might'. An eerie, morbid hive of unfocussed sound, with an anaemic male voice bled dry of will, 'Mother Might' captures the appalling allure of being engulfed and enwombed. Their next EP, *Half Life* (1990), featured the image of an unborn baby on its sleeve, eyes closed, suspended in amniotic fluid, with the image's edges fringed in crystalline snowflakes. Songs like 'half-life, remembered' and 'Baby Maker' seemed like lamentations for the plight of being born; the latter mourned the impossibility of never knowing, let alone recovering, 'what you left behind'.

Rave 'til Mother Dawn

Pink Floyd's legacy materialised elsewhere in the early 1990s, in more improbable circumstances. One of Pink Floyd's earliest London gigs was at an event called the All-Night Rave (the band specialised in performances that went on until sunrise). Later, they recorded the soundtrack to *More*, a movie about drug fiends on the long-time hippy island of Ibiza. In the late 1980s, a new psychedelic movement – rave culture – was born in Ibiza, created by British holidaymakers who had such a good time dancing to acid house music while tripping on Ecstasy that they didn't stop when they got back to the UK. Rave culture shares lots of aspects with the Floyd experience: dazzling, psychotropic lightshows, an obsession with 3-dimensional sound, and transcendental imagery. Giant, all-night raves held illegally in the English countryside revived the pagan impulses of the counterculture; 1988 and 1989 were celebrated as replays of 1967's original Summer of Love.

By 1990, acid house's brisk pace was mellowing and bands started to make music to accompany and enhance the feeling of 'coming down' as the sun rose. The Beloved's 'The Sun Rising' (with its beatific, madrigal-like female vocal), 808 State's 'Sunrise', Blue Pearl's 'Mother Dawn', the Orb's 'Perpetual Dawn': this music was designed to capture the elegiac euphoria of the all-night rave's end. The genre came to be known variously as New Age house, ambient house or 'chill-out'. That's when the Pink Floyd influence kicked in. Innocence's 'Natural Thing' sampled a curlicue of radiant guitar from Floyd's Syd Barrett tribute 'Shine On You Crazy Diamond'; the KLF rushed out an album called *Chill Out* whose cover picture – sheep ruminating in a pasture – was a homage, at once ironic and affectionate, to *Atom Heart Mother*.

Soon the theory emerged that rave culture as a whole, and ambient house in particular, was the expression of a new Gaia-consciousness: ravers were in synch with the bio-rhythms of Mother Nature. Alex Paterson of the Orb declared that the 1990s would be 'a decade of rainforest consciousness, a backlash against the rape of Mother Earth'.[12] The Shamen formulated a vision of rave culture as a revival of 'archaic consciousness'. This was a concept invented by Terence McKenna, a proselytiser for naturally-occurring hallucinogens like psilocybin mushrooms and DMT. McKenna believes psychedelic plants can reawaken mankind's sense of connection to the planetary ecosystem and that the resulting revolution in consciousness will help us to outgrow our 'toxic' lifestyles, returning mankind to the symbiosis with nature we once enjoyed.[13]

McKenna was an original hippy who was blown away by the fact that the whole psychedelic project was being rehabilitated by rave culture, not to mention other emergent forms of cyberdelic culture (virtual reality, etc). Another former hippy turned 'zippy' (a hippy who thinks technology has a friendly, liberating potential) is Fraser Clark, who created *Evolution* magazine in order to evangelise for the techno-pagan promise of rave culture. Clark argues that house music's 120 beats-per-minute is the same as 'the baby's heartbeat in the womb.... Imagine twenty-thousand young westerners dervish-dancing to 120 bpm all night till the sun comes up. You get to feeling you're in the same womb.'[14]

Musically, ambient house harked back to the crystal-clear tranquillity of progressive rockers like Steve Hillage and synth-symphonists Tangerine Dream; to the galactic/Gaia imagery of jazz-rock fusionists like Weather Report, Return To Forever and Mahavishnu Orchestra. There were obvious links to New Age music, with its sonic simulation of soothing spa waters, or the way its fans used the music to help them recover from the stress-ridden rigours of urban life. Ambient house sacrificed pace for peace. Where faster brands of rave music had a voodoo intensity, ambient house was influenced not by Africa but by the idea of the Pacific as paradise – 'the really motherly, soporific hemisphere', as Paul Oldfield put it.[15] You could trace a line from the Hawaiian guitar on *Atom Heart Mother* and *Meddle* and the mellow blues of Fleetwood Mac's' *Albatross*', through early 1980s funk-pagans 23 Skidoo's 'Easter Island' and dreampopsters Cocteau Twins' 'Aikea-Guinea', all the way to 1990s tracks like 808 State's 'Pacific State' and Future Sound of London's 'Papua New Guinea'.

While the beatific indolence of ambient house endured as a genre, rave music grew more frantic again as the 1990s progressed and Ecstasy got cut with amphetamine. But the techno-pagan spirit persisted and evolved, with the resurgence of illegal raves in the English countryside, instigated by anarcho-mystic outfits like Spiral Tribe and by neo-hippy travellers on the 'free festival' circuit. Spiral Tribe preached a creed they called Terra-Technic, arguing that ravers' non-stop ritual dancing reconnected mankind with the primordial energy of the Earth.

Even in urban dance scenes like the speed-freak subculture 'ardkore, pagan and tribalistic motifs abound (one 'ardkore subgenre is called 'jungle'). Witness the astonishing similarities between the structure of the working-class raver's weekend and the elements that make up the dance rites practised by prehistoric Great Mother Goddess cults (as re-imagined by John Moore in his monograph *Anarchy & Ecstasy: Visions of Halcyon Days*). According to Moore, various techniques to disorientate and to weaken defences were practised to make the pagan adept vulnerable to a state of mystic rapture he calls 'bewilderness' – including sleeplessness (all-night raving), fasting (ravers know an empty stomach makes the Ecstasy come on quicker and stronger), and 'enraptured abandonment to a syncopated musical beat'. Dance, says Moore, erodes inhibitions and psychic/bodily 'rigidities', opening the individual up for 'possession by the sacred wilderness'.[16]

The pagan dancers entered 'labyrinthine structures, often caves or underground passages' (not unlike your average nightclub). Here, aided by the contemplation of sacred mandalas (similar to the fractals and kaleidoscopic projections at raves), and by hallucinogens administered by hierophants (dealers!), the adepts are 'deranged into an ecstatic synaesthesia.... Both physically and spiritually, they enter the underworld, the womb of Mother Earth'. In the delirium of sacred ecstasy, 'the initiate becomes androgynous, unconcerned with the artificial distinctions of gender.... Encountering total saturation, individuals transcend their ego boundaries and their mortality in successive waves of ecstasy'. Moore's trance-dancers literally lived in Eden, a matriarchal peace-loving society that lived off fruit-gathering; their Gaia-attuned lifestyle was eventually shattered by the emergence of warfaring, patriarchal, meat-eating tribes. *Anarchy & Ecstasy* was published just before the rise of rave culture, but could it be that the experience of dancefloor communion that rave offers is actually a faint echo of the lost Edenic rites which Moore mourns and yearns to revive?

Skyclad

Ambient music chooses a different route to get to the same feeling of oneness with the Cosmos: not Dionysian freak-out, but a gently enfolding sound-bath. Abolishing the gap between foreground and background, ambient aims to unfocus your perceptions, blur all sense of being separate from the music. You can listen attentively or do something else altogether, because ambient is music you live inside.

Ambient music should be considered a descendant of psychedelia because it shares three of its defining attributes. First, it's spatial music: Brian Eno developed echo and reverb in order to create an imaginary 'psycho-acoustic space'. 'I wanted to be situated inside a large field of loosely-knit sound, rather than placed before a tightly organised monolith', he wrote in the sleevenotes to *On Land* (1982). Like psychedelic/cosmic rock, ambient is wombing. Second and third, ambient tends to be pastoral and fixated on childhood. With *On Land*, Eno was obsessed with recapturing childhood memories of specific places. 'Lizard Point', 'A Clearing', 'Dunwich Beach, Autumn, 1960', 'Unfamiliar Winds (Leeks Hills)', 'Lantern Marsh' all refer to places near where Eno grew up in East Anglia. And like Floyd on 'Granchester Meadows', Eno used real animal noises (rooks, frogs, insects) as musical elements.

Ambient music has much in common with the most innovatory aspects of house/techno production: it plays with the normal ranking of instruments in the mix, disorientating the listener. And it refuses rock's thrust-and-climax narrative structure in favour of a more 'feminine' economy of pleasure, i.e. plateau after plateau, an endlessly deferred climax.

If one band joins the dots between Pink Floyd-style cosmic rock, ambient, and rave culture, it's the Orb. The group's key member Alex Paterson used to work for E.G., the label that put out Eno's ambient albums; the Orb's debut *Adventures Beyond the Ultraworld* (1990) paid tribute to Pink Floyd with titles like 'Back Side of the Moon' and artwork that spoofed the cover of the Floyd's *Animals*; the Orb's music is the unabashed return of cosmic rock, layering serene washes of synth and spangly guitars over a laidback dance beat. Their sound is an aural counterpart of the visual pun that climaxes *2001: A Space Odyssey*, where an Earth-like planet turns out to be, on closer inspection, a gigantic foetus sky-clad in swirly blue.

The Orb revived many of the psychedelic tropes we saw with the Incredible String Band: infantilism verging on the twee, as in 'Little Fluffy Clouds', which samples Rickie Lee Jones recalling, in an adenoidal coo, how she gasped in wonder as a child at the Arizona skyline; worship of Mother Nature in 'Earth (Gaia)'; a longing for the embrace of eternity in 'Supernova at the End of the Universe'; 'Back Side of the Moon' is a simulacrum of heaven, all clusters of seraphic harmony, cascades of stardust, shimmery sounds like magic wands working wonders. But the Orb's most beautiful song is the whimsically titled 'A Huge Evergrowing Pulsating Brain That Rules from the Centre of the Ultraworld'. Ever widening ripples of synth conjure a mood of brain-blasted, heart-in-mouth

euphoria; in and out of the dazed haze weave church bells, splashing pebbles, choral ascents, jet-plane vapour trails. It's a *hive of
passivity*.

The Orb also explored the links between ambient and dub reggae. Around the same time that Eno was first formulating the idea
of ambient, dub reggae pioneers like King Tubby and Lee Perry
were also using echo and reverb to conjure a vast 'psycho-acoustic
space'. Like ambient and house, dub is based around a decentered
soundscape: instruments drop out of the mix for long periods, reap-
pearing as reverb-drenched mirages that loom, then dissipate like
mist. Like ambient and house, dub has aspirations to the eternal:
mostly instrumental, its meditational air sometimes give it a medieval aura. And, like ambient and house, dub is wombadelic music:
the music floats out to enfold you, the bass penetrates and subsumes
your body. In 1995 the dub-influenced trip hop outfit Smith and
Mighty released a track entitled 'Bass Is Maternal'. The Orb's music
is for stay-at-home ravers, clubbers chilling out after a night of
frenzy, and spliff-heads. A mystical appreciation of the divine weed
– marijuana, ganja, pot, whatever you care to call it – is *the* common
denominator between psychedelia, dub, and rave. When high, the
listener hears all forms of music with increased fidelity and dimension. But dub reggae, with its echo-drenched spatiality, is *designed* to
be enhanced by marijuana. Dope has many properties that work
well with 'mystical' music. It decreases the sense of distance between source and listener; it encourages synaesthesia (so that the
listener 'sees' the music); it weakens the interpretive and associative
functions of the mind, and diminishes both memory and future-
focused anxiety, all of which enables the listener to become utterly
absorbed by the present moment, 'lost in music'.[17]

With dub, sound becomes incense or fragrance, filling the gaps
between listener and speakers. Swathed in this 'holy smoke', the
listener sinks into a sacred stupor, achieves the state of grace that is
total de-activation. For the Rastafarian, this nirvana is a glimpse of
Jah's kingdom of righteousness. Like psychedelia, dub is nostalgic,
a music of homesickness and exile: Rastas dream of a return to Zion,
the ambrosial, golden realm that beckons all the lost tribes of the
African diaspora. But could it be that this lost utopia is really a
subconscious memory of the 'inner ocean' of the womb, where the
foetus hears everything refracted, reverberant, *dubbed-up*, via the
fleshly amplifier of the mother's body? The post-Orb, 'ambient dub'
band Original Rockers suggested as much with the title of their 1993

single 'The Underwater World of Jah Cousteau'.

The magical, mystical aura of reverberations is a musical thread that connects psychedelia, dub, ambient, the New Age subgenre of 'resonant music' (recorded in temples, cathedrals and giant cisterns), and even easy-listening artists like Mantovani. Joseph Lanza, author of *Elevator Music: A Surreal History of Muzak, Easy-Listening, and Other Moodsongs*, argues that 'the cathedral-like reverb Mantovani put on his orchestral strings, it reminds you're enclosed. It's like you're in a huge space but you're cloaked by God. It's ceiling-assurance, it allows you to cope with infinity'.[18] One explanation for the spiritual aura imparted by echo is that it harks back to when our prehistoric ancestors enacted rites in caves and grottoes. But the womb-theory – reverb as a primordial echo of our personal prehistory in the amniotic sea—may be more fundamental. It's not for nothing that studio engineers talk of a recording being 'dry' when it's devoid of echo or reverb.

Although the Orb brought out the links between house, cosmic rock, dub and ambient, it took another group to go all the way and record the first pastoral techno album (seemingly a contradiction in terms, given techno's inorganic, urban, futurist sound). On Ultramarine's *Every Man and Woman Is A Star* (1992), techno is transformed into the sound of tranquillity, solitary communion with Nature. On songs like 'British Summertime' and 'Skyclad', owl hoots, chirping crickets and babbling brooks mingle with acid house bass-squelches and chattering sequencers; cascades of acoustic guitar and dolorous fiddles intertwine with electronic bleeps and undulating rhythm loops. Ultramarine's music is techno infused with the folky-jazzy ambience of Robert Wyatt, Kevin Ayers, Joni Mitchell, and other pre-punk influences like soft country rock (the Eagles, America) and rustic prog-rock (Mike Oldfield's *Hergest Ridge*).

The duo, Paul Hammond and Ian Cooper, came from rural Essex, a part of the English countryside very similar to where Eno grew up, with its desolate estuaries and marshes. And their methodology was similar to Eno's *On Land*. 'When we write songs, we think in terms of landscapes', said Hammond. *Every Man and Woman Is A Star* was a soundtrack to an imaginary canoe-trip across the USA. Along with the pastoralism, Ultramarine expounded a Zen philosophy of trance dance. 'Stella' sampled a performance artist theorising about how dance enabled her to shed confining dogmas and fixed ideas, and 'find that emptiness where I can begin again': a sacred expanse in which she was able to connect her innermost self with outermost infinity.

'Intimate immensity' is how the philosopher Gaston Bachelard characterised this sensation – a feeling of oneness with the universe that brings together body and horizon.[19] In *Civilisation and Its Discontents*, Freud wrote of a long-lost selfless self, the phase of 'primary narcissism' in which the infant does not distinguish between itself, the mother and the world. 'Originally the ego includes everything.... the ego-feeling we are aware of now is.... only a shrunken vestige of a far more extensive feeling – a feeling which embraced the universe and expressed an inseparable connection of the ego with the external world'.[20] Psychedelia's strategies of regression and deactivation endeavour to unlock this diffuse but majestic self-without-contours, the 'royal we' of the infant/mother dyad, or of the lost kingdom of the womb. In the psychedelic imagination, the pastoral, the cosmic and the oceanic merge into a continuum, because they all induce such a sense of benign, all-enfolding vastness; a vastness that seems to promise an end to our separateness and the recovery of a lost continuity.

(This is an expanded and updated version of a chapter from the psychedelia section of Simon Reynolds and Joy Press *The Sex Revolts: Gender, Rebellion and Rock'n'Roll*, London: Serpent's Tail, 1995, and Cambridge, Mass: Harvard University Press, 1995.)

Notes

1. Grinspoon, L. and Hedbloom, P. (1975) *The Speed Culture: Amphetamine Use and Abuse in America.* Cambridge, Mass.: Harvard University Press, p 291.
2. Marinetti, F. T. (1973) 'Geometric and Mechanical Splendour and the Numerical Sensibility', reprinted in Appolonio, U. (ed.) (1973) *Futurist Manifestoes.* London: Thames and Hudson, p 154.
3. Incredible String Band interview in Melody Maker, 30 September 1967.
4. Paglia, C. (1992) *Sexual Personae: Art and Decadence from Nefertiti to Emily Dickinson.* New Haven: Yale University Press, pp 187-8.

5. Brown, O. N. (1966) *Love's Body*. New York: Random House, p 47.
6. Mark, M. 'It's Too Late To Stop Now', in Greil Marcus (ed.) (1979) *Stranded: Rock 'n' Roll For A Desert Island*. New York: Alfred A. Knopf, p 15.
7. Mark, *ibid*, p 12.
8. Nick Kent on Syd Barrett in *NME*, 13 April 1974. Reprinted in Kent, N. (1994) *The Dark Stuff*. Harmondsworth: Penguin.
9. Grahame, K. (1992) The Wind In The Willows. Ware: Wordsworth, p 151.
10. Nick Mason quoted in Schaffner, M. (1991) *Saucerful of Secrets: The Pink Floyd Odyssey*. New York: Harmony Books, p 146.
11. Saint Francois de Sales, quoted in James, W. (1985), *The Varieties of Religious Experience*. Cambridge, Mass: Harvard University Press, p 18 (note).
12. Alex Paterson from Melody Maker, 10 March 1990.
13. McKenna, T. (1992) *Food Of The Gods: The Search For The Original Tree of Knowledge – A Radical History of Plants, Drugs and Human Evolution*. London: Rider, passim.
14. Fraser Clark quoted in Rucker, R., Sirius R. U. and Queen Mu (eds.) *Mondo 2000: A User's Guide to the New Edge*. (publisher not known) pp 142-3.
15. Paul Oldfield from *Melody Maker*, 10 March 1990.
16. Moore, J. (1988) *Anarchy and Ecstasy: Visions of Halcyon Days*. London: Aporia Press, pp 29-31.
17. Marijuana's properties: Arthur C. Hastings, 'The Effects of Marijuana on Consciousness', reprinted in Tart, C. (ed) (1990) *Altered States of Consciousness*, New York: Harper Collins, pp 407-431.
18. Joseph Lanza, interview by the author, 'The Sound of Muzak', *Melody Maker*, 27 May 1995.
19. Bachelard, G. (1969) *The Poetics of Space*. Trans. Maria Jolas. Boston: Beacon Press, pp 182-210.
20. Sigmund Freud, *Civilisation and Its Discontents*. Quoted in Brown, *op. cit.*, p 141.

PSYCHEDELIC WARRIORS AND ECSTASY EVANGELISTS

Stuart Metcalfe

The aim of this essay is to map the route that the psychedelic Amphetamine Ecstasy (3,4 Methylenedioxymethamphetamine or MDMA) has taken on its journey from being an obscure slimming aid and under-used psychoanalysts' tool to being the most talked about 'recreational' drug of the 1990s. In doing so, this essay explains why Ecstasy is the drug of choice for British youth, and why the histories of British House music and Ecstasy are inseparable.

The seemingly unstoppable rise of Ecstasy in Britain can be traced back to the summer of 1987 and the west Mediterranean tourist resort of Ibiza. In this Spanish island lie the genealogical roots of the musical culture of 'Acid House', where, in nightclubs such as Pasha and Amnesia, British holiday-makers first experienced the heady combination of Ecstasy and electronic dance music. Influenced by their summertime psychedelic experimentations, an exclusive coterie of upwardly-mobile working-class clubbers took their memories home and attempted to recreate their ecstatic summer holidays in London nightclubs such as Shoom and Future. 'E' culture was being born, and born to illustrious parents at that, with many of the budding music entrepreneurs of this small drug-orientated scene becoming the superstars of contemporary British House music. The likes of Paul Oakenfold and Danny Rampling, pivotal figures in the fledgling scene of 1987, now regularly command huge sums for their DJing and production skills.

As this Ecstasy-based club culture grew, it became attached to a musical style that directly referenced its Iberian origins; the aptly named 'Balearic Beat'. Attempts at defining this genre in musical terms have since proved difficult. This is because the phrase 'Balearic' was used to describe not a specific musical style, but a musical eclecticism and an experimentation that drew upon British Indie music, American Hip-Hop, and Chicago-based House music. Whilst mainstream British pop culture was stagnating amidst a plethora of mutually antagonistic and segregated musical genres, Acid House and the Balearic style signalled that the modernist/postmodern collage aesthetic was here to stay, and that popular music was about to make a great leap forward.

Technological advances within music production had gathered pace throughout the 1980s, and by 1987 the previously rigid boundaries between musical production and consumption were starting to disintegrate. Centred within this development was a new lease of life for the club DJ. Unlike his traditional British counterpart, the Balearic DJ did not merely play one record after another, interspersing the mix with inane banter, but was required to mix two or three records together at the same time, creating a unique collage of sounds and rhythms. With an impressive degree of manual dexterity, the best DJs would perform all manner of turntable tricks, turning a box of records into more than the sum of its parts, providing a complex soundtrack for a night of dancing.

After the Acid House winter of 1987, the so-called 'Second Summer of Love' of 1988 was a magnificent musical heyday that broke down the sterile divisions between musical genres. A significant facet of early rave culture was its success in weakening established gender, race and class barriers. These changes were symbolically reflected in a shift in the dress codes of British youth. In came casual sports wear that had only previously been championed by a football-attending urban underclass. Crucially, this newly popularised style of clothing excluded no-one. The 'baggy' clothing style as worn by Mancunian groups such as The Happy Mondays became increasingly popular, with both men and women sporting dungarees, loose fitting t-shirts and floppy hats. Dance culture was turning its back upon its previous incarnation as a space where sexual partners were sought after. In a mass refusal of sexuality, previous dress codes were abandoned, and the message was dress not to impress, but simply to sweat.

This second Summer of Love saw British youth using Ecstasy to enhance the rave experience; enriching the sensation of dancing to an eclectic soundtrack, and providing what Steve Redhead termed 'a politics of pleasure, a hedonism (in hard times) – a pleasure for its own sake in times when moral regulation of youth [was] pervasive and deep economic recession [was] rife'.[1] Whilst the Acid House culture of the winter of 1987 drew some influence from the use of Ecstasy and other psychedelics, such drugs were not seen as essential to enjoyment of the scene, and most ravers viewed Ecstasy use as a relatively harmless form of escapism, a way of mentally recovering from the rigours of recession-hit Britain.

By the summer of 1988 Ecstasy use had mushroomed, and elements within rave culture declared that British youth would pick up the psychedelic mantle of 1967 and once again rock society's foundations. A new form of Psychedelic Warrior was born; drawing influence from the role LSD was alleged to have taken in the political changes in the late 1960s, the Ecstasy Evangelists set about their attempt to help history repeat itself, but with Ecstasy instead of LSD as its spiritual fuel.

Spurred on by the liberatory possibilities that Acid House culture had glimpsed, Ecstasy-consuming dancers with a few hundred pounds in the bank could invest in twin record decks and a mixer; thereby creating their own musical creations, turning the DJ into what Grandmaster Flash has called 'the human sampler'. Equally, the experience of Acid House meant that many were inspired to purchase cheap sampling and sequencing equipment, and began to make their own records.

In doing so, Ecstasy-consuming musicians began to pay close attention to one specific psychopharmacological property of Ecstasy,[2] namely its ability to encourage repetitive behaviour by stimulating the 1b receptor in the brain. Add Ecstasy to the sequenced kick drum crotchet beat of House (and its 1990s Techno variant) and you have a dance floor full of Ecstasy consumers who appear to have entirely synchronised their bodies to the music. Many of these new Ecstasy Evangelists suggested that, as well as permanently changing gender, class and racial boundaries, Ecstasy use had led to the discovery of the part of the brain that makes the *Homo sapiens* species want to dance.

The psychedelic missionaries had found a drug that directly matched the formal properties of sequenced House music, a drug that 'fitted' a musical genre as a hand fits a glove. Slowly but surely the Balearic spirit was abandoned, out went the hip-hop influences, with their 'awkward' emphases on the first two beats of the bar, and out went any rock influences that disrupted the beat. In came a form of perfectly-sequenced 'four to the floor' British House that appeared to liberate music from the stifling restrictions of the male-dominated music scene.

Another psychopharmacological property of Ecstasy is that it acts as an empathogen, encouraging the user to 'enter' and understand the feelings of others. As a result of this rave culture began a phase where the pop audience, previously used to facing forwards at concerts and 'worshipping' the live band and lead singer, turned to each other and indulged in an Ecstasy-inspired embrace. The rave scene developed a makeshift verb to describe the intense emotional bonds formed by E consuming dancers: 'loved up'. The Evangelists suggested that Ecstasy, combined with a computer technology that threatened to remove the egotistical lead signer and 'cock rock' guitarist from the musical equation, had broken the divide between audience and 'star'. The dancer was as much a star at a rave event as the DJ or stage-bound performer. Mirroring this development was the DIY ethic whereby collectives of 'faceless' DJs and musicians played music to a scene that was not interested in who they were, merely the rhythms that they produced. The suggestion was that rave culture had found a drug that simply made things better; music, dancing, sex, and life in general were to be transformed if only enough people could be persuaded to imbibe Ecstasy, and experience its heady cocktail of effects.

The empathogenic qualities of Ecstasy led to suggestions that E could, and would, irrevocably alter the consciousness of British youth culture. According to some, Acid House and rave culture signalled the dawn of a new post-capitalist age of communal co-operation, or alternatively the revival of a pre-historical shamanic order. The Ecstasy Evangelists were gaining strength, prescribing psychedelic drugs as the be-all and end-all of youth culture, as a cure for everything from moral authoritarianism to football hooliganism.

Whilst on their journey to the new Enlightenment, the Evangelists dismissed any warning signs that suggested that all was not as it should be in the Acid House garden of Eden. Overlooking the Thatcherite entrepreneurial talents of the very drug-dealers who supplied them with their E, and ignoring an influx of 'Acid Teds' (working-class hedonists who held the ideals of Acid House in disdain), the Ecstasy crusaders saw Acid House as a greed-free culture, a blueprint upon which to build their utopian dreams. British society had, at last, found a way out of its late-twentieth century malaise. Amidst these pipe dreams, the Evangelists ignored the central reasons which led to the demise of the hippy 1960s, which crashed down around them at the tragedy of Altamont.

For those intent upon spreading the E word, the next step towards the psychedelic revolution was the production of music that overtly encouraged the use of psychedelic drugs. For these initiates the 'white-label' 12 inch record, pressed up by individuals and sold in small quantities to record shops or out of the back of a van, could bypass the traditional moral regulators; the government, record companies and global capitalism. There was rash of individuals and groups releasing their own Ecstasy-inspired records, and the loved up vibe continued through 1989 and into 1990. One typical example of an Ecstasy-inspired record from this period is the white-label 12 inch produced by the Liverpudlian group Mind, Body and Soul. Whilst the band's name referred to a brand of LSD particularly popular in Liverpool in the late 1980s, the song, a version of Jefferson Airplane's psychedelic anthem 'White Rabbit', sampled the Acid guru Timothy Leary's call to arms 'Turn On, Tune In, and Drop Out', prefacing it with a sampled voice saying simply 'Ecstasy'. The track also included a spoken reading of the rhyme sent by the English psychiatrist Humphrey Osmond to Aldous Huxley in 1955 that suggested a name for the group of drugs that both had been experimenting with: 'to fathom hell or soar angelic, just take a pinch of psychedelic'.[3]

The comparisons were obvious, the second psychedelic wave was upon us. As it was in the 1960s, it would be the job of musicians to go forth and proclaim the truth to the world. During the first period of mass psychedelic drug use it was Tim Leary himself who emphasised pop music's role in spreading the word about LSD; writing in 1967 Leary suggested that 'I've dropped out completely myself. I'm already an anachronism in the LSD movement anyway. The Beatles have taken my place. That latest album – a complete celebration of LSD' (Leary, 1967). Leary went on to rename The Beatles 'the Four Evangelists'. For the likes of Mind, Body and Soul, the 1960s were alive and well, and the lesson to be learnt was a simple one; drop an E, take Acid, and everything was going to be all right.

May 1990 saw the same story being told in Manchester, with Factory Records latest signing Northside offering up a paean to LSD with the track 'Shall We Take A Trip'. Again, direct connections were made within the song's lyrics to the 1960s psychedelic revolution, and the whole tone of the piece echoed the somewhat naïve attitudes of the original tripsters:

> L, S, D
> Shall we take a trip down memory lane?
> Head in the clouds into the Acid rain
> time means nothing, I can smell the trees
> chase that rainbow in the summer breeze

> (©Factory Records)

There are many examples from this period of the proselytising zeal of the new Psychedelic Warriors, with one of the more humorous being the controversial behaviour of the British deputation to the New Music Seminar, in New York in 1990. Keith Allen, an anarchic British comedian, introduced himself to a perplexed audience of American music bosses as 'Dr' Keith Allen of the Post-Freudian Therapy Centre in Geneva and a world expert on drugs:

> the basic psychology was in 1987 in a club called Schoom [sic], I had a load of Ecstasy topped off with a little amyl-nitrate [a stimulant famed for its ability to enhance sexual arousal]... and I would give people one of these tablets and they would give me £20. That's psychology![4]

Attempting to get the seminar onto a more intellectual footing, Tony Wilson, boss of Factory Records and part owner of The Haçienda nightclub in Manchester explained the grip that Ecstasy was beginning to hold on British music:

> if you're a rock group and you cannot play rock music in the style to which you can dance and with the rhythms that have come out of America but have been ignored here, then you aren't a rock group that matters... I went into my club, The Haçienda, two weeks ago and one-and-a-half thousand 18-year-old kids were going mental,

> dancing like crazy to Northside, to Mondays, to Marshall
> Jefferson, to Derrick May, to Pink Floyd, to The Beatles...
> I've never seen anything like it in my life and I felt old for
> the first time. The wave is that strong.[5]

If Ecstasy and dancing were to change the world, the psychedelic
warriors would require DJs who were able to maintain a continuity
of tempo and rhythm throughout the night, so that there was no
interruption in the beat that would interfere with the Ecstasy high
(a drop in tempo brings the E user down from their trip, a drop in
intensity that allows the light of reality to shine on the dance floor).

The demand for continual 4/4 House music throughout the early
1990s meant that dance music's relationship with Ecstasy fundamentally altered. Whereas for most ravers Ecstasy was perceived to
be an added bonus to the liberatory atmosphere in clubs and at
raves, for the Evangelists it became an essential ingredient of an
average night out. Whereas Ecstasy was previously used to enhance
the sounds and textures of dance music, the situation reversed, the
continuous DJ set was used by Ecstasy consumers to heighten their
weekend drug trip. The increasing status of both the DJ and Ecstasy
itself led to the pivotal importance of the 'DJ remix', a version of a
dance track that emphasises sequenced beats exactly on the bar, thus
enabling the DJ to complete a seamless switch between records.
Gradually the Balearic spirit of adventure was muted, and DJ sets
began to resemble a gradual and inevitable journey towards the
peak of the Ecstasy consumers' trip. As more Ecstasy was consumed, the demand for, and eventual supply of, Ecstasy-inspired
music grew and grew.

As Ecstasy consumers became Ecstasy Evangelists, and as more
and more Evangelists became DJs and musicians, the situation arose
whereby Ecstasy-influenced producers were making music solely
for Ecstasy consumers. Experimentation was squeezed out of the
scene, leading to a dance music that was directly derived from the
psychopharmacological properties of Ecstasy, a music that facilitated the much talked about 'trance dancing' that the
Ecstasy-consuming elite saw as the first step to the New Age. Whereas
Tabloid scare stories emphasised the supposedly sexual hedonism
of E-inspired British dance culture, the Evangelists suggested that
the Ecstasy experience went beyond mere pleasure and sensuality,
beyond the weekend thrill. Ecstasy could and would change the
world.

In 1990 bands with an unashamedly 'rock' past, bands who had previously traded upon a macho image (such as Pop Will Eat Itself and Primal Scream), scrambled onto the bandwagon, eager for a piece of the action. The Soup Dragons, previously a group allied to the British indie guitar scene, had a summer hit with the dance track 'I'm Free', and summed up the prevailing mood:

> I'm free
> to do what I want
> any of the time,
> because I love you, need you,
> love you, need you
> because I'm free

> (©Raw TV Products)

It was that simple, no effort was needed. Whereas a previous generation had sung The Beastie Boys chorus of 'you've gotta fight for your right to party', the swollen ranks of the Ecstasy Evangelists left it all up to the drug. The Entertainments (Increased Penalties) Act of 1990 came and went with little opposition, thereby increasing the penalties for organising unlicensed raves for profit. Overtly political attempts to halt the moral authoritarianism of parliamentary legislation were sneered at by the zealots. Hundreds of ravers were being arrested at illegal raves, but these events were viewed as teething troubles at the dawn of a new paradise. If the whole world could be changed by Ecstasy and by dancing, why on earth did you need to engage with boring old politics.

Dance music had become 'mental food' for Ecstasy consumers, and those who saw Ecstasy as the start of a Brave New World were in raptures. However, things were starting to go badly wrong, and the new hippy dream was gradually turning into a nightmare. In 1991 nightclub and rave entrance prices rose at an alarming rate, and violence crept onto the scene. But for the Psychedelic Warriors this did not signal the end of their dreams, for the problem could be cured simply by consuming more Ecstasy. The Evangelists had forgotten their history lessons. Just as the social battles won in the sixties were a result of political struggle, the liberatory atmosphere of early raves, and the implied communal politics of dancing, were not solely caused by Ecstasy consumption, but were the result of hard work and determination, the result of a direct political opposition that stated that everyone had the right to party, irrespective of gender, sexuality, colour or creed.

In 1992 the beat continued, Ecstasy consumption increased, and more and more dance records contained lyrics seemingly encouraging people to take an E. The Shamen's 'Ebeneezer Goode' is a classic example of a dance track whose lyrics directly referred to the Ecstasy experience, yet were oblique enough to avoid direct censorship:

> Ebeneezer Goode's the leading light of the scene,
> know what I mean
> he created the vibe
> he takes you for a ride, and as if by design
> the party ignites like he's coming alive
> he takes you to the top
> shakes you all around and back down...
>
> A gentleman of leisure,
> he's there for your pleasure
> But go easy on old Eezer
> he's the kind of geezer who should never be abused
>
> [chorus] Eezer Goode, Eezer Goode, he's Ebeneezer Goode.
>
> (© One Little Indian Records)

By this time Ecstasy use was no longer the preserve of a small bohemian elite, it had been democratised to include even the most commercial dance floors. The summer of 1992 saw the traditional Roxy and Mecca discotheques, the last bastions of pre-Acid dance music, resonating to dance floors singing 'Es are good, Es are good' to the chorus of The Shamen's number one hit.

Ecstasy had become as essential to the dance experience as music itself. Home Office statistics suggested that 1.5 million Ecstasy tablets were consumed every weekend in 1995.[6] A survey of 700 young people aged between 14 and 16, compiled by Manchester University, suggested that 51% of those questioned had taken drugs, whilst 76% had been offered them. This did not go unheeded by the British press, with for instance The Guardian correctly interpreting this development as meaning that 'drug-taking has become an integral part of youth culture'.[7] Many reports suggested that, within certain geographical areas, the majority of school-leavers had, at some point, consumed an illegal drug.[8]

Whereas the drug-users of previous generations were marginalised and demonised, even by their peers (in the pre-punk 1970s, drug-users were dismissed as hippies by 'ordinary' young people) the new Ecstasy politics have led to the stage whereby it is the non-drug takers who are the deviants within dance culture, in the sense that they deviate from the norm of drug consumption within British youth culture. Howard Parker would appear to agree: 'over the next few years, and certainly in urban areas, non-drug-trying adolescents will be in a minority group. In one sense, they will be the deviants'.[9]

Whilst psychedelic drug consumption has spiralled upwards, the predicted outcomes of the Ecstasy propagandists have not material-ised. In particular the heady days of Acid House, with their liberatory atmosphere, have all but vanished. Whilst Acid House was sup-posed to lead to a situation whereby the old gender relationships of the dance floor disappeared, this has not occurred. The 'refusal of sexuality' has been gradually abandoned, and the dance scene of the mid-1990s has become as rigidly demarcated as the early 1980s. Visit any of the biggest British dance clubs: Cream in Liverpool, The Ministry of Sound in London, or The Haçienda in Manchester, and you'll find mating grounds not dissimilar to the Roxys and Meccas of previous youth cultures. Advertising strategies that employ what some suggest are sexist images are increasingly common. Photo-graphs of semi-naked women abound on flyers and in magazines devoted to dance culture. One the biggest dance floor smashes of 1995 was Nush's 'U Girls'. With a chorus line of 'you girls look so sexy' and a promotional video featuring a procession of 'club babes', Nush's track marked the return of dance as sexual display. Racism has also resurfaced, with segregated scenes, and intolerance sim-mering beneath the surface. Gay clubs have strengthened their door policies, claiming that Ecstasy-consuming heterosexuals often fake homosexuality in order to gain entry into clubs, but have a less than tolerant attitude to gay men and women whilst inside. Political apathy amongst Ecstasy users has meant that the free party scene has been criminalised with little resistance,[10] and even legal raves such as the 1996 Tribal Gathering in Oxfordshire have been aborted after local political pressure. Tales of stabbings and shootings at clubs and raves are now increasingly common. Class barriers have returned, primarily due to the somewhat excessive door prices of the more prestigious clubs. Few low-paid clubbers can afford the expense of a couple of Es and a ticket for a World of Dance event (£25 + booking fee), or entrance to the 1995/6 New Year's Eve party at The Haçienda (£40 + booking fee). And it's not just the profiteering of promoters and club owners who have pushed the price of dance culture out of the hands of poorer clubbers. Whilst Acid House promised to break down the barriers between producers and consumers, nowadays dance musicians are as idolised as the rock stars of previous generations. If the top DJ also has a pretty face then he (and it is invariably 'he' in a male-dominated industry) is nothing short of a God. The days of the anonymous DJ getting on with his job are no more and artists such as Todd Terry can command £20,000 for a single performance. Whereas in Acid House the DJ was practically invisible, hidden behind his decks, nowadays DJ boxes resemble altars, with dancers continually looking upwards in the hope of catching a glimpse of the DJ deity.

The psychopharmacological repetition of the E trip has continued to have an influence on dance culture, as well as dance music, but not in the positive manner predicted by the Psychedelic Warriors. Contemporary dance culture has become a culture of the 'weekender'. Unlike the Evangelists, ordinary Ecstasy-users do not believe that psychedelic drugs will change the world, they merely use them to escape from the stresses and strains of modern life. Many of the current wave of clubbers merely live for the weekend, when they can be temporarily free from the reality of their day to day existence. During the week many of these Ecstasy-users work, if work is available, in what have been termed 'McJobs',[11] boring, repetitive work, requiring little concentration. Those that have managed to find skilled employment also describe their jobs as repetitive and boring. The cure prescribed by those remaining Evangelists for low pay, unemployment and poverty is, of course, more Ecstasy. Dance/Ecstasy culture (for they now amount to the same thing) has become as repetitive as the music. Rather than being a release from the repetition of unfulfilling jobs, Ecstasy consumption has become a repetitive act in itself. Flowered Up, an enthusiastic group of hedonists who never fell for the Evangelical party line, saw the warnings back in 1992, and summed up the situation well with their single Weekender:

> I see you everyday, you walk the same way
> weekender
> you go to work, Friday is Payday
> weekender
> give it up, give your life up
> weekender

... just live a little (have a good time)

... no work just party, party!
you got a new shirt, you got a new suit
saved your life for a two day flirt
you pay the price coz Monday sure does hurt
tell at work your weekend tale
still need the pleasure of a dirty sale
Monday's back, what can you do?

(© Sony Music Entertainment)

Monday's back, nothing has changed, and you've got a drug hangover from hell. Ecstasy hasn't changed the world. What it has done is turn hedonism into ritual, creating a functionalist dance music the sole of aim of which is to increase the Ecstasy high. Whilst experimentation with Ecstasy has reached an all time high, experimentation within House and Techno music has reached an all time low.

With some ravers taking 20 Ecstasy tablets in one weekend, something has had to give way. In 1991 and 1992 the rave scene splintered and shattered into small groupings of socially-opposed musical subgenres. As the 'tolerance levels' of regular Ecstasy-users grew (overuse of Ecstasy means that with each consecutive trip more and more E is required to achieve a satisfactory high), they began to supplement their tablets with amphetamine sulphate. As a result rave begat, amongst other music sub-genres, Gabber, an aggressive and fast amphetamine-inspired dance music that eschews the peaceful character of Acid House. Pronounced 'habber' in its native Dutch, this style of Techno revels in apocalyptic imagery, with, for example, the Dutch group Wedlock calling one of their singles 'I'm The Fuck You Man'. A night spent at a Gabber event can be a disconcerting experience, where young working-class skinheads punch the air and throw their bodies around with an alarming ferocity. Gabber is a subgenre that seems a long way from the loved up music of the late eighties, and is a musical form that disconcertingly resembles Heavy Metal, with a lyrical and musical emphasis on violence and destruction.

But all is not lost within the contemporary music scene. In the other direction from Gabber pulled a musical genre that has almost single-handedly saved dance music from Ecstasy-related stagnation. Jungle (recently renamed by some as 'drum and bass') consists of a frenetic hi-hat percussion track at around 320 beats per minute, a second percussion track at around 160 beats per minute, and an irregular and shifting bass line at around 80 beats per minute. The 160 b.p.m. drum track invariably has an erratic beat emphasis, thereby directly rejecting the 'four to the floor' basis of House and Techno music. An example might be where the first beat of each bar is on the beat, and the rest are syncopated (off the beat). Vocals, strings and synthesised sounds are sandwiched between percussion and bass.

Jungle, whilst still based upon a 4/4 time signature, firmly eschews the crotchet beat that characterises British House and Techno music. Instead of the 4/4 kick drum, jungle relies upon sped up 'break beats', either sampled from American hip-hop records,[12] or programmed using sequencing software such as Steinberg's Cubase©, which allow each drum hit to be graphically represented and edited on screen. The origin of the breakbeat is generally accepted to be the Bronx, New York in the early 1970s, where a DJ would mix two records together, extending the mix at the point of a drum break by cross-cutting between the two records using an audio mixer. Jungle takes these break beats and digitally 'chops' them so that each four bar structure is different. There is no Ecstasy-inspired repetition at the heart of jungle, instead there are never-ending circles of change and difference. Hours and hours of skilled programming mark a return to musicians taking care when they make music, a return to intelligence.

Whereas House and Techno clubs still prosper, and remain soaked in Ecstasy, amphetamine sulphate, and more recently cocaine, contemporary jungle clubs are relatively drug-free (beyond the occasional whiff of a cannabis joint). In particular there is a noticeable lack of 'gurners' in jungle clubs. Gurning is a side-effect of Ecstasy where facial muscles are contorted. During the early 1990s gurning was seen to be part of the 'habitus' of the average raver, part of the grammar of actions that allowed ravers to differentiate between Ecstasy consumers and 'outsiders'.

Whereas the psychopharmacological structure of Ecstasy matches the musical structure of 4/4 House and Techno, the musical structure of jungle discourages Ecstasy use. Jungle's frantic percussion and irregular bass line mitigate against the bodily synchronisation felt by the Ecstasy-user when dancing to House. Shorn of a sequenced beat on each bar, jungle dancers either stay rooted to the spot, moving their arms and gyrating their hips, or frenetically jump up and down. There appears to be less of the tension visible in those who dance to, in particular, Techno, and more of a relaxed fluidity in their movements.

House and Techno fans are ignoring the long-term risks of Ecstasy consumption, with many taking a potentially brain-frying quantity each and every weekend. Whilst Ecstasy is now deemed to be essential for the full enjoyment of House and Techno music, this is not the case with jungle. The complex relationship between drug (Ecstasy) and music (House rhythms) has broken down. This breakdown has been caused by something as seemingly insignificant as the beat emphasis on a record.

Once the psychopharmacological effects of Ecstasy have been removed from the youth cultural equation, the whole culture surrounding dance music changes. Whereas House and Techno cultures have become stale and repetitive, and seem to lack innovation, jungle appears to be facing up to reality. Even some of the Ecstasy Evangelists are jumping over the fence. Mary Anna Wright, researcher on the Ecstasy Evangelists' bible, *Ecstasy and the Dance Culture* by Nicholas Saunders, now allies herself with the jungle scene, suggesting that the reason for this is that 'it doesn't lie; there's none of the "Everything's gonna be alright" stuff in the lyrics'.[13]

Whereas the repetitive kick of the House drum is the order of the day for your average Ecstasy consumer, jungle's manic percussion track is widely considered to reflect, or alternatively to originate from, the frantic pace of inner-city life. This is made explicit in one of the rarest of things; a lyric in a jungle record, entitled 'Inner-city Life' by the artist Goldie:

> Inner city life
> inner city pressure
> taking over me
> I won't let go no no

> (© FFrr Records)

This emphasis on fast urban lifestyles is also combined with an emphasis on 'darkness', which, whilst simultaneously highlighting the largely black origins of jungle, also underlines the shadow cast by the urban and suburban poverty-traps in which so many jungle consumers find themselves situated. There is no suggestion in jungle music that societal change is imminent, there is no Evangelism suggesting that psychedelics such as Ecstasy and LSD will change the world. Rather there is an overwhelming melancholy, a recognition that things like unemployment, racism, and poverty matter, and to pretend that these things will disappear in an Ecstasy haze is wrong. Steve Shapiro acknowledges this, suggesting that the British jungle experience is:

> ... less about a utopian vision, less about escaping through the music, and more about an acknowledged temporary hiatus from the difficulties of real life. Nothing will have changed after a night out, but for a moment, a good time will be had... Frankly, rave and House music seems to have a predominantly white middle-class audience, whereas jungle has a much stronger presence of black people. They have a mode of representation and cultural referents based on a very different experience of life. This experience is something shared by many working class and poor young people. They share a common existential experience of urban and suburban ghettos.[14]

Jungle's sense of darkness means that the Acid House generation has grown up, and that growing up in an accelerated culture can lead to a sense of disenfranchisement from the core of British society. Britain's underclass feels that it has not got the financial resources to keep up with the ever-changing consumerist mainstream. It is no coincidence that the most critically acclaimed jungle club in Britain in 1995 was called Speed, and the primary musical precursor of jungle was known as 'the darkside'.

Having said that the most important musical form since Acid House is not a drug-driven culture, there are still plenty of young teenagers willing to experiment with the thrills and delights that Ecstasy use can bring. Ecstasy use within House and Techno cultures is seen by clubbers as a way out of their repetitive lives, but ends up becoming a repetitive act in itself. With youth unemployment running high, and career structures hard to come by, E appears to be a logical and cheap[15] solution to a very real problem. Egged on by the Evangelists, Ecstasy consumption has become the be-all and end-all of House culture. The liberatory relations fought for by Acid House have been ignored, and intolerance has been allowed to seep in through the back door.

Ecstasy-related rallying cries such as 'Peace, Love, Unity and

Respect' can still be heard within contemporary House culture. Visit any British House club and you will find that the majority of dancers are under the influence of Ecstasy, even if many of them also have a bottle of beer in hand. Original scene makers such as Paul Oakenfold and Danny Rampling have gradually distanced themselves from the musical eclecticism and spirit of adventure present in early Acid House. Interestingly, both DJs now champion the 'Goa Trance' movement, a scene within a scene where Leary-esque hippy platitudes abound. Goa Trance is itself currently merging with 'Dream House', a variant of House with extended string-laden intros designed to increase Ecstasy's empathogenic qualities. It is no coincidence that Dream House bears more than a passing similarity to the Acidhead's Progressive Rock of the 1970s, and is derided by many as a retrogressive musical form.

Whilst the above tale might seem pessimistic, this should not necessarily be the case. Let us not forget that Ecstasy is a relatively safe drug. Ecstasy kills very few people compared with, say alcohol, and blame for the vast majority of fatalities lies fairly and squarely at government unwillingness to provide impartial risk-minimalisation information, and at nightclubs who are unwilling to invest in air-conditioning and free water supplies (Ecstasy, combined with hours of dancing, can lead to bodily dehydration). Whereas alcohol-driven music scenes are narcissistic and violent, some Ecstasy-orientated dance clubs do still feel full of love. But for every free-spirited and adventurous club, there are several money-grabbing, violent, and intimidatory scenes. Whilst not wishing to sound like an Ecstasy Evangelist, the effects of good quality E can be the foundation of a marvellous night out. Even the government agrees that rave culture and Ecstasy use are inseparable; under pressure from their liquor-producing sponsors (alcohol consumption amongst British youth has dropped in the 1990s) and the powerful farming lobby (fearful of their land being used for raves) the Conservative government have effectively banned outdoor raves with The Criminal Justice and Public Order Act of 1995. This act criminalises both the participants and organisers of events at which are played, in the (immortal) words of the act, 'sounds wholly or predominantly characterised by the emission of a succession of repetitive beats'.

Elements within British youth culture appear to have grown out of reckless hedonism, and as such British musical culture is entering a more mature phase. This process is not aided by books such as the aforementioned *Ecstasy and the Dance Culture*. In this book, Nicholas Saunders, a refugee from the 1960s whose enthusiasm for Ecstasy borders on the obsessive, suggests that Ecstasy, as well as enlivening and enriching dance culture, can improve sexual and family relationships, cure chronic depression, improve problem solving, increase physical fitness, advance sporting prowess, relieve pain and even lead to better job prospects.[16] Such talk is dangerous. If society is to create a music and culture that can bring about change, if youth culture is to progress and to diversify, then simply following in the footsteps of the 1960s will not suffice. Recreational drugs and psychedelic experimentation amount to no more than beautiful eyelid movies, an inner entertainment that must never be allowed to become the be-all and end-all of life itself.

Notes

1. Redhead, 1993, p 7.
2. Dr. Martin Paulus, Resident in Psychiatry, University of California at San Diego, offers a more scientific account:
    > One basis of the rave phenomenon is the music synchronising people's behaviour to an underlying rhythm. When you move to that rhythm you essentially do one type of behaviour – demands on your behaviour are to do the same thing over and over again; you're taking a drug that does the same thing over and over again, and it seems to fit perfectly together (quoted in MacDougal Craig, 1995).
3. Cited in Stevens, 1987, p 94.
4. Quoted in Sutherland, 1990.
5. Quoted in Sutherland, 1990.
6. Cited in Wroe *et al*, 1995, p 18.
7. 15 August 1995, p 10.
8. See for instance Parker *et al*, 1995.
9. Quoted in Boseley, 1995, p 2.
10. Honourable exceptions must be made at this point. The Exodus Collective in Luton have continually opposed government interference. The Reclaim the Streets group have also been active, with their 'Rave Against The Machine' protest bringing a six-lane major road in North London to a standstill. United Systems and Advance Party, both organisations campaigning for the right to hold raves,

have attempted to muster some political action. However the point stands, the vast majority of dance culture has allowed Government legislation to be passed without protest, and have witnessed the destruction of the liberatory atmosphere of early Acid House raves.

11. 'low-pay, low-prestige, low-dignity, low-benefit, no-future job in the service sector' Coupland, D (1992) *Generation X: Tales for an Accelerated Culture.* London: Abacus, p. 5. Although originally a term used to describe American youth, the publication of Coupland's book in Britain in 1992 popularised the term here.

12. It is this origin that led to jungle's frequent emphasis on the first two beats of the bar, the traditional waltz beat that characterises hip-hop, which can contrasted with House's 4/4 march emphasis.

13. Quoted in McKay, 1996, p 109.

14. Shapiro, 1995.

15. One result of the phenomenal demand for Ecstasy in Britain has been the professionalisation of its supply. Whereas in the late 1980s Ecstasy production was a relatively expensive process, nowadays European Ecstasy laboratories are commercial drug factories pumping out more and more of the drug. As a result of this the price of Ecstasy has fallen dramatically, from between £15 and £20 in 1987 to as little as £7 in 1996.

16. See Saunders, 1995, pp 106-23.

Bibliography

Boseley, S. (1995) 'Drug culture opening new generation gap' in *The Guardian*, 25th July, p.2.

Coupland, D. (1992) *Generation X: Tales for an Accelerated Culture.* London: Abacus.

- (1995) 'An infantile political debate, Why can't we have a sensible discussion about drugtaking?' in *The Guardian*, Tuesday, 15th August, p.10.

Leary, T. (1967) Interview in *Look*, 8th August.

MacDougal, C. (1995) Transcript for Equinox: Rave New World, Channel 4, London.

McKay, G. (1996) *Senseless Acts of Beauty: Cultures of Resistance since the Sixties.* London: Verso.

Parker, H., Measham, F., and Aldridge, J. (1995) *Drugs Futures: Changing Patterns of Drug Use amongst English Youth.* London: Institute for the Study of Drug Dependence.

Redhead, S. (1993) 'The Politics of Ecstasy' in Redhead, S. (ed.) Rave *Off: Politics and Deviance in Contemporary Youth Culture*. Aldershot: Avebury.

Saunders, N. (1993) *Ecstasy and the Dance Culture*. London: Neals Yard DTP Studio.

Shapiro, S. (1995) 'Jungle Critical Analysis' in http://www.facl.mcgill.ca/jungle/analysis.html, (n.p.)

Stevens, J. (1987) *Storming Heaven: LSD and the American Dream*. London: Paladin.

Sutherland, S. (1990) 'Wake Up America, You're Dead!' in Melody Maker, 4th August.

Wroe, M., Mills, E., and Spillius, A. (1995) 'Heaven, Hell and Ecstasy' in *The Guardian*, 19th November.

Discography

Flowered Up (1992) 'Weekender', Heavenly/Columbia Records/Sony Music Entertainment (UK) Ltd., London, HVN 16.

Goldie (1995) 'Timeless: Inner City Life' on Timeless, Ffrr/London Records, London, PY 900.

Mind, Body and Soul (1989) 'White Rabbit', white label, MBS 001.

Northside (1990) 'Shall We Take A Trip?', Factory Records, FAC 268.

The Shamen (1992) 'Ebeneezer Goode', One Little Indian Records, 78TP12.

The Soup Dragons (1990) 'I'm Free', Raw TV Products, RTV9.

THE FINAL WORD ON DRUGS

Fraser Clark

This is a development of a theory of the Archaic Revival *conceived by Terence McKenna.*

A Short History of Drugs from the Monkey to the Twentieth Century

You won't understand history if you think you already do. Understanding (and then tuning into) our evolutionary nature is the *fundamental question and answer* before we can tackle *anything* else. We 'know' so little of history, especially our earlier history, that the best policy when trying to understand the motives and behaviour of our forebears, *no matter what the surrounding circumstances*, remains extrapolating from *personal experience*. Which is all that 'scientists' have been doing. The personal experience *they* bring to the task, unfortunately, is as paltry as the information itself. For, after living the grossly unnatural lives that humankind has been reduced to, and dealing only with measurable quantities in extremely limited models, they are far less likely than the average, open-minded Joe Blowjob to have yet come up with an accurate, rounded picture.

Despite decades of propaganda, then, *all the important questions remain to be answered!* For example: constructing the 'set' on which we must try to innerstand the lives of our early ancestors with the scant information we presently possess is like, say, trying to work out our own evolution in the last century of the second millennium from the following information:

- that it took place against a background of a global one degree rise in temperature
- that seven species of butterflies and five of fish became extinct during the period
- and that studies of well-preserved bodies of late twentieth Century man show a rapid weight increase

Current competing theories of evolution would be represented by arguments as to whether the warmer sunshine, by improving agricultural productivity, produced *Homo sapiens's* weight increase, or whether it was all those fish and butterflies they must have consumed to extinction, or whether it was due to a cultural explosion of international communication and trade that is not on our list.

So, in considering the ideas below, dismiss from your mind the opinions you have been fed all your life, admit that the little information we have been led to think we possess is as likely to be a hinderance as a help, and judge their likelihood by whether your personal experience resonates 'street cred' or not.

Who Dunnit? Who Stepped on the Evolutionary Accelerator?

The major challenge for all evolutionary theories is to explain what is far and away the most spectacularly dramatic leap-forward that has occurred since the single-celled amoeba. The evolutionary fortnight it took our ancestors to swap the ocean for dry land, for example, is *lackadaisical* beside the Cosmic Second it took a monkey species swinging in the African jungles to evolve to the global internet, nuclear technology and off-planet space travel.

Since such sudden an acceleration is so totally unlike anything else in history as to suggest outside interference, it is certainly no wonder that world religions have grown up to explain it, nor that visitors from outer space have been seriously suggested. While we can certainly not discount such theories, let's be truly scientific and look for a simpler explanation from our own personal experience.

Are we aware of anything today that can bring about such changes? Science's offerings of the discovery of fire, the wheel, agriculture or language don't much resonate with anything I'm aware of, what do *you* think? A change of diet perhaps? Now *that* feels closer. We all know that a switch to health foods can greatly improve one's general vitality and even intelligence. But still, it would take something much stronger than raw aloe vera juice to cause such a unique evolutionary explosion.

Well, in my lifetime's experience, I've only known behavioural modifications as fundamental as swapping tree-swinging for rocket building to be caused by two things – religious conversion... and drugs. And the biggest of these is... *religious conversion through drugs.*

The Mushroom Monkey Mix

According to McKenna's theory, as the African rainforests retreated and the great grass plains appeared an evolutionary imperative forced the tree-dwelling apes to quit the trees, stand up on their own two feet, and go check out the grasslands for fresh food and possibilities.

This is the 'set', then, into which we must try to imagine ourselves. And the story I am about to tell must have happened many times, over many monkey generations. See if it rings true to your personal experience of life on this planet.

So here we are, you and me and a couple of the others have climbed fearfully down to the ground and, ignoring the shouted warnings of the tribe up in the branches and indeed the genetically encoded taboos in our very brains, are heading, partly already on back legs, towards the sheen of brilliant light that announces the forest's end. We're joshing, warning each other to keep a careful eye out for predators – and, of course, once the trees lie too far behind for even a quick dash to safety, our chattered fears increase. We don't go too far the first time, grab a few scarce delicacies and head thankfully home. But, when we return to the rest of the worried, disapproving tribe, everything has changed. We're in such high spirits that their arguments leave us untouched: 'you're setting the kids a bad example!' 'Great grandfather Adam tried that years ago and never came back!' And so on.

Don't the elders know that the times they are a' changing?! Don't they realise that food's getting scarcer, that in such situations it's the *duty* of the red-blooded males to explore pastures new?! And besides, everybody's heard the rumours of apes who've been to the grasslands so often by now that they're even starting to 'walk' on their hind legs! Didn't Charlie see a band of them last year down by the great waterfall? It's like some new kind of religion or something, and it's affecting the youth mostly, those with no social position to maintain.

> 'It's just a phase, Martha. It'll pass, you'll see, and he'll end up the best climber in the pack.'

The primary activity of the modern equivalents of these apes in north Africa, as they explore the grasslands, is scavenging and nibbling at everything that looks interesting. It's inevitable, then, as McKenna says, that our ancestors must have sooner or later encountered the giant psilocybin mushroom which can stand nine inches high.

Compare the image of the monkey nibbling the ice-cream-cone-looking mushroom with the ape swinging a club in the film 2001 and search your own experience for which lies deeper in our psyche. Both happened in our history, yes, but which was more spermatic to our development? I'd guess that a branch breaking off in a monkey's hand would have been common in our tree stage, and therefore clearly not very important. The mushroom's first appearance, on the other hand, is so perfectly timed as to suggest outside planning. Here, just when individual ego is most in danger of being aroused by this new walking on back legs away from the social enclosure of the tribe – bang – the ego-dissolving psychedelic appears!

And once they've actually chewed on a psychedelic mushroom? What then? What actual changes do mushrooms bring about in us, and would have brought about in *them*?

Monkey's First Trip

Historians would murder for a record of that missing link, forgetting for a moment that stoned monkey had no language to describe it, even to himself. For the staggering vision in that first trip, if our theory is true, would have been a blistering, eye-opening and yet blinding vista of the sudden evolutionary acceleration forwards to star travel. Certainly we can say that it would have been a *religious experience* in its widest and deepest sense. Would unquestionably have stimulated self-awareness, with all the ramifications ensuing – like expulsion from the garden?

However, since the species would have already learned to try any new plant in slightly increasing increments, we must ask first: how do small doses of psilocybin affect the brain? The subjective feeling is of a state of restlessness, of alertness. Indeed modern research has shown that human subjects administered low doses spot small variations in length, breadth and movement *better* than undosed subjects. Crucially useful, then, for our monkeys when travelling far from the safety of their treetop womb.

It is pure theory but more than just possible, then, that some of these early bands of roving explorers might have adopted a strategy of survival-friendly, low-level 'pick-me-up' use – like athletes today or students popping a little benzedrine – especially for a situation where they were far from the screeching but reassuring back-up cacophony of jungle family life.

And in larger doses? Well, full tripping must surely be linked to the development of higher conceptualising skills, self consciousness, language and spirituality (as in arousing the questions of who am I and what is all this?). It would surely have helped develop simultaneously more personal independence of identity from the petty village nationalisms of the local tribe, and more universal feelings and reverence for the great brother/sisterhood of the ape family and of planetary life itself. And would surely have led to the discovery of fire, the wheel and eventually to the shamanic need for agriculture, but that's to run ahead of our story.

Mushroom-tripping also seems able to plug us into a mythological past and also affords us a grand, if hard to understand, vision of the future. I'd suggest that the past which those apes envisioned would be of the link between all monkeys, even a reverence for all life, the perception that in a real but higher sense we are All One. Or at least all one family.

And the vision of the future? The mind boggles. Certainly a separated personal vision quite unlike anything that had occurred to them before. And a vision of a new race? Of a psychedelicised monkey society, spreading across the plains, speaking in tongues, mastering new forces like fire – indeed a vision of the *human! Homo sapiens*, indeed, and a blurred vision of belonging to some kind of chosen race amidst the merely instinctual boom and chatter of the rest of nature's species. Why me? Why us? What special purpose? What awesome destiny?

Imagine the bond – telepathic and other – that must have been created among the stand-up-tall, psychedelicised brothers! (and sisters, since only speed to escape was called for here). A far, far deeper bonding than, say, 1960s hippies felt when surrounded by angry straights.

I can and often do imagine our now merry band of psychic pioneers, already fusing molecularly into a terrestrial tribe (as opposed to 'of the trees'!), tripped off their faces down on the forest floor, dancing on their back legs in a kind of group-identity fashion statement, maybe even fucking in the missionary position for the first time! While up in the trees the elders, the parents, the more cautious and the infirm yell and scream warnings, condemnations and even curses on our pagan heretics below. *'Get back up here before it's too late!' 'You'll be sorry!' 'If nature had intended us to walk she'd never have given us trees to swing in!'* While our heroes drawl back: *'Aw, come on down and join the party! It's safe. It's brilliant! We love you!'*

This particular image is very strong in me. I can almost see/hear its echoes in my genes. And I can find its fractal in my own experience.

A Society of 'Love 'n' Peace' Human Apes

And so, gradually, there arose and evolved a species of psychedelicised apes which left the trees and walked forth on its hind legs to adapt to the new evolutionary imperative – life on the plains. And gradually they spread out from north-west Africa, around the Middle East at least as far as India and, in my opinion, as far as the west coast of Ireland where stones depicting moon worship (as opposed to the later sun worship) have been discovered.

And the majority who stayed in the trees? They're still there, our conservative, nay-saying cousins, undeveloped in their own little evolutionary niche! (making this theory eminently testable, and I can certainly personally confirm that, in the mushroom areas of South America, monkeys can be spotted occasionally picking and eating the magic mushrooms.)

What nature of a society was it at its most developed? Clearly a shamanic one (though the shaman himself had not yet made his entry), built as it must have been around the 'teaching' of the mushroom. By the way, though McKenna does not deal with this at all, the most important question remains: how did the wisdom get into the mushroom *in the first place?* But that is a 'spiritual' argument, with no place here except to wonder if such a question must originally have been stimulated during our psychedelicised stage of evolution.

(One wholistic argument would be that since the monkeys are made up of planetary material, then higher centres would exist in their brains corresponding with what is in the earth – but already we're straying too far into the mystical for our modern civilisation.)

The crucial question is: *what does the mushroom do to individuals who consume it?* And again we must look inside ourselves to find the answers. McKenna is brilliant on this, and I go along wholeheartedly with him: mushrooms, psychedelics *dissolve ego.* And regular ritual ingestion of mushrooms from birth or a young age (for these apes would have quickly discovered the security problems around mushroom ingestion and formalised the taking of them) would prevent the growth of ego!

Indeed we know enough from the scraps of habit and cultural myths that have been preserved to this day to be certain that it was a tribal society, that all major decisions were made on a unanimous basis, by group mind, that they 'humped in a heap' so that children were held in common (because the fathers would not be known, leading eventually to the matriarchal stage which is well established historically as predating patriarchy). And now we infer that they achieved this state by members gathering for a few days around the full moon to ritually ingest the mushrooms. They would have been peace-loving, open minded and friendly to other 'walking' strangers, recognising them as brothers and sisters with a common parentage. Does this stir deep ancestral memories of a time when humans did not hate and distrust other groups (let alone enslave, destroy and economically exploit them)?

And so this psychedelicised 'ego-free' ape civilisation spread as far as Ireland and India, apparently reaching its finest cultural flowering around the Tassili caves in Southern Algeria, where a whole mushroom-worshipping culture has left cave paintings of mushroom-headed gods and shaman figures from whose bodies distinct mushroom shapes can be seen emanating. These date from around 6000 BC, and show they had developed a high level of art, and certainly language, and the whole panoply of herbal medicine and 'allies'.

Suppose that the whole spread of this *true* civilisation of increasingly humanoid beings was in constant, communal telepathic communication (as some maintain the animal world still is)... the 'noble savage' long dismissed by the de-natured, anthropology 'experts'... Atlantis – the folk memory of a previous super civilisation found in the mythologies of so many peoples of the planet. And still in each of our hearts like a genetic memory – unless you maintain (unscientifically – because involving more than necessary assumptions) that 'the still quiet voice' of your natural conscience, almost like a memory deep in the heart of how things *were* or *were meant to be*) came 'from God' or 'from alien landings'.

'Fuck This Circle Lark, I'll Do It My Way!'

All right, we've come up with an explanation of that sudden, meteoric standing-start evolution. Now we must answer the most important question: *how and when did things go wrong?* How, after such a promising breakthrough, did we get to the terrible mess we're in today? And, because it allows an answer, finally, to this all important question, this is where the monkey-mushroom theory gets *really* interesting. All important because, if we can find out what went wrong, we can possibly return to that wrong choice and make another one. Before it's too late!

The answer, if it's true, should send a chill down your spine and ring echoes in your genes. For, unlike the first mushroom trip which was a positive evolutionary vision, this moment would be the most traumatic in the entire history of the tribe. For this is where our species (and perhaps evolution of the planet itself) took a wrong path which it has been following ever since.

(You could argue, of course, that it was a Great Mistake we had to make in order to learn the ecological lesson of community, but, in my opinion, it was far too costly a mistake and, in fact, not necessary, though the process was unstoppable and inevitable once begun.)

We must imagine a time and a place: the place is probably in a colder northern area to which psychedelicised ape-human society had spread. The time is the full moon.

Something terrible has happened! *There are no mushrooms for the tribal ritual!!* Now this must have happened many times before, which is why the shaman had arisen, specifically tasked by the community to avoid such a situation. Other than the shaman, no concept of 'leader' had yet emerged, although something of a hunter/ warrior caste must have arisen to deal with security problems, and herbal lore would have slowly become the expertise of the women. There are reasons for believing, indeed, that the early shamans were mostly females.

By this moment, over many generations, the shaman had developed a means for preserving the mushrooms, first by drying them, and then by preserving them in honey. He had also researched and discovered other drugs which could, in a crisis, be substituted. Perhaps, this time, they tried a brew of various herbs the shaman had laid aside for just such a situation. Perhaps they even drank the honey in which the previous month's mushrooms had been stored. Certainly mead (fermented honey) is found later as part of the staple diet of the northern peoples.

And so the full moon ritual passed without too much mishap. But things were more serious than might be supposed. Let us say that the end of the summer was approaching and the tribe had to decide whether to go north and spend the winter hunting caribou, or to head to the warmer southlands and fish. Group decisions, of course, had to be unanimous, had to 'emerge' from the 'sacred circle' of group mind, and only long psychedelicised talking and swapping of folk tales, legends and wisdoms could pull all the various personal opinions into group harmony.

So another month had to pass. Now the weather's getting colder and a decision has to emerge soon. But still the shaman, despite his best efforts and those of the whole tribe, is unable to obtain the correct material for the ritual, necessitating another full moon with little chance of a group decision. Individual egos are popping up like cancers, arguments are simmering just below or already on the surface, factions have even started appearing, and the only hope of the wiser elders (for holding together the threatened sacred unity of the tribe) is to put full energy into obtaining enough mushrooms to heal the situation. Scouts are sent out to visit other nearby tribes but there seems to be a general shortage.

Let's suppose then (as must have happened one time) that their plans fall through and yet a third mushroom-less full moon appears. Winter is by now very much upon them, and, huddled in their sacred circle around the campfire, they discuss things deep into the night, trying for a group decision. Without the mushrooms to dissolve personal egos, however, bitter, angry arguments break out. Let's say that they have drunk the 'mead' and some of the younger males are getting more and more frustrated (as well as drunk) until... *FINALLY*... totally infuriated by the same argument going round, round and round with no appearance of a group decision 'emerging' (and God knows, anyone who has sat in a rainbow-type gathering today knows how frustrating such circles can be when even the village idiot has to be listened to respectfully) a young male warrior leaps to his feet:

> *'What a fucking way to run a railway! I'm the best of the warriors and a master at hunting the caribou, and I say: if we piss about another month making this decision we shall lose the caribou spoor and stand no chance of a good hunt. I've been talking to the other warriors and most of them will go with me. So make your choice now. Fuck this sacred circle lark, I'm heading North!'*

And, so saying, he turns from the fire and the circle, and stomps off towards the suddenly threatening darkness when (as I imagine it) a very old crone monkey-human (perhaps the shaman herself) cries out in a terrible voice that has echoed down the generations since: *'WE MUST NOT BREAK THE SACRED CIRCLE!'*

Our furious teenager stops in his stride. He whirls: *'oh, yeah? why not?!'* Whereupon, into the head of the old crone, unused to this new, shouting, competitive style of conversation, and anyway not so good at this public speaking business, flood a whole host of wholistic-style reasons, none of which she is able to marshall together for such a climactic, traumatic moment. She looks around for help from the others but none is forthcoming. Perhaps they are drunk, perhaps exhausted by the bickering. Perhaps, even, no language for it had yet developed. And finally she says: *'You'll see... You'll see!'* ...

And our adolescent male strides contemptuously off into the night and into an unknown future – followed by several other young males and their favourite mates, each possibly remembering that previous, and by now genetically imprinted, climax in their history when the young had led the first apes out of the forest towards their new destiny.

History is Bunk, and Nearly all Crime

And so, from what has come down to us as the Fall, begins what we call 'history', the history of ego (ego being a cancerous growth in the brain of our species), the chrono-logical cascade of inevitable repercussions of that young male's choice. Follow it through (as humanity has done) – once competition starts, it can only develop until the entire planet is ruled by the most efficiently competitive group. But the beauty (the horror) of it is that the theatre of our Story's unfolding is not an infinite plain, but a finite planet. Karma-creation, carried on long enough, eventually must catch up and teach us its lesson. The old crone's lesson in this case, *'You'll see... You'll see!'*

These young males initiated a whole new breed. My innate and objective sense of shame at the increasingly competitive ego-systems flowing from their actions – doubtless an evolutionary throwback to our psychedelicised past! – inhibits me from calling such a gigantically murderous fuck-up a 'culture' though the optimist in me insists that I must. A whole new species evolved (or more accurately devolved) that was founded on physical strength, lying (its psychic equivalent) and a hysterical fear of the natural and of 'letting go', which shows up in our current mania about the effects of 'drugs'.

For, with all hope of trust lost in the breaking of the sacred circle of community, this new military race proceeded, by the inevitable anti-raising process fundamental to competition, to bully, plunder, enslave and finally commit genocide against the gentler species till the psychic fabric of the original telepathic net was irretrievably ruptured, leaving only small outlying remnant pockets that have barely managed to survive up to the present moment, with virtually all but their myths and ideas (what we might call 'buried con-science') wiped from 'history'.

Can you, as I can, imagine the terrible depth of this 'Original Sin', the subconscious guilt for the beauty these new alpha males soon realised they had destroyed? How it must have driven them mad with rage and hatred! The unavoidable ritualising of the group's behaviour, the social layering, the codes of social repression of spon-taneity necessitated by the otherwise uncheckable violence and social upheaval such activity might unleash. Private property, patriarchy, the suppression of the weak, the female, the animal, sex, and ... drugs. No wonder we modern humans use only a tenth of our brain's capacity!

For here we had a dominant 'culture' terrified of the ego-melting effect of the mushroom (a large percentage of our population today is mycophobic!) and indeed totally abhorring all forms of mysticism. Luckily not every trace of the old culture was completely wiped out, surviving, even to the present day, in small pockets with long, long lineages stretching back to the original 'noble savages'. Perhaps, even, the Tassili cave civilisation didn't blossom in 6000BC but survived *as late as* 6000BC? Nevertheless, history clearly shows that, though preserved in diminishing fractal forms as the seer, oracle or joker whose 'inspired' pronouncements could still rouse uneasy psychedelic (larger than mere physical brain) echoes of respect in the very genes of the new leader/king alpha male and indeed of the rest of the tribe, the shaman gave way to the priest for that very reason – being perceived as a threat to the 'new world order'. In decreasing fractals the priest then garbles the degenerating religious dogmas to ever less impressed followers until the present day when either full karma is achieved in species – and even planet-suicide (*'you'll see, you'll see!'*), or the empty husks are swept successfully away by a rebirth of the shamanic spirit of communion with all life.

The very planet is now threatened by this competitive culture, by ego pure and simple. For now we have run out of places to avoid it. Now the whole world is threatened and we are seeing the wisdom of the words of that old crone. Yes, we *shall* see. We are seeing why the sacred circle must not be broken.

The question now is: *can we re-make, are we re-making, a culture based in shamanism and the sacred circle before we all perish?*

Drugs, Shamanism and the Sacred Circle as we Enter the Third Millennium

By 1997 British society, by re-integrating shamanism, has moved beyond the drug issue. A rapidly and *truly* evolving culture (which it must be as we hurtle through the final nanosecond of 'history') does not proceed merely in a repetitive circle of expansion/reaction/expansion, though it surely continues to do that on one level. It also moves in an evolutionary spiral where social issues and patterns repeat but on a higher level. Such a model involves, however, no possibility of breakthrough – say, to a new dimension altogether. Like leaving the ocean, the trees, or the planet. Nor, as in this case, of reintegrating a previously lost level of understanding to produce a qualitatively new mix.

Chaos science shows clearly another model of evolution where each level of the seeming spiral, while retaining certain essential self-similarities, iterates and expands further and further from the original central forcefield, with apparently trivial cause/effects often turning out to be hugely significant (like the just-surviving strains of late middle-history pagan cults in Europe and the more ancient wisdom paths of the East which began to re-enter our culture in the 20th century, accelerating in the 1960s and exploding exponentially in the 1990s) until, finally, with the very next fractal (the hundredth as in the hundredth monkey?), the whole project expands clean out of the old paradigm and falls under the gravitational influence of a new 'strange attractor'.

For simplicity's sake, let us assume that the whole competitive path was a necessary exploration in order to allow our species to evolve to a higher level of community. The only question remaining and worth asking, then, is this: *Is the species actually learning the lesson? Is it re-incorporating the shamanic spirit and, with that, the sacred circle of community?* I'd say: yes, and one of the main signs is that, with three years to go, it is already clear that drugs will no longer be an 'issue' in the third millennium; here's why.

Though psychic spontaneity and adventure have always threatened the dominant ego-culture on this planet, drugs first became a frontline, media issue in the 1960s, up there with war, social equality and several other issues headed by sex. Well, Vietnam's long gone and its modern equivalent Iraq could not be sold to the gene pool for more than a month. Equality looks like a lost issue, though it's actually starting to cook *nicely* on the back burner of the new ecology issue (which is part of the sacred circle of community with all life). The sex war was won *during* the hippy thing, the new cultural theme cascading chronologically outwards across the global society's synapses until the sex 'issue' today has become an utterly safe way of appearing 'revolutionary'.

Leaving drugs to become the next and possibly (hundredth?) great social fractal until the explosive dominance of the rave scene – a very 'strange attractor – indeed, settled the issue once and for all in the mid 1990s.

... Maybe like Last Time, Baby Soft Sex Will Turn out to be Okay

As a 'free love believer' at college in the very early 1960s, when sex was becoming an 'issue', I remember all too clearly the fundamental, irrational anti-sex argument we believers ultimately and always ran up against. Almost impossible to credit today, let alone take seriously, goddess knows it was parrotted at me often enough that I still wake up sweating sometimes, it was this: *'release the taboos against sex and people will start fucking all the time, they won't go to work... and civilisation as we know it will disappear.'* With that argument having collapsed by the early 1970s under the weight of a large enough number of personal experiences (the only way anything ever changes despite appearances to the contrary), and with the next looming frontier issue becoming drugs, the same argument made its reappearance: *'if we decriminalise drugs, people will be helpless before them, they'll do them all the time, stop going to the office and civilisation will collapse.'* Adding mournfully, since these anti-mysticism, anti-nature conservatives are the same people who resisted every other recent change (one of the essential self-similarities of the fractal): ' – *if it's not already collapsed anyway!'*

Notice that, although in the last half of the 1970s and the first half of the 1980s the drug issue largely disappeared from public view, like the hippies themselves or the witches before them, the number of personal experiences continued to grow inexorably, as did the alternative culture itself, with its increasing connections to the old pagan (and ancient shamanic traditions), popping up sporadically into public view via punks and Stonehenge, and their combination the new age travellers.

With the advent of Rave, and its deep infusion by the old hippy/punk scene, the sheer number of personal experiences ensured that, by the mid 1990s, the drug war was won, bar the official shouting. For the new generation, the subject today has shifted from being an issue to being close to a mere *topic*, like sex has become, and dancing, and petting, and nudity, and all the rest of it during our recent long, slow, ambient evolutionary 'return march' through the final nano-second of outdated 'history'.

So many and so subtle are the pathways of change that we notice them only occasionally, in an emotional rush of *possibilities*. Is it not truly remarkable, for example, how today in Britain nobody actually bothers any more to advocate the total eradication of drugs? All the talk now is of *'holding the line'*, and even just *'slowing the spread'*. Finally in Britain (which leads hopefully to America, the transmitter to the rest of the planet) everyone's suddenly agreed that the name of the game is *information*. Don't, for goddess' sake, miss the depth of significance coded in *'information'* – it's taken three decades (and a whole week of evolution!) to get to here. What *'information'* means is that it's now OK, and even *responsible*, to describe the *beneficial* aspects of drugs (without which, obviously, we'll never get to a sane personal and social attitude to drugs and shamanism).

Basically the official position has shifted to the defensive. Right now you can spot the old dinosaurs on TV as they begin to glimmer that there's a new majority in town, or an unstoppable momentum of ideas, personal experiences, research and scientific breakthroughs towards it (designer drugs, smart drugs, therapeutic drugs, illegal class As manufactured in the pineal gland etc, etc) as to make *any* fixed position dinosaur-like. Suddenly the holy fire in their bellies feels like irascibility and intolerance even to *them*. They've shifted from 'no, *you* don't' to 'no, *we* won't'. *We* won't take the 'soft drugs' option, *we* won't allow drug testing equipment outside clubs, *we* won't look at this, *we* won't admit that, and so on. But nobody bothers to say 'you won't!' any more.

Yes, People, it's Human Culture but not as We've Known it These Last few Millennia

Fractally rehearsed, then, by the 1960s hippies, the drug war was finally won by the 1990s ravers as the qualitative 'breakout' predicted by chaos theory looms closer. And the process of re-assimilating the natural allies into our cultural bloodstream is the final fractal leap out of the old forcefield and into the ambit of the strange attractor of becoming a fully technologised, shamanic, global community. With mysticism back at the heart of Europe (whether the head realises it yet or not), we are now embarked on a new path: learning from our ancient shamanic wisdom for our joint psychic journey ahead.

'Oh, not that word shaman again' I hear you say (but doesn't that prove the point?!). Certainly the word needs some definition. Not the usual distanced 'historical' anthropological one, but in the personal everyday sense. Could we, for example, have become a shamanic culture again without realising it? The most important point to bear in mind, as we compare notes, is that the shaman came late in our evolutionary voyage, and only among those tribes lacking an abundance of mushrooms. Elsewhere and hitherto people would have certainly collected their own supply as granted by the goddess, and the shaman role would not have developed. So 'shamanic' really means 'self-administering of higher natural energies'.

Our future is a huge subject, still in full tide, and my argument, at this moment in the mid 1990s, will necessarily be mostly composed of jottings and notes. Notes jotted between tree swings and paradigm jumps on 'tiny' but fastforwardly cascading cultural changes.

> 'Come on down! Get out of your mind – and back into
> your heart and body!'

I first consciously noticed the shift towards a new strange attractor at a free festival a couple of years before rave burst on the scene. After a day of monkey-surfing, I was huddled deliciously exhaustedly round a campfire with a group of hippy types (which I suppose I'd define as belonging to a rebel, pilgrim, somewhat luddite caste at that time), absentmindedly tracking what I was very aware was the usual kind of conversation, when it suddenly occurred to me that a nineteenth century anthropologist could only conclude that he was witnessing a shamanic culture!

The values of this dominant-culture-to-be (not obviously more than a subcult then, but carrying the monkey's baton with which the coming rave culture could *win the HUMAN RACE!*) were quite, quite different from the threatening, self-destructing, competitive, ego-based 'culture' around them. Indeed, only my habit of serially inhabiting both (which later gave birth to my vision of the zippy) anthropologically enabled me to see it.

The hippy 'tribe' (culture) possessed its own quite separate conception of human social history which reached further and further back to the witches, the Egyptians, and ultimately to the shaman; plus its own theories of evolution and the future. They spent, for example, little time discussing incomes, personal materialistic ambitions or achievements, other than the immediate and practical. Rather, their tales and conversations were about their own or the general level of consciousness, and their desired or actual states of mind, drug-related for the most part, certainly, but by no means exclusively. Where a 'straight' (competitive monkey/dinosaur) might have talked of the latest model of car or the TV commercial or the speed in numbers at which he'd driven to get there, or the cost of any such item, or just general factual information, the outsider rebel pilgrim luddites spoke of an alien they'd seen in a dream/vision or the higher emotional state they'd been in last week, or the Herman Hesse novel they were reading.

Now, perhaps like you, I dismissed this first observation for some time as equivalent competitive hippy *'my car got even higher than yours'* stuff until I was forced by honesty to admit that, though such *self-similarities* certainly ran through it, nevertheless what was being valued (and striven for) demonstrated a wholly different model of reality. Their personal memory maps would be of conscious insights, visions and emotional highs (and lows). Indeed how different could any two evolutionary models *be*!? Much of the conversation was of the means for altering these states, involving much discussion of legend, rumour, scientific and anthropological breakthroughs, theories of evolution and so on. Particularly striking, as hinted above, was the general attitude to heroes and leaders. Despite their apparent cross-overlap in the 'new age' movement, where each can talk of reaching new levels of enlightenment and self understanding, the stark chasm between the two cultures is demonstrated by 'straight' society's most new age conception of an evolved human ape: the *lone yogi individual pursuing her personal evolution*. For the alternative community, in so far as leaders were accepted at all, they were conceived as shamans, *selflessly committed to the welfare of the tribe*, preserving its true valuables (and values) for all.

What Rave did in Britain in the 1990s was to transform the new age, an essentially bourgeois lifestyle, into a national movement towards shamanic group mind and away from purely personal liberation. Forget Jesus, by the way, the priests deified the dead shaman for their own competitive reasons and no Christian seriously presents him as an actual exemplar.

Another cross-overlap is the internet where instant global communication increasingly resembles telepathy and a skin of psychic communion like an aura around the egg we share. And are there signs of shamanism appearing in the overground culture? They're everywhere, see if you can spot them: the breakdown of social stratification in the spread and dominance of the 'middle class', the resurgence of the female, the increasing rejection of war as the extreme end of 'conversation' and so on and on. Even in politics we glimpse a return to 'the good man', 'the moral man', the all-round man (the shaman) rather than the expert, the corporate man, let alone the absentminded professor or the royal upper class with the fruity accent.

Demand an Altered State!

If the details of our liberation are as hard to perceive and number as the individual raindrops in a storm, the overall evolutionary direction is perfectly clear. Our culture, from a 'standing' start, and after a very long and dangerously unhealthy (or just possibly necessary and therefore healthy) *detour* into personal, competitive ego, is now accelerating deeper and deeper, faster and faster, into a technologised, shamanic, sacred circle of community. And our future is as clear and as unclear as that monkey ancestor's first trip. But don't take *my* word for it. Be your own shaman and... *ask the mushroom!*

Further Reading

Most of the works relating to the use of psychedelics in a British context can be found listed in the previous essays, especially those of Melechi and Sandison. Some more general publications have been included in the following bibliography.

Aaranson, B. and Osmond, H. (eds.) (1971) *Psychedelics*. London: Hogarth Press.

Artaud, A. (1976) *The Peyote Dance*. New York: Farrar, Strauss and Giroux.

Baudelaire, C. (1971) *Artificial Paradise: On Wine and Hashish as Means of Expanding Individuality*. New York: Herder and Herder.

Braden, W. (1967) *The Private Sea: LSD and the search for God*. London: Pall Mall Press.

Casteneda, C. (1970) *The Teachings of Don Juan: A Yaqui Way of Knowledge*. Harmondsworth: Penguin.

De Bold, R. and Leaf, R. (eds.) (1969) *LSD, Man and Society*. London: Faber and Faber.

DeRopp, S. R. (1958) *Drugs and the Mind*. London: Gollancz.

Fallowell, D. (ed.) (1979) *Drug Tales*. London: Hamish Hamilton.

Harner, M. (ed.) (1973) *Hallucinogens and Shamanism*. London: Oxford University Press.

Harner, M. (1990) *The Way of the Shaman*. San Francisco: HarperSanFrancisco.

Hayter, A. (1968) *Opium and the Romantic Imagination*. London: Faber and Faber.

Hoffer, A. and Osmond, H. (1967) *The Hallucinogens*. New York: Academic Press.

Kluver, H. (1968) *Mescal and Mechanisms of Hallucination*. Chicago: University of Chicago Press.

Leary, T. et al. (eds.) (1993) *The Psychedelic Reader*. New York: Citadel Press.

Le Barre, W. (1969) *The Peyote Cult*. New York: Schocken Books.

Lee, A. M. and Shlain, B. (1985) *Acid Dreams: The CIA, LSD and the Sixties Rebellion*. New York: Grove Press.

Lewin, L. (1964) *Phantastica, Narcotic and Stimulating drugs: their Use and Abuse*. London: Routledge. Original German edition, 1924.

Lewis, I. M. (1971) *Ecstatic Religion: Anthropological Study of Spirit possession and Shamanism.* Harmondsworth: Penguin.

Ludlow, F. (1857) *The Hasheesh Eater.* New York: Harper and Brothers.

Michaux, H. (1964) *Light Through Darkness: Explorations Amongst Drugs.* London: Bodley Head.

Michaux, H. (1972) *Miserable Miracle.* San Francisco: City Lights.

Michaux, H. (1975) *Infinite Turbulence.* London: Calder and Boyars.

Moreau, J. J. (1973) *Hashish and Mental Illness.* New York: Raven Press. Original French edition, 1845.

Newland, C. (1963) *Exploring Inner Space: Personal Experiences under LSD-25.* London: Victor Gollancz.

Petrullo, V. (1975) *The Diabolic Root: A Study of Peyotism, The New Indian Religion, Among the Delawares.* New York: Octagon Books.

Rudgley, R. (1993) *The Alchemy of Culture.* London: British Museum Press.

Slotkin, J. S. (1956) *The Peyote Religion.* Glencoe: Free Press.

Solomon, D. (ed.) (1968) *The Marihuana Papers.* New York: New American Library.

Strasbaugh, J. and Blaise, D. (eds.) (1991) *The Drug User: Documents 1840-1960.* New York: Blast Books.

Tart, C. (ed.) (1990) *Altered States of Consciousness (Third Edition).* San Francisco: HarperSanFrancisco.

Wells, B. (1973) *Psychedelic Drugs.* Harmondsworth: Penguin.

Zaehner, R. C. (1957) *Drugs, Mysticism and Make-Believe.* London: Collins.

Contributors

Michael Carmichael received a degree in Modern History at the University of North Carolina in 1968, and went on to become a research consultant and adviser to five American presidential campaigns. He lives in Oxford, where he is the founder of the Theatrum Chemicum Britannicum, a private academic society for the history and archaeology of psychoactive substances.

Fraser Clark hit the beatnik road out of Scotland in 1965, after completing a degree in psychology. He was still on the road, editing and publishing *Encyclopaedia Psychedelia International*, when Rave exploded in Britain. He has produced rave singles with Timothy Leary, albums with Terence Mckenna, Genesis P Orridge and The Shamen (Shamanarchy In The UK), and he created the club, Megatripolis. He now lives in London, where he has just finished writing a *BOOK OF RAVeLATIONS*.

Antonio Melechi is currently undertaking doctoral research on the intellectual history of the drug experience at the University of York. He is now collecting testimonies for an anthology of drug tales and would like to hear from readers who have their own heavenly, hellish or absurd experiences to recount. The anthology will cover all drugs – from anaesthetics to amphetamines, cannabis to cocaine. Please write to: A. Melechi (Drug Tales), Department of Sociology, University of York, Heslington, York, YO1 5DD; or e-mail: melechi@compuserve.com

Stuart Metcalfe is Associate Lecturer in Media and Cultural Studies at Liverpool John Moores University.

Simon Reynolds writes about music and pop culture for *Artforum*, *The New York Times*, *Village Voice*, *Melody Maker*, *The Wire*, *Rolling Stone*, *Mojo*, *Frieze* and *i-D*. He is the author of *Blissed Out: The Raptures of Rock* (Serpent's Tail, 1990) and co-author, with Joy Press, of *Sex Revolts: Gender, Rebellion and Rock 'n' Roll* (Serpent's Tail, 1995).

Ronald Sandison worked as a consultant psychiatrist at Powick Hospital, Worcester, from 1951 to 1964, where he pioneered the use of LSD as a therapeutic tool for the treatment of a range of non-psychotic disorders. Since 1964, he has worked a consultant psychotherapist and lectured in psychotherapy at the University of Aberdeen. In recent years he has worked at the Margaret Pyke Centre in Soho, and in private practice in Herefordshire where he now lives.

Alexander Trocchi is best known as the author of *Cain's Book* (1960), a graphic account of his own struggle with heroin addiction. After leaving Scotland for Paris in the early 1950s, Trocchi edited the literary journal *Merlin* and became a member of the Situationist International. Arrested on drugs charges in New York in 1960, Trocchi jumped bail and arrived in London the following year, becoming a central figure in the emergent counter-culture – his own project sigma bringing together various disparate strands of the underground. Trocchi died in 1984.

Sheila Whiteley is the head of Popular Music Research and Post-graduate Studies at University College Salford. She is the author of *The Space Between The Notes* (Routledge, 1992), has published many articles on the production and consumption of popular music and is currently editing an anthology of essays on gender and pop, *Sexing The Groove* (Routledge, forthcoming).

Andrew Wilson is an art historian, curator, and writer on contemporary culture and art. He is currently completing a PhD at the Courtauld Institute of Art. His books include *Paul Graham* (Phaidon Press, 1996) and *Blast! Vorticism – The First Avante Garde in England 1914-1918* (Sprengel Museum, Hanover 1996). He works for *Art Monthly*, London.

Index